CIPA GUIDE
PATENTS ACTS

EIGHTH EDITION

SECOND SUPPLEMENT

CIPA GUIDE TO THE PATENTS ACTS

EIGHTH EDITION

SECOND SUPPLEMENT

Up to date to 1 October 2017

EDITED BY

PAUL G. COLE

and

RICHARD DAVIS

FOR
THE CHARTERED INSTITUTE
OF PATENT ATTORNEYS

Founded 1882
Royal Charter 1891

SWEET & MAXWELL   THOMSON REUTERS

First Edition 1980
Second Edition 1984
Third Edition 1990
Fourth Edition 1995
Fifth Edition 2001
Sixth Edition 2009
Seventh Edition 2011
Eighth Edition 2016

Published in 2017 by Thomson Reuters,
trading as Sweet & Maxwell. Registered in England & Wales, Company
No.1679046. Registered Office and address for service: 5 Canada Square,
Canary Wharf, London, E14 5AQ.

For further information on our products and services,
visit *http://www.sweetandmaxwell.co.uk*

Typeset by Sweet & Maxwell Ltd, 5 Canada Square, Canary Wharf,
London, E14 5AQ
Printed and bound by CPI Group (UK) Ltd, Croydon, CRO 4YY

No natural forests were destroyed to make this product; only farmed
timber was used and re-planted

A CIP catalogue record for this book is available from the British Library

ISBN 978 0 414 06546 8

Notice to Readers

CIPA GUIDE TO THE PATENTS ACTS

EDITORS
Paul G. Cole
Chartered Patent Attorney
Lucas & Co

Richard Davis
Barrister
Hogarth Chambers

The supplement to the "Black Book" has been produced by the Editors listed above, with the help of a team of contributors, acknowledged in alphabetical order below, each of whom has contributed subject matter for one or more individual sections. Barristers, solicitors and patent attorneys have all served as members of the team.

James Anderson, Elkington and Fife LLP
Sophy Denny, Elkington and Fife LLP
Zoe Butler, Powell Gilbert LLP
Sam Carter, Hogarth Chambers
Paul Casbon, Lucas & Co
Alison Firth, Professor Emeritus, University of Surrey
Nicholas Fox, Simmons & Simmons LLP
Anoop Joshi, Brodies LLP
Gill Grassie, Brodies LLP
Anna Hatt, Beck Greener
John Hull, Beck Greener
Jonathan Markham, Beck Greener
Jamie Muir Wood, Hogarth Chambers
David Pearce, Barker Brettell LLP
James Peel, J. P. Peel & Co
Thomas Phillips, Ministry of Defence
Tim Roberts, Brookes Batchellor LLP
Ashley Roughton, Barrister, Nabarro LLP
Vicki Salmon, IP Asset
Mike Snodin, Park Grove IP
Nick Wallin, Withers & Rogers LLP
Philip Walters, Celldex Therapeutics
Trevor Cook, WilmerHale

CIPA Guide to the Patents Acts

EIGHTH EDITION

Second Supplement

INTRODUCTION

This Supplement is cumulative and reviews legislative changes enacted and legal opinions handed down after the text for the Eighth Edition was finalised. It attempts to state the law comprehensively up to 1 October 2017. Text added since the first Supplement was published is indicated by ■.

Attention is drawn to a statistical chart shown by Ms Heli Pihlajamaa, Director, Patent Law at the EPO at the 2017 CIPA congress, and which is reproduced below:

Origin of European patent applications

Analysis showing the geographic origin of first-named applicants, based on European patent applications filed with the EPO (direct European applications and international (PCT) applications entering the European phase).

© European Patent Office 2017

Although economies differ as between the EU member states, it is not immediately apparent why the number of UK-originating inventions deserving protection should be only 19% of that for Germany, 43% of that for France and less than those for Switzerland and the Netherlands which have smaller populations. The more likely explanation is that UK researchers and management are insufficiently aware of the benefits provided by the patent system, and that there are substantial but still untapped reserves of UK inventions that could usefully be addressed. If there have been disincentives e.g. the level of litigation costs, it is submitted that these should be investigated and appropriately addressed.

The future of the European Unitary Patent and the United Patent Court is an issue of strategic importance to readers. The final statutory instruments to allow UK ratification are now before the Westminster and Holyrood Parliaments. So UK ratification could happen by the end of 2017. Currently the programme is being held up by a challenge in the German Constitutional Court which has delayed ratification by Germany. Further information on that challenge is expected in late 2017.

Eligibility remains an issue of strategic importance, especially for software/business method inventions and for inventions in the field of life sciences and both for UK/Europe and for the US. In Europe, the legal position in both fields is relatively stable notwithstanding controversy over plant or animal products resulting from conventional breeding operations. It remains in a state of considerable flux in the US, where a continuing sequence of adverse eligibility decisions is creating consternation amongst the US profession and is of relevance to UK and European practitioners whose clients are seeking or are likely to seek US patent protection.

Experience both in the US and in the UK demonstrates judicial resistance to claims that are of undue breadth in the software/business method field, often by claiming a result without specifying the technical features by which the result can be achieved and in the life sciences field often by undue speculation. For example, in life sciences, the generic Markush claim format has been standard practice for many decades notwithstanding that such fields may be less predictable than some chemical fields e.g. dyestuffs. Instances where such claims have been held valid and covering a compound whose synthesis and testing is not described in the specification are hard to find. An extreme example is found in *Merck Sharp and Dohme v Shionogi* discussed below. Such broad claims may lack credibility for want of supporting data or for want of a disclosed rationale for the prediction, and this may apply both to the range of compounds covered and to the range of new medical indications for a known compound as in the *Warner Lambert* case now before the UK Supreme Court. Readers will be aware that it is futile to prosecute claims to grant that are unlikely to survive due diligence enquiry or litigation, and recent US experience especially as to the eligibility of subject matter in the software/business method field shows the loss of credibility that flows from main claims held invalid and the consequential risk of dependent claims being treated somewhat dismissively.

Recent years have shown increasing exchanges and collaboration between UK practitioners and their overseas colleagues, especially those in the US. Three papers on inventive step and on claim interpretation presented at the 2017 annual meeting of AIPLA by Brantley C. Shumaker, Warren D. Woessner and Suzannah

K. Sundby enable significant similarities and differences between UK/EPO law and US law and are considered in this Supplement.

As previously, each entry in this Supplement has a marginal reference in bold type to the numbered section and paragraph number of the Eighth Edition ["the Main Work"] to which it relates e.g. §125.23, and is identified by headings (e.g. "Extent of invention") and sub-headings (e.g. "Claims containing numerical limits") corresponding to those in the Main Work. The Supplement also contains Supplementary Tables which are to be read in conjunction with the corresponding Tables in the Main Work.

As previously, in this Supplement there is an introductory paragraph for many sections entitled "Contents" and numbered e.g. §14.00. Although only some paragraphs within a section may be referred to in this Supplement, it includes in its list all the other paragraphs of that section that appear in the Main Work. Although the Guide has a comprehensive Index, awareness of relevant material and ease of navigation in a work of the present length and complexity are important considerations, and it is hoped that these introductory paragraphs will be useful both for navigating this Supplement and also for navigating the Main Work. For example, Section 15 has the title "Date of filing application" which appears in the Act, from which it was by no means obvious to the reader, and is now apparent from the contents paragraph, that the commentary discusses such topics of day-to-day importance to practitioners as missing parts of documents, time limits, divisional applications and the compliance period. Gathering together the titles of the commentary paragraphs and presenting them in an ordered sequence highlights the underlying logical structure which has evolved, e.g. for Novelty the key issues of completeness, certainty and substance §§2.20–2.22, and it is hoped that this will also be useful for readers.

It should once again be acknowledged that the Guide is a team effort. Special thanks are due to my co-editor Richard Davis. In addition to Richard and myself, contributors in the accompanying list are acknowledged with thanks. Tibor Gold is once again to be thanked for proofreading this Supplement, as also is Matt Ashdown. The editors are, as ever, grateful for the help and encouragement of Kristiina Kojamo and the editorial team at Sweet & Maxwell, including in particular Lewis Ward, and for the support of the Chartered Institute of Patent Attorneys through its Textbooks and Publications Committee.

Paul Cole
October 2017

TABLE OF CASES

References are to section (§) numbers.
An additional table of EPO Decisions arranged in numerical order follows this Table
These decisions are also included in the Table below,
arranged under the proprietor's name.

xi

TABLE OF EPO DECISIONS

(This Table is a list of decisions of the Appeal Boards of the European Patent Office and is arranged in numerical order. When the name of the patent proprietor is given, the decisions in this Table are also included within the alphabetical listing in the main Table of Cases. The references are to section (§) numbers. Decisions marked as "Unreported" are available on the "Espace-Legal" CD-Rom produced by the EPO and, for recent decisions also on the EPO website, see http://www.epo.org

TABLE OF STATUTES

(References are to section numbers.)

TABLE OF STATUTORY INSTRUMENTS

References are to section numbers.

TABLE OF COURT RULES

(References are to section numbers.)

Ancillary Practice Directions

TABLE OF INTERNATIONAL CONVENTIONS, TREATIES AND RELATED RULES AND REGULATIONS

(References are to section numbers.)

TABLE OF EUROPEAN PATENT OFFICE GUIDELINES

(References are to section numbers.)

TABLE OF ABBREVIATIONS

(Supplementary to the Table of Abbreviations contained in the Main Work.)

BRI	BROADEST REASONABLE INTERPRETATION
CAT	COMPETITION APPEAL TRIBUNAL
CGK	COMMON GENERAL KNOWLEDGE
CJEU	COURT OF JUSTICE OF THE EUROPEAN UNION
CRO	CIVIL RESTRAINT ORDER
CVD	CHEMICAL VAPOUR DEPOSITION
EFTA	EUROPEAN FREE TRADE ASSOCIATION
FRAND	FAIR REASONABLE AND NON-DISCRIMINATORY
GCRO	GENERAL CIVIL RESTRAINT ORDER
GUI	GRAPHICAL USER INTERFACE
INN	INTERNATIONAL NONPROPRIETARY NAME
PKTWO	PROTECTING KIDS THE WORLD OVER
PSA	PROBLEM/SOLUTION ANALYSIS
PTAB	PATENT TRIAL AND APPEAL BOARD
SEP	STANDARD ESSENTIAL PATENT
TTS	TRUSTED TRANSACTION SERVER
UPC	UNIFIED PATENT COURT
USPTO	UNITED STATES PATENT AND TRADEMARK OFFICE

Patents Act 1977 (c.37)

PART I [Sections 1-76A]—NEW DOMESTIC LAW

Patentability [Sections 1-6]

SECTION 1—Patentable inventions

Add new paragraph 1.00:   **1.00**

Contents

COMMENTARY ON SECTION 1

Scope of the section

1.04   *After the nineteenth paragraph (beginning "The ramifications of Bilski, Prometheus, Myriad and particularly Alice"), add new paragraphs:*

The predictions of continuing difficulty in the US foreshadowed in the Main Work have so far proved largely correct. Developments in relation to life sciences inventions are discussed at new §76A.03A. In the domain of software and business methods it is also important that UK and European practitioners should maintain awareness of current developments. That awareness is needed both for UK or European inventions intended for future patenting in the USA and for incoming applications to the UK-IPO or to the EPO, for which an awareness of the difficulties faced by our US colleagues is important background information.

In relation to software/business method inventions developments have largely continued along existing lines with subject-matter held ineligible that would be difficult to success-fully prosecute to grant in the UK or at the EPO. However, recent cases indicate more favourable types of analysis in some instances. Leslie A. McDonell and Amanda K. Murphy, "Section 101 guidance" [2016] 10 *CIPA* 66 review guidance recently issued by the USPTO including a number of additional examples which they consider offers patent applicants a more positive outlook than previous guidance.

An objection under s.101 was rejected in *Enfish, LLC v Microsoft Corp* 822 F.3d 1327 (Fed. Cir. 2016) which concerned a self-referential database and in which the court's key reasoning is of wide significance:

> "... the first step in the *Alice* inquiry in this case asks whether the focus of the claims is on the specific asserted improvement in computer capabilities... or, instead, on a process that qualifies as an "abstract idea" for which computers are invoked merely as a tool. As noted *infra*, in *Bilski* and *Alice* and virtually all of the computer-related §101 cases we have issued in light of those Supreme Court decisions, it was clear that the claims were of the latter type—requiring that the analysis proceed to the second step of the *Alice* inquiry, which asks if nevertheless there is some inventive concept in the application of the abstract idea, see *Alice*, 134 S. Ct. at 2355, 2357.59. In this case, however, the plain focus of the claims is on an improvement to computer functionality itself, not on economic or other tasks for which a computer is used in its ordinary capacity.
>
> Accordingly, we find that the claims at issue in this appeal are not directed to an abstract idea within the meaning of *Alice*. Rather, they are directed to a specific improvement to the way computers operate..."

The court went on to warn that describing claims at a high level of abstraction all but ensures that the exceptions to s.101 swallow the rule. Neither the invention's ability to run on a general purpose computer nor the fact that the improvement was not defined by reference to "physical" components should doom the claims, otherwise there would be a risk of resurrecting the bright-line machine-or-transformation test. In conclusion the court observed that:

> "Much of the advancement made in computer technology consists of improvements to software that, by their very nature, may not be defined by particular physical features but rather by logical structures and processes. We do not see in *Bilski* or *Alice*, or our cases, an exclusion to patenting this large field of technological progress... we are not faced with a situation where general-purpose computer components are added *post-hoc* to a fundamental economic practice or mathematical equation. Rather, the claims are directed to a specific implementation of a solution to a problem in the software arts. Accordingly, we find the claims at issue are not directed to an abstract idea."

McRO, Inc v Bandai Namco Games America Inc (Fed. Cir. 2016) concerned a method for automatically animating lip synchronization and facial expression of animated characters. It was held that the ordered combination of claimed steps, using unconventional rules that related sub-sequences of phonemes, timings, and morph weight sets, was not directed to an abstract idea and was therefore patent-eligible subject-matter under s.101. In reversing the decision of the district court, the Federal Circuit held that an over-simplified interpre-tation had been adopted that failed to account for the specific requirements of the claims.

In *Iron Gate Security, Inc v Lowe's Companies, Inc* (S.D.N.Y. 2016) the court held that the first step of the *Alice* enquiry was to determine whether the claim moves beyond a long-understood concept or simply seeks to monopolize one by masking it through the medium of technology. To do this, a court must ask whether the claims are directed to a specific implementation to a solution to a problem. With regard to the second step:

> "... the objective is to determine whether the claims provide a solution to a problem, the following questions being relevant to the step two inquiry: (1) Is there an improvement recited? (2) Is there a benefit recited? (3) Is something new recited? (4) Does the patent have one or more particular applications? (5) What are the steps and limits to be followed in applying the invention?"

The defendant's high-level description of the claims was again criticised as having mischaracterized the invention, and the invention was designed to solve a problem that existed within the technological realm, rather than just implementing an abstract idea.

■ Arguably a paradigm instance of mischaracterization occurred in *Recognicorp LLC v Nintendo Co* (Fed Cir. 2017) in which the claimed method concerned creation of a composite facial image that started by selecting facial features on one display and ended with a composite image reproduced on a second display. The panel in *Recognicorp* held that the method was directed to encoding and decoding image data, both starting with data and ending with a new form of data. It is difficult to reconcile this holding with the claim language which recited a method starting and ending with displayed images. In a denied petition for *en banc* review, an amicus brief pointed out the contrast with the landmark EPO decision in T 208/84 *VICOM/Computer-related invention* and the need for the "all elements" rule of claim interpretation to be considered.

■ In contrast, positive eligibility was found for a computer memory system in *Visual Memory LLC v NVIDIA Corp* (Fed. Cir. 2017) and for accessing files in a data storage system in *Speedtrack Inc v Amazon.com* (N.D. Cal. 2017). It should nevertheless be emphasized that legacy patents issued under the practice resulting from *State Street Bank* continue to be litigated, resulting in a continuing flow of adverse eligibility decisions for computer-implemented software and business method inventions.

In drafting descriptions and claims with a view to future filing in the US, it is desirable to recite features which so far as possible fit the subject-matter positively into one or more of the statutory categories of 35 USC 101. That effort can be regarded as analogous to ensuring that the described invention is industrially applicable within the meaning of s.1(1)(c) and s.1(1)(d) of the Act and the corresponding provisions of the PCT and EPC. Readers will recall that Note 5 to TRIPS art.27 equates "useful" in US terminology with "capable of industrial application" under s.1 of the UK Act, the PCT and the EPC and that r.5.1(vi) requires that the description shall indicate explicitly, when it is not obvious from the description or nature of the invention, the way in which the invention is capable of exploitation in industry, the term "industry" being understood in its broadest sense as in the Paris Convention.

The s.101 categories likely to be relevant to software or business method inventions are "process", "machine" and "manufacture". As explained more fully in §76A.03 a process, including in this context a program to be run on a computer, is a mode of treatment of certain materials to produce a given result and is an act, or a series of acts, performed upon the subject-matter to be transformed and reduced to a different state or thing. A machine, including in this context a programmed computer, can include every mechanical device or combination of mechanical powers and devices to perform some function and produce a certain effect or result, see *Corning v Burden* 56 US 252, 267, 14 L. Ed. 683 (1854). A manufacture, explained more fully in §76A.03 and also in this context including a programmed computer, is an article produced from raw or prepared materials by giving to these materials new forms, qualities, properties, or combinations, whether by hand labour or by machinery. It follows, therefore, that (following the general analysis in *Iron Gate*) features or combinations of features helpful in fitting positively into s.101 are those which produce a useful new effect, result or quality and are of a real world transformative nature, such features also being helpful for establishing eligibility in the UK and Europe.

Computer programs—further UK opinions

1.10   *After the fourth paragraph (beginning "Gale's Application [1991] R.P.C. 305 concerned"), add new paragraph:*

The UK *Manual of Patent Examining Procedure* was updated at 1.15 in April 2015 to make it clear that it is not a single embodiment of an invention which is important when determining eligibility but the nature of the central idea or invention which is embodied in the claims, and whether it comprises an advance that lies in a non-excluded field. On the reasoning in *Merrill Lynch's Application* [1989] R.P.C. 561 at [569] and in *Bloomberg LLP and Cappellini's Applications* [2007] EWHC 476 (Pat) at [9] merely including claims to a program or a program in a computer or on a carrier such as a compact disc ("*Beauregard* claims") will not make an otherwise excluded invention patentable. However, such claims are considered allowable where corresponding method and apparatus claims (or notional such claims if none exist) would be allowable on application of the *Aerotel/Macrossan* test. Thus claims to a computer program for generating a system or for producing a product e.g. of the form: "a computer program comprising computer-readable code for generating a system as claimed in X" or "storage medium having encoded thereon code for making a system as claimed in Y" or "machine-readable medium having software thereon to produce the item of claim Z on a 3D printer") will not normally be allowable unless, following *Astron Clinica*, the computer program would cause an otherwise patentable process to be performed when run.

Add new paragraphs at end:

The Boeing Company's Application BL O/312/15 concerned a maintenance procedure for aircraft in which an individual component was identified as a rogue component by generating an operating parameter from a history of health management data, the data being linked to a specific component using a unique identifier scanned from the component, and by determining if the operating parameter deviated from a baseline operating parameter, which was representative of components of the same type. The contribution was the application to aircraft system maintenance of known analytical techniques for identifying potentially faulty components and of the use of known scanning procedures to track those components. The contribution was not in the analysis of data and the subsequent identification of potentially faulty parts, but in the application of these techniques to aircraft maintenance procedures. The aircraft system was not part of the computer since the maintenance of an aircraft system was a process carried out outside the computer and the identification of potentially faulty parts had an effect on that process including extending the life of the aircraft and improving the safety of the aircraft which were technical effects. The identified contribution was therefore technical and was not a computer program as such. The application was subsequently ordered to be granted, see BL O/026/16.

The above decision may be contrasted with *Hitachi Ltd's Application* BL O/597/15 which concerned simulating movements of, and planning timetables for, trains. In this case, there was no application of data analysis and no direct controlling link between the timetables and the actual movement of trains. That would not be changed by adding a feature of implementing the new timetable by instructing trains to move accordingly, as was proposed in an auxiliary request. There was a fundamental disconnect between a timetable and the movement of trains that may be moved according to that timetable. The latter may well be technical but it was concluded that the former is the output of a program for a computer as such. Both of the patents in issue fell within the computer program exception.

The Boeing Company's Application BL O/002/16 concerned a computer-based system and method for estimating the cost of moving fuel from one location to another using vehicles and associated personnel. The technical contribution was held to be a tool including a graphical user interface (GUI) for enabling an operator to estimate the costs involved in using various combinations of vehicles and associated personnel to move a quantity of fuel from one location to another including, if necessary, specifying design options for new vehicles to help perform the task, which tool was configured to warn the user if the user input did not meet vehicle ability parameters and safety requirements. Any "warning" function provided in this invention was more an input verification step and different from the sort of alarm-generating function that was at the heart of the invention in *Protecting Kids the World Over* (PKTWO) so that this case differed from PKTWO on the facts. The invention fell squarely in excluded matter as a computer-implemented business method, the task performed by the computer program being a logistical activity of the sort found to be excluded in *Cappellini* [2007] EWHC 476 (Pat). None of the signposts pointed to the existence of any technical contribution and accordingly the application was refused.

Intuit Inc's Application BL O/023/16 concerned a programming system that enabled users to group certain computer program modules with related functionality together so that they could be used as a group and/or shared with other users. Once a group had been created the user could reopen all the modules together without having to activate them individually and make the links between them. The Hearing Officer found that the contribution of the invention related entirely to a computer program, as such and the application was refused.

In *Emerson Process Management Power and Water Solutions Inc's Applications* BL O124/16 a parent and divisional application were considered, with both applications relating to the provision of better abstract models of a process control system by determining compensation and error models. The contributions were found not to extend beyond the abstract models per se and hence were excluded as computer programs.

In *Fisher-Rosemount Systems Inc's Application* BL O/320/16 a contribution whereby process control routines were effectively tested during normal operation while an associated process was running was held to be a program for a computer as such, and the application refused.

A user interface related invention was considered in *Micro Focus IP Development Ltd's Applications* BL O/136/16. Two applications, one parent and one divisional, were considered, both entitled "Interfacing systems and methods". The parent application described a system for extracting text-based information from a host computer system using a rules-based configuration of components to determine, combine and present visual control objects, such as selection boxes, tables and location information within a graphical user interface. This "emulation" of the underlying host application was achieved without changing the host code or infrastructure. The divisional application additionally displayed the user interface on remote devices using web sockets for asynchronous communication over a network. Whilst neither application was found to relate to the presentation of information, both were instead refused because they related only to a program for a computer as such.

Apple Inc's Application BL O/137/16 concerned linking a software application that is pre-installed on a client device with a user account. The claimed method was concerned with the problem of managing updates and installations of applications that had been pre-installed on a device. It entailed a server verifying that the installed application was distributable by the server and verifying that the application had not been previously linked. The latter step was carried out by retrieving a unique identifier from metadata associated with the installed application, the metadata being stored at the server, and verifying that the unique identifier had not been associated with any user account. Following verification, the application was linked to a user account which configured downloads, re-downloads and updates to one or more client devices associated with the user account. In the outcome, it was held that the application did not make a technical improvement in the installation and updating of applications, but instead was an administrative improvement in the way the installation and updating of applications was managed which merely circumvented problems of usability. The subject-matter therefore fell within the computer program and business method exclusions.

A further circumvention case is *Lionel Wolovitz's Application* BL O353/16. The invention concerned a system and method for brokering a transaction, for example a money transaction, between a first party and a second party by use of a trusted transaction server (TTS). The system was arranged so that the two parties did not need to share sensitive information with each other via a non-secure channel, such as the internet. Instead each party was authenticated with the TTS via a trusted communication channel, and only a non-sensitive transaction code was passed directly between the parties via the non-secure channel, the TTS then brokering the transaction. Refusing the application on the ground that the invention was no more than a computer program per se, the Hearing Officer concluded that the contribution made by the invention lay not in providing a new or more secure system or network overall, but instead in the protocol defining the order in which the information was exchanged, thereby circumventing, rather than solving, the identified problems with passing sensitive data over a non-secure channel.

The contribution in *Blyk Services Oy's Application* BL O/253/16 was held to be a multimedia message delivery platform configured to inform the user or users of wireless communication devices of the availability of multimedia content by a notification message sent via a short messaging service centre, to receive a request for the multimedia content from a user device via a response message and provide either the requested or alternative multimedia content to the user device on the basis of when the response message was received. No technical contribution could be discerned and the application was refused on the basis of the computer program and business method exclusions, although the alternative objection of lack of inventive step was not made out.

In *Validsoft UK Ltd's Application* BL O/291/16 the contribution was held to be a method of authenticating a transaction in which user location information was received by a computer server, separate from the mobile network, from an application operating on the user's mobile device in response to a change of location of that mobile device, and a request for authenticating a point of sale or ATM transaction including transaction location information was received from an authentication server. The received location information was compared and the generated authentication data was communicated to the authentication server. The method provided for quicker authentication than obtaining location information from the mobile network. However, any increase in speed was not the result of the computer itself being quicker in the sense it was in *Symbian* or *Gale*. It did not come from the solution of a technical problem within the computer or system but rather from changing what the system was doing, more particularly changing the process so that location information was not obtained from the normal communication network but rather from a separate server which was fed the information by an application on the mobile device. The invention differed from *Lantana* or *Gemstar* because authenticating financial transactions was not a technical field. The computer here was not operating more efficiently or effectively: instead it was operating in much the same way as before albeit it was being asked to do something different. Accordingly, the application was excluded as a computer program or business method.

An invention relating to reducing the computation time needed to transform data sources into an object model using a transformation script which initially included errors was considered in *Palantir Technologies Inc's Application* BL O/309/16. The result was achieved by providing validation notices as the errors arose when the transformation script was run, so that a user or developer could then fix the error in the transformation script before running the transformation script again. The Hearing Officer found the contribution to relate to a computer program as such. In *Palantir Technologies, Inc's Application* BL O/358/16 three applications that related to selecting data records from a data set by matching attributes of the data were considered. In particular, one of the applications related to a method for selecting, from a larger dataset, a subset of records that were related to a common entity by using a classifier which produced a matching probability value for each record in the larger dataset, and comparing the probability value to a set threshold. The other applications related to methods of comparing every record in a dataset with each of the other records, the comparison made only for selected attributes of each record. In all three cases the claimed methods were said to be particularly suited for very large datasets. All three inventions were found by the Hearing Officer to relate solely to excluded matter, namely to computer programs as such. The applications were refused.

6

■ Often an excluded invention will fall into two or more of the exceptions, in which case the Comptroller will refuse an application therefor on the plural grounds. However, there remain those cases where the only exclusion that can be made to apply is the computer program *as such* exclusion. Recent UK cases where applications were refused solely for being a computer program as such include *Fisher-Rosemount Systems Inc's Application* BL O/320/16, *Palantir Technologies Inc's Applications* BL O/358/16 and BL O/259/17, *Kube Partner's Ltd's Application* BL O/193/17, *Cadio Inc's Application* BL O/297/17, *Ford Global Technologies, Inc's Application* BL O/299/17, and *Thoughtwire Holdings Corp's Application* BL O/349/17. Whilst the decisions on such cases turn on the facts of the inventions, there are some cases where the negative decision on patentable subject-matter is a matter of a very fine judgment—*Cloudera Inc's Application* BL O/440/16 relating to a method of performing queries on stored data in a distributed computing environment which provided the benefits of both known "schema-on-read" and "schema-on-write" (previously alternatives to each other) in one system being one such example.

Computer programs—further EPO opinions

Add new paragraphs at end: **1.11**

In T 1370/11 *MICROSOFT/On-demand property system* the Board held that the argument that a computer program or computer-implemented method is inventive because it is faster than an earlier one is on its own insufficient to establish an inventive step. More specifically, the improved speed of a computer program is not by itself a technical contribution to the art, and because the computing time does not contribute to the technical character of the computer program, it cannot support the presence of inventive step of a corresponding computer-implemented method.

Case T 543/14 *APPLE/Touch interface configuration* concerned a portable electronic device having a touch sensitive display and a stored program. The Appeal Board noted that providing a visual indication of technical conditions of a machine is a technical feature, according to the case law of the boards of appeal (see T 528/07 *ACCENTURE/ Portal System*, T 781/10 *SAMSUNG/Portable device and method of providing menu items* and T 887/12 *RECKITT/Hydrophobic stain remover*). It further held that features recited in the main claim were not related to a computer program as such but rather to a user's gestural interactions with the portable electronic device and the subsequent specific response of the device, and therefore had a technical character, citing inter alia T 0781/10, T 1900/09 *SYNAPTICS/Object position detector* and T 852/10 *RESEARCH IN MOTION/Detecting user-selected input*. In particular, the following features were technical:

- instructions for, in the normal mode of operation, activating an application by tapping on an icon at a first location on the touch-sensitive display;
- instructions for, in response to detecting the first finger contact on the application icon at the first location held for more than the predefined time-period, initiating a predefined user interface reconfiguration mode, distinct from the normal mode of operation, that allows a user to reposition one or more displayed application icons;
- instructions for detecting movement of the first finger contact from the first position on the touch-sensitive display to a second position on the touch-sensitive display while in the interface reconfiguration mode;
- instructions for, in response to detecting movement of the first finger contact from the first position on the touch-sensitive display to the second position on the touch-sensitive display while in the interface reconfiguration mode, moving the application icon to the second position on the touch-sensitive display;
- instructions for detecting a second predefined user action, separate from the first predefined user action, after moving the first application icon to the second position on the touch sensitive display; and
- instructions for, in response to detecting the second predefined user action, fixing a

7

position of the application icon at the second position, and terminating the user interface reconfiguration mode.

The Opposition Division took the view in T 485/11 *DIESSE/Identification of sample containers* that labelling of a sample container at the stage of production or packaging was merely an administrative measure devoid of any technical aspects and should thus not be taken into consideration in assessing inventive step. The Appeal Board noted that the identification code contained data relating to the type of analysis for which the container was intended, so that placing it at the time of production or packaging could prevent a medical operator at the time of use from choosing a container which could be inappropriate for the intended analysis of a patient sample. Therefore, this feature could be considered as a technical feature solving the technical problem of avoiding label misplacement with respect to the kind of container to be used for a given type of analysis.

■ In T 339/13 *IMMERSION/Interacting with virtual pets*, the Board accepted as a technical problem in the context of virtual pets achieving the reliable and reproducible perception of a physical interaction with a real pet. It also accepted that the problem had been solved by technical features of the device interface. These were a reciprocating cursor movement and haptic feedback.

—Scheme, rule or method for doing business—UK opinions

1.12   *Add new paragraphs at end:*

In *BAE Systems Plc's Applications* BL O/111/16 three applications relating to improvements to energy management systems used on sites which were connected to a power grid but also had their own on on-site power sources were considered together. The various claims related to methods and associated apparatus to more efficiently manage power production and distribution based on criteria associated with each discrete producer and consumer in the network. The Hearing Officer found the contributions to be computer implemented business methods which were not technical in nature.

■ Additional cases where applications were refused because the invention was considered to be a method of doing business include *Validsoft UK Ltd's Application* BL O/291/16, *Blyk Services Oy's Application* BL O/253/16, *Apple Inc's Application* BL O/137/16, and *The Boeing Company's Application* BL O/002/16, all discussed at §1.10. More recent decisions include *The Boeing Company's Application* BL O/392/16, *Lim's Application* BL O/465/16, *Global Analytics Inc's Application* BL O/535/16, *Ohlson's Application* BL O/565/16, *Trillium Technology AB's Application* BL O/210/17, *Barclay's Bank Plc's Application* BL O/268/17, and *Geodesixs Inc's Application* BL O/344/17, all of which were refused for being both methods for doing business and computer programs. For recent examples of cases where applications were refused for being business methods only, *Synchronous Technologies Inc's Application* BL O/528/16, *Tata Consultancy Services Ltd's Application* BL O/255/17, and *Hay's Application* BL O/276/17 provide examples.

■ An application where the claimed subject-matter was a mixture of technical and non-technical features was considered in T 1463/11 *CARDINAL COMMERCE/Universal merchant platform* which was concerned with online shopping. Customer identification was conventionally by means of "plug-ins" which were pieces of software in the merchant server specific to the particular authenticating authority and to the needs of the authentication process, there being a plug-in for each of the different means of payment, e.g. for each type of credit-card and for each direct transfer from a particular bank. The invention was to install the plug-ins no longer in each online shop but in a central server accessible by several online shops, thereby relieving the shop's server from the installation and upkeep of the plug-ins. It was held that there were technical considerations that spoke against relocating the plug-ins and that established a prima facie case for technical prejudice against relocating the plug-ins to a centralised server. These were the potential for an increase in latency, possible reductions in the number of transactions that could be processed in a given time period, and the increase in the number of points at which communications could be subject to hacking. Accordingly, there was nothing that stood in the way of grant of a European patent.

—Presentation of information

After the thirteenth paragraph (beginning "In HTC Europe v Apple [2012] EWHC **1.15**
1789 (Pat)"), add new paragraphs:

■ *Fisher Rosemount Systems Inc's Applications* considered in BL O/490/16 and BL
O/146/17, both related to displaying process control information for a control plant, but in
both cases the Hearing Officer found the inventions to relate to no more than a presentation of information as well as a computer program as such. In contrast, *Bennett's Application* BL O/361/17, discussed at §1.16, gives an example of an invention that is ineligible
for being a presentation of information and an aesthetic creation.

■ *Fisher Rosemount Systems Inc's Application* had a different result in BL O/246/17,
however. In this case the contribution was assessed to be a process plant display and
control system which provided a user configurable display, editable during runtime,
wherein control of the process plant was dependent upon process plant data received at
user configured portions of the display. The Hearing Officer considered such a contribution to provide a "direct link" between information being displayed to an operator on the
screen and the operator then generating (either manually or automatically) updated control
data which is then transmitted to the process plant in order to control the plant. The
provision of such a "direct link" meant that the invention was really concerned with direct
control of a process plant, which direct control the Hearing Officer had no doubt was
technical in nature, and hence the objection of excluded subject-matter was overcome.

■ A 3D radar sampling system used to continuously monitor and statistically character-
ize the airborne target activity within a surveillance volume for aviation safety and security
was considered in *Accipiter Radar Technologies Inc's Application* BL O/390/17, the
system including an airborne-bird activity illustrator which statistically characterized bird
activity in the airspace for users, allowing them at a glance to understand and appreciate a
new hazardous situation. The contribution was held to be in a 3D radar system which
provided information unavailable from prior systems and although involving the presentation of this information to its users, was not limited to that presentation per se but instead
extended to the capture and generation of this information as a whole. Similarly, although
the invention relied on a computer program for its realization, the contribution made by
the invention went beyond that. Accordingly, the application was remitted to the Examiner
for completion of the examination process. Another case with a similar outcome is found
in T 651/12 *XANAVI Informatics/Map database device* in which ergonomics, understood
as the applied science of refining the design of products to optimize them for human use,
was held to be a technical field in the context of a map display, and displaying a
three-dimensional bird's-eye view map was thus considered to provide a technical solution
to a technical problem. In the present case, the three-dimensional bird's-eye view did not
provide merely a more orderly or appealing presentation of map data, but a presentation
which was ergonomically adapted to the needs of the user, e.g. a driver of a car.

■ Further ergonomics-related decisions have also been handed down. In T 862/10
MICROSOFT/Notification system it was held that choosing the location of a display object
depending on the urgency of the message was non-technical and hence did not contribute
an inventive step. However, using sound localization methods to localize an audio signal
associated with the display object in a position at or near the location of the physical
rendering of the display object solved the objective problem of making it easier for the
user quickly to locate the position of the display object on the display screen. Both the
problem and the means to solve it were considered technical since they did not depend on
psychological or other subjective factors but on technical parameters (based, inter alia, on
human physiology) that could be precisely defined. In T 2461/11 *INNOVATIVE
SOLUTIONS & SUPPORT/Facilitating entry of manually-adjustable data* the problem
faced by the skilled person was that a pilot having to enter manually-adjustable data
settings imaged on a display in an aircraft cockpit had to devote unusual attention to
entering the desired setting in order to avoid inadvertent, potentially disastrous errors.
Enlarging the image of the data setting on the display, maintaining the enlarged image and

reducing the enlarged image as defined in dependence of the sensed manipulation of a control by the user credibly assisted the pilot and contributed a technical solution to the technical problem.

■ Similarly, T 690/11 *BAXTER/Dialysis system* related to an automated peritoneal dialysis system configured to display a plurality of dialysis therapy set-up procedure screens that required an operator input, and to display a plurality of dialysis treatment screens that graphically illustrated the progress of the dialysis therapy in real time. The Board held that the claimed display of set-up procedure screens and treatment screens related to the interaction between the system and the operator and hence implied technical means for the transmission and handling of respective signals contributing to the correct operation of the system, which related to the internal state of the system and conferred a technical character on the claimed features.

—Aesthetic creations: literary, dramatic, musical or artistic works

1.16   *After the third paragraph (beginning "The invention in Milliken and Co's Application BL O/498/12"), add new paragraphs:*

■ Another case where an application was refused for being an aesthetic creation only (without also being a computer program, for example) is *Bennett's Application* BL O/361/17. In this case the inventor claimed a new form of eyewear in the form of "shutter glasses" where the lenses are replaced by horizontal strut members. The glasses had oversized wings upon which specific logos or branding could be applied. The prior art showed shutter glasses with similar oversized wings, but without the logos or branding thereon. The Hearing Officer therefore assessed the contribution as being the application of logos or branding to parts of otherwise conventional shutter glasses, and found that such a contribution was both an aesthetic creation and a presentation of information.

■ An invention relating to a fusible bead toy based on beads of transparent water-soluble resin and a bead tray with indentations slightly smaller than the bead size so that the beads contacted one another was considered in *Epoch Co Ltd v Character Options Ltd* [2017] EWHC 556 (IPEC). In use, water was sprayed on so that the beads fused to one another and when dry formed a block of beads melded together to form an image. It was held, following T 686/90 *HETTLING-DENKER/Translucent building materials* [2004] E.P.O.R. 5 and distinguishing *Gram Engineering Pty Ltd's Application* BL O/275/08 that the contribution to the art in the present case could also reasonably be described as an aesthetic effect imparted by a fusible bead toy but not an ineligible aesthetic creation.

—Scheme, rule or method for playing a game

1.20   *Add new paragraph at end:*

■ *Curtis' Application* BL O/260/17 and *Anderson's Application* BL O/298/17 are both examples where the Hearing Officer found the contribution to relate to the rules for playing a game per se, and hence refused the applications.

SECTION 2—Novelty

2.00   *Add new paragraph 2.00:*

Contents

The state of the art (subss.(1)–(2))

—Documents in public places and/or that can be inspected as of right—Internet Publications

After the thirteenth paragraph (beginning "Operation of the EPO standard of proof "up to the hilt" is illustrated"), add new paragraph: **2.04**

■ For a recent review of the standard of proof in relation to internet publications see T 545/08 *ORACLE INTERNATIONAL/Change capture for data warehousing* in which the correctness of the explanation in the *EPO Guidelines* G-IV, 7.5.2 was affirmed that the standard is not mere probability but conviction that the publication date is correct. In the present case, the cited document had been retrieved more than 18 months after the application date, it was not self-evident that disclosure must have happened before that date e.g. from the reliability of the website or information in the document itself, and no explanation was given why the document was considered to have been made available before that date. The Examining Division simply relied on a date "January 2002" appearing on the front page of the retrieved document, but this date was imprecise and unqualified, and the commercial website from which it was retrieved was not a source generally deemed to provide reliable publication dates. There was therefore no prima facie evidence to rely on, and the Examining Division was not entitled to rely on that document as prior art. A similar fact pattern occurred in T 526/12 *NUANCE/Method for creating dictation macros*, in which the alleged prior publication was a downloaded internal manual of a university and bore a date which appeared to be a date of author's revision rather than a publication date. Its unfinished nature suggested that it had not been intended for publication.

Add new paragraph at end:
■ Time of publication was critical in *Unwired Planet International Ltd v Huawei Technologies Co Ltd* [2015] EWHC 3366 (Pat). The priority document was filed in the USPTO on 8 January 2008. The frame of reference of the USPTO was the correct one, i.e. Eastern Standard Time. The reference relied on was made available to the public at 02.36 on 8 January 2008 EST and was therefore not made available to the public before the priority date. The fact that at the same instant the date was still 7 January in other places in the world such as Hawaii was irrelevant. This decision was affirmed [2017] EWCA Civ 266, holding [161] that a publication is not part of the state of the art unless it was published before the priority date, which is the 24-hour period of the day on which filing took place in the time zone of the patent office where it was filed. The publication must occur before that day, on a time basis, by reference to the time zone of the patent office of filing. Simultaneous filings in the US and Japan simply illustrate that the two filings give different windows of protection against prior publication. That is inevitable in the date-based system for actual prior publications under art.54(2), for which a time-based system would have created other difficulties. Policy considerations differ as between art.54(2) and art.54(3) which deals with deemed publication, so that no question of a document in fact being made available in different time zones can arise.

Prior public use

2.07   *In the second paragraph, after the sentence ending "... since nobody had the opportunity of stopping the cars and asking to look at them.", add:*
■ A similar fact pattern arose in T 1410/14 *SIEMENS/Passenger transport vehicle* with a similar outcome.

After the tenth paragraph (beginning "In PCME v Goyen Controls [1999] F.S.R. 801"), add new paragraph:
■ An argument that a commercially available computer program was effectively a "black box" not revealing the underlying algorithms was rejected in T 2440/12 *SIMCON/Fluid flow simulation* in which, *before* the filing date of the opposed patent, Simcon had already commercialised its software product Cadmould. As defendant in patent infringement proceedings in Germany, Simcon planned to disclose the method embodied in the Cadmould software in order to demonstrate that it was based on its own development and did not infringe the appellant's patent. Since the respondent did not wish that the disclosed information be unprotected, it decided to file its own application which resulted in the opposed patent. However, the Board held that any interested person who acquired Cadmould and used it for the purpose for which it was commercialised automatically executed the method steps as defined the patent, which was novelty-destroying. Simcon argued that disassembly of the program as sold would only result in a low-level language output which would not have conveyed to a skilled person the subject-matter now being claimed. In rejecting this argument, the Board held that what the skilled person obtained from a disassembled code or from the stepwise execution of a software product was an "alternative" description, albeit very concrete and detailed (= low-level), of the method embodied by the software. If the machine code of the software could be translated into human-readable language, the two representations of the method should, in principle, be considered as two different forms of disclosure of the same method which were equally available to the public.

After the eighteenth paragraph (beginning "A general statement of the standard of proof required"), add new paragraph:
In T 2451/13 *NUTRICIA/Sensoric imprinting* it was held that if the publication date of a

document originating from an opponent was in dispute, although the onus on the opponent was proof "up to the hilt" that yardstick was "beyond reasonable doubt" rather than "absolute certainty".

The requirement for a novelty-destroying disclosure to have an "enabling" character

To the end of the ninth paragraph (beginning "The doctrine of non-enablement has so far been applied"), add: **2.09**

■ The *ICI/Pyridine herbicides* decision was followed in T 719/12 *LONZA/Beta-amino alcohols* in which it was reaffirmed that a compound disclosed by name in prior art was not available to the public when no method for its preparation was available at publication date of that prior art. The cited document merely postulated the relevant compound as a potential theoretical product of a Mannich reaction or the steam distillation of the corresponding tertiary amine, but categorically stated that said compound could neither be isolated nor obtained when said reactions were actually carried out, in spite of the use of conditions which were considered favourable for its formation. The Board held that in view of this categorical statement the skilled person, at the date of publication of the cited document would not have seriously contemplated repeating its teaching in order to undertake further investigations as to whether the compound was formed after all, and that an experimental repetition by opponents involved additional steps resulting from ex post facto considerations. If the compound had been produced in crude form but its presence remained undetected by a skilled person, that would not suffice to make it available to the public. A similar finding was also made more recently in T 437/14 *THE TRUSTEES OF PRINCETON UNIVERSITY AND THE UNIVERSITY OF SOUTHERN CALIFORNIA/ Complexes of form L2IrX*, the relevant compound being a transient intermediate postulated in a prior art document, but not a discrete product that disappeared only after a further step was taken, it then not being relevant whether the skilled person had any particular reason to stop the process at that point; see also T 327/92 *ALLIED SIGNAL/Oriented film laminates* (monoaxially stretched laminate existing for only 60 seconds before being converted to biaxially stretched laminate; citable) and T 392/06 *CIBA/Triazinylaminostilbene* (intermediate slurry prior to washing and drying; citable).

Add new paragraph at end:

In *Hospira UK Ltd v Cubist Pharmaceuticals LLC* [2016] EWHC 1285 (Pat) the claimed subject-matter was the use of daptomycin for the manufacture of a medicament for treating bacterial infection using a particular dosage regime. After the earliest priority date but before a second subsequent priority date, the patentees issued a press release indicating that patients in Phase III clinical trials would receive a dose of daptomycin within the specified range. It transpired that the claimed subject-matter was not entitled to that earliest date, so that the press release was a citable document and the issue under s.2 became whether it amounted to an anticipation. The defendants argued that the requirement for disclosure of efficacy had been met because the fact that the Phase III trials were taking place indicated that efficacy must have been demonstrated in earlier Phase II trials. However, it was held that this point was relevant to obviousness, see §3.30, but was not sufficient to establish anticipation. The therapeutic effect was a functional technical feature of the claim and should be taken into account when assessing its novelty, see *Regeneron Pharmaceuticals Inc & Bayer Pharma AG v Genentech Inc* [2013] EWCA Civ 93; [2013] R.P.C. 28 at [56], T 609/02 *SALT INSTITUTE/AP-1 complex* and *Hospira v Genentech* [2015] EWHC 1796. The objection of anticipation should not succeed because the press release was forward-looking and did not disclose that the clinical trials had actually taken place or that the proposed treatment was effective.

2.18   *After the eleventh paragraph (beginning "Parts of a document may not be arbitrarily isolated"), add new paragraph:*

■ A further instance in which novelty was established over an apparent earlier publication on the ground that the earlier drawings were no more than schematic illustrations and not necessarily to scale is found in T 205/14 *FRANKISCHE ROHWERKE /Publication of relative dimensions in drawings*, citing T 204/83 *CHARBONNAGES/Venturi* and T 748/91 *MIBA/Composite plain bearings.*

—Completeness as a necessary attribute of anticipation

2.20   *To the end of the first paragraph, add:*

■ It was explained in *Edwards Lifesciences LLC v Boston Scientific Scimed Inc* [2017] EWHC 405 (Pat) at [139] that: "It is not essential that an item of prior art should expressly disclose all the features of an invention for that prior art to deprive the invention of novelty. It may be that one or more integers are disclosed by inference. But this must be an inevitable inference drawn by the skilled person reading the prior art." If the prior art allows even for the possibility that its performance would not result in the claimed invention, it will not deprive that invention of novelty, see *Synthon BV v SmithKline Beecham Plc (No.2)* [2005] UKHL 59; [2006] R.P.C. 10 at [22], [23].

■ In the EPO, an approach consistent with settled law e.g. as explained in T 312/94 *PHILIPS/Reactive ion etching* was adopted in T 1658/12 *ZITO/User-specific dispensing*, in which the Board explained [3.8]:

"In determining what is made available to the public within the meaning of Article 54(2) EPC by a prior art patent document, such as International Application D2, it must be borne in mind that it is the description which chiefly serves to disclose the invention in a manner that it may be carried out, whereas the chief function of the claims is to define the subject-matter for which protection is sought. Where a combination of features is found only in the claims (or only in the claims and a "Summary of the Invention" which merely recites the features of the claims), it must be very carefully considered whether this combination truly corresponds to the technical teaching of the document as it would be understood by a skilled person, or whether it is merely an artefact of the claim drafting process aimed at obtaining maximal scope of protection.

This applies all the more in the case of unexamined applications such as document D2."

—Certainty as a necessary attribute of anticipation

2.21   *After the first paragraph, add new paragraphs:*

The relative standards of proof needed to show firstly that it was likely that prior art would be set up in a particular way to achieve a specified result or secondly that the prior art being set up in a particular way a specified result would be achieved was considered in *Actavis Group PTC EHF v ICOS Corp & Eli Lilly and Co* [2016] EWHC 1955 (Pat). Cases considering the standard of proof in the former situation include *General Tire & Rubber Co Ltd v Firestone Tyre & Rubber Co Ltd (No.1)* [1972] R.P.C 457, *Inhale v Quadrant* [2002] R.P.C. 21 and *Synthon v SmithKline Beecham* [2005] UKHL 59; [2006] R.P.C. 10. Birss J agreed with Laddie J in *Inhale* that even if it was overwhelmingly likely that an experiment would be set up in such a way that the result achieved would be within a patent claim, that was not enough for anticipation. That followed as a matter of principle and was what the word "inevitable" was seeking to exclude. The result might be obvious but if the issue was anticipation by novelty-only art that was of no significance. That situation should be contrasted with the situation in *Actavis v Janssen* [2008] EWHC 1422; [2008] F.S.R. 35 in which Floyd J had to decide if a product would have the relevant property, held that it was overwhelmingly likely that it would and then said that in this situation the court should be concerned to establish what on the balance of probabilities would in fact occur, the inevitable result test not requiring proof to a quasi-criminal standard. Birss J explained [401] that:

> "If a claim covers something which is the truly inevitable result of carrying out a prior teaching then that claim is monopolizing something which was available to the skilled person without any knowledge contributed by the inventors. It makes sense that the public should not have to worry about such a patent. It lacks novelty. However when a skilled person is given the patent, they have a new teaching and a new goal in view. Knowledge of that goal is likely to influence how they follow the teaching in the document. Even if they miss the target on the first shot, the patent has told them where to aim and, with straightforward trials and knowledge of the goal, they may reach the target. If so then the invention will still have been sufficiently disclosed even if the first shot at putting the invention into practice may be wide of the mark."

In the present case, the question was whether a composition made to a particular particle size necessarily had the claimed pharmacokinetics. Evidence established that it was highly likely that it would, and the relevant claim therefore lacked novelty.

Add new paragraph at end:
■ Novelty for a range overlapping the prior art but not involving a conventional selection situation was considered in *Jushi Group v OCV Intellectual Capital* [2017] EWHC 171 (IPEC) 68. A spectrum of possibilities could be envisaged. The smaller the overlap, the more likely it was that this part of the prior art disclosure was "so submerged in it as not to be available", see *H Lundbeck A/S v Norpharma SpA* [2011] EWHC 907 (Pat); [2011] R.P.C. 23 at [88](b) and T 666/89 *UNILEVER/Washing Composition* [1992] E.P.O.R. 501, 507. In the present case, the TBA criterion of "serious contemplation" would be adopted and it was observed that:

> "If a party wishes to argue that a patent lacks novelty pursuant to the application of the 'serious contemplation' criterion, it must provide evidence of the relevant overall area of overlap, not in terms of the nearest percentage necessarily, but enough to give the court a sufficiently accurate impression of where it is and how large it is. This may best be done in the Grounds of Invalidity. Then in the normal course expert evidence will be directed to whether the skilled person would seriously contemplate using the information disclosed in the prior art to perform the invention in that identified area of overlap. The party alleging invalidity bears both the legal and evidential burden of proof."

In the outcome, that burden was not met and lack of novelty was not established.

—Novelty of purpose

To the end of the eighth paragraph (beginning "The Board held in T 1049/99 L'OREAL/ **2.23**
Composition cosmétique filtrante"), add:
■ Similarly, in T 151/13 *BLUE CUBE/Conversion process* it was held that the purpose of a particular reagent in a known chemical process is not a functional technical feature in the sense of G 2/88 and does not render said process novel, the additional information not teaching the skilled person to do anything over and above what is already disclosed and not being a new use which exploits the relevant discovery for some new technical purpose.

Selection inventions

To the end of the seventh paragraph (beginning "The EPO approach to selection **2.24**
inventions is set out in EPO Guidelines"), add:
The correctness of the two-list principle, at least under UK law, was doubted in *Gareth Kevin Glass v Freyssinet Ltd* [2015] EWHC 2972 (IPEC) where it was observed that if, for instance, a single prior art document discloses two lists of constituents and states clearly and unambiguously that any one from the first list may be combined with any one from the second list, then this is exactly the same disclosure as setting out all possible combinations seriatim in a single list. In any event, the court was bound by *Ranbaxy UK*

Ltd v Warner-Lambert Co [2006] EWCA Civ 876; [2007] R.P.C. 4, at [36]–[41] where there had been a finding of lack of novelty despite a first selection of one of three listed optical isomers and a second selection of one of seven pharmaceutically acceptable metal salts, alighting on the claimed compound being merely one of the alternatives explicitly taught by the cited art and not a case of any adaptation of it. The important question in determining whether a combination from within a single item of prior art deprives a subsequent claim to that combination of novelty was whether there is clear and unambiguous teaching, taking the prior art as a whole, that the relevant combination could be made. The question was left open what was the necessary number of alternatives, presented as a single list or unambiguously signalled combinations, consistently with the law on selection inventions for none of them to be deemed individually disclosed.

■ In *Jushi Group v OCV Intellectual Capital* [2017] EWHC 171 (IPEC) 68 which involved overlapping ranges, only that part which was involved in overlap could be a selection invention, the remainder being novel in a conventional sense. The cited document provided no individualised description of any product falling within the claims of the patent. The claimed products had a technical advantage. The overlapping subject-matter could therefore be characterised as a selection invention, both being novel and involving an inventive step.

SECTION 3—Inventive step

3.00 *Add new paragraph 3.00:*

Contents

COMMENTARY ON SECTION 3

Introduction and background

—Historical development of the concept of obviousness—tests used by the UK and US within the common law and problem/solution analysis (PSA) used by the EPO

At new paragraph at end: 3.04

It will be recalled that in *HTC v Apple* [2012] EWHC 1789 (Pat); [2013] EWCA Civ 451 a patent covering the "slide to unlock" switch feature found in iPhones and involving detecting contact with a touch-sensitive display of a portable electronic device while the device is in a user interface lock state and unlocking the device by moving an unlock image along a predefined displayed path on the touch-sensitive display in accordance with the contact was held to be invalid for lack of inventive step. A contrary conclusion was reached on the equivalent US patent by the Court of Appeal for the Federal Circuit in an *en banc* opinion in *Apple v Samsung* (7 October 2016). The fact that the same key prior art was relied on in both jurisdictions makes comparison of the evidence adduced and the consequential legal reasoning particularly relevant, as also is the fact, noted in the dissenting opinion of Judge Dyk, that this was the first time that the Federal Circuit had considered an obviousness case *en banc* in the 26 years since *In re Dillon* 919 F.2d 688 (1990) so that the importance of this recent decision ranks second only to the Supreme Court opinions in *Graham* and *KSR*. The problem with which the invention was concerned was to provide a user-friendly solution to accidental activation of mobile touchscreen devices (e.g., "pocket dialling"), the claimed solution being to provide an unlock image as a graphical user interface object which a user moves from a first predefined location on the touchscreen to a predefined unlock region. Although technical considerations and expert evidence featured in both the UK and the US opinions, see §3.06, those in the UK focused more closely on the expert reports (that of the defendant's expert being considered the more credible), whereas the contrary US opinion of the panel majority was supported by detailed secondary evidence including long-felt but unmet need, industry praise, copying, and commercial success, see the discussion of this case at §§3.32 and 3.33. As explained in the Main Work at §3.39, following the dictum in *Glaverbel SA v British Coal* [1995] R.P.C. 155 CA that secondary evidence should be kept in its place there has been a tendency to treat such evidence as of lower probative value and to adduce it with caution. However, its value in appropriate cases is apparent e.g. from *Haberman v Jackel International* [1999] F.S.R. 683 and from the Federal Circuit decision here. It is interesting to speculate whether if some or indeed more of the secondary evidence adduced in the US had also found its way into the UK proceedings the relatively dismissive opinions both at first instance and on appeal would have been modified and a different outcome reached, the hindsight approach of the UK courts being difficult to reconcile with the contemporaneous audience applause for the claimed feature at the iPhone launch event.

The preliminary question—field of the invention

—The art or field of endeavour in which the invention arises—disclaimer practice

3.06   *After the third paragraph, add new paragraph:*

In both the UK proceedings in *HTC v Apple* and the corresponding US proceedings in *Apple v Samsung* the claims were limited to portable electronic devices e.g. an iPhone. In the UK, both at first instance and on appeal the claimed subject-matter was held to be obvious over a paper by Plaisant et al. That paper concerned an experiment to determine which control ("toggles") users preferred on wall-mounted controllers for "entertainment, security, and climate control systems." The authors presented to a group of students six alternative unlocking mechanisms including a "slider toggle" where a user could activate the controller by grabbing the pointer and sliding it to the other side. The students preferred "toggles that were pushed" over "toggles that slide," and ranked the slider fifth of the six alternatives. It was argued in the US that it was obvious to combine the sliders of Plaisant with a mobile phone described in a reference called Neonode and that taking the ideas in Plaisant and putting them on the Neonode was just a routine thing to think about in terms of interaction design. However, the panel majority in the Federal Circuit concluded that the combination was not obvious and that to conclude otherwise would be to give in to hindsight, against which the Supreme Court cautioned in *Graham* and *KSR*. Though the prior art references each related to touchscreens, it would not have been obvious for a skilled artisan, seeking an unlock mechanism that would be both intuitive to use and solve the pocket dialling problem for cell phones, to look to a wall-mounted controller for an air conditioner, and still less so to choose the slider toggle, which the study found rated fifth out of six options in usability.

The skilled person or team and his or their characteristics

—The person skilled in the art

To the end of the last paragraph, add: **3.07**

In *Norbrook v Bimeda* BL O/243/15 applicants for revocation attempted to establish that the claimed subject-matter was obvious by an independent reconstruction exercise in which their expert was tasked to improve on the prior art without any prior knowledge of the patent. A first reason that the attempt was unsuccessful was that the starting point given to the expert was held not in fact to be part of the common general knowledge of the skilled person. A second reason was that the expert was on his own admission "a naturally inventive person" and was the named inventor in nearly seventy patent applications. Although his evidence as to what was common general knowledge was accepted, in the reconstruction exercise he was unable to distance himself from his own inventive nature when required to assume the mantle of the notional skilled unimaginative person, so that the solutions he devised were not an indication of obviousness.

—Characteristics of a skilled person

Add new paragraph at end: **3.08**

It was argued in *Unwired Planet International v Huawei Technologies* [2016] EWHC 94 (Pat) at [155] that the sparse nature of the disclosure in the specification to support the implementation of the claimed invention meant that the patent assumed a high level of skill on the part of the skilled person so that for obviousness a higher level of skill on the part of the skilled person should also be applied. It was held that this proposition was wrong in principle because it was the properly construed patent claim that counted, not the content of the specification. Otherwise two claims for the same invention over the same prior art would be judged differently for obviousness depending on whether one patent contained a worked example and the other did not. Borrowing in part the words of Lord Hoffmann in *Conor Medsystems Inc v Angiotech Pharmaceuticals Inc* [2008] UKHL 49; [2008] R.P.C. 28 at [19], a patentee is entitled to have the question of obviousness determined by reference to the claim and the objectively determined skilled person, not by reference to the extent of the disclosure in the description.

—The skilled team

After the fourth paragraph (beginning "In Minnesota Mining v AT! Atlas"), add new **3.09**
paragraphs:

In *Accord Healthcare v Medac* [2016] EWHC 24 (Pat) Birss J referred to the "trap identified by the Court of Appeal in *Schlumberger v EMGS* [2010] EWCA Civ 819 in that it may involve hindsight to postulate a team consisting of two distinct disciplines which had not been put together in reality before the priority date". In the present case, the patent was addressed to a team in which a clinician and a formulator were working together. For the purpose of obviousness there was evidence that such teams existed in reality, and this was not a case where the invention was "art-changing" or brought together two disparate fields. In contrast, in *Sartex France v Hexcel Reinforcements* [2016] EWHC 966 (IPEC) it was held that a skilled team was neither needed nor appropriate, and that only one skilled person was required.

■ Carr J commented in *Fujifilm Kyowa Kirin Biologics Co Ltd v Abbvie Biotechnology Ltd* [2017] EWHC 395 (Pat) at [128], [129] that there had been a lively, but ultimately pointless, debate between the parties about the identity of the skilled person. The reason why the debate was pointless was because what mattered was the skill-set of the team, not whether that skill-set was to be found in one or two individuals.

The knowledge attributed to the skilled team

—Common general knowledge in the art

3.11   *To the end of the fourth paragraph (beginning "In Generics trading as Mylan v Warner Lambert [2015] EWHC 2548 (Pat)"), add:*
■ It was observed in *Yo! Homes Ltd's Application* BL 0/272/17 that the territorial aspect of common general knowledge is complicated by the omnipresence of the internet and the World Wide Web, and that modern architecture is undoubtedly a global business with an international perspective, with the leading lights in the field being responsible for designs all over the world, so that the relevant knowledge was not exclusively UK knowledge but was international.

After the sixth paragraph (beginning "In HTC Europe Co Ltd v Apple Inc [2013] EWCA Civ 451"), add new paragraphs:
■ The same point as in *HTC Europe* arose in *Sony Communications International v SSH Communications Security Corp* [2016] EWHC 2584 (Pat) in which it was observed that the lack of a starting point for the assessment of obviousness is a particular problem with obviousness over the CGK. Once a starting point is identified, questions can properly be asked about how the invention could have been arrived at, taking into account the specifics of that starting point and whether it suggested the invention or even lent itself to the invention. It was observed at [94] that:

> "Without any idea of the application that existed at the priority date that is said to be a starting point for making the invention, one cannot properly consider 'motive', 'number of alternative approaches' or the kinds of problems that might have been caused by seeking to apply the invention. It is not possible to apply the *Pozzoli* questions, particularly the third question which involves identifying the difference between the prior art and the invention of the Patent, without first identifying a starting point. I accept that the *Pozzoli* approach may not be suitable for all cases but, in this case, the fact that there is no identifiable starting point is indicative of a fatal flaw in the attack based solely on CGK."

■ In the outcome, the claims in issue were held to be obvious over specific pleaded items of prior art.

Prior art acknowledged in the specification

—Routine further investigations

3.16   *After the third paragraph (beginning "The relevant legal principles were reviewed by Arnold J. in KCI Licensing v Smith & Nephew"), add new paragraph:*
■ An argument that the correct starting point is the cited prior art read in the light of the common general knowledge, which may extend to documents cross-referenced in the cited prior art, but no wider was rejected in *Fujifilm Kyowa Kirin Biologics Co Ltd v Abbvie Biotechnology Ltd* [2017] EWHC 395 (Pat), the court preferring the position set out by Arnold J in *KCI Licensing* that there may be material which is not common general knowledge, which nonetheless, as a matter of routine, the skilled person would look for and find when approaching a particular problem.

To the end of the last paragraph, add:
The above opinion was upheld in *Generics (UK) Ltd (t/a Mylan) v Richter Gedeon Vegyészeti Gyár RT* [2016] EWCA Civ 410, Jacob LJ concluding that there was no logical distinction between looking something up and asking a question about a published document. In both cases the prior art spurred the action of finding out in a non-inventive

way. However, the facts here were unusual—a clearly obvious error, a clear source to ask what the correct figure was and a clear finding not only that an answer would be given but that it would be unambiguous. It did not follow that "the skilled person would ask" route to obviousness would follow for cases where the facts were not so precise or certain. Floyd LJ, concurring, held that where it is established that the skilled person would have been prompted by the state of the art to ask for a specific piece of information from a source which would be obvious, and that the information requested would have been freely given, a finding of lack of inventive step was properly open.

The inventive concept

—The collocation/combination test and its relevance to inventive concept

After the fourth paragraph (beginning "In Schlumberger v Electromagnetic Geoservices **3.19**
(above)"), add new paragraph:

■ For a recent example where the *Sabaf* approach was followed, see *Thoratec Europe Ltd v Ais GmbH Aachen Innovative Solutions* [2016] EWHC 2637 (Pat), where the specification did not explain how the first and second sets of features interacted to produce the identified benefits [146], and on the face of the specification it appeared that each of them produced its own benefits independent of the other. The *Sabaf* decision was distinguished on the facts in *Silixa Ltd's Application* BL O/112/16. In *Sabaf*, the features under consideration were two distinct parts of a gas burner, each functioning independently with no interaction with the other. The steps in the claimed invention were inextricably linked and had a combined effect so that the Examiner's argument that there was no synergy between them was rejected. Similarly, in *Epoch Co Ltd v Character Options Ltd* [2017] EWHC 556 (IPEC) it was held that synergy between transparency, polyhedral beads and their use in a fusible bead toy gave rise to a new toy that was more attractive to children than the old ones and that by common consent this had not been done before the priority date. Therefore, the claimed subject-matter could not be dismissed as a mere juxtaposition of features. However, it was subsequently held to lack inventive character over cited prior art, change of the shape of known beads from spherical to gem-like polyhedral not being of inventive significance.

Add new paragraph at end:

■ The significance of the test in the USA is apparent from many decisions and from USPTO *MPEP* §2141 in which the following particularly rationales are given supporting a finding that a person having ordinary skill in the art ("PHOSITA") would have been motivated to combine the references, all but one of them expressly or implicitly involving the test:

(a) combining prior art elements according to known methods to yield predictable results;

(b) simple substitution of one known element for another to obtain predictable results;

(c) use of known technique to improve similar devices (methods, or products) in the same way;

(d) applying a known technique to a known device (method, or product) ready for improvement to yield predictable results;

(e) "obvious to try"—choosing from a finite number of identified, predictable solutions, without a reasonable expectation for success;

(f) known work in one field of endeavour may prompt variations of it for use in either the same field or a different one based on design incentives or other market forces if the variations are predictable to one of ordinary skill in the art; and

(g) some teaching, suggestion, or motivation in the prior art that would have led one of ordinary skill to modify the prior art reference or to combine prior art reference teachings to arrive at the claimed invention [see the *KSR* decision of the US Supreme Court and e.g. *In re NuVasive, Inc.*, 842 F.3d 1376, 1379 (Fed. Cir. 2016)].

Teachings, or combinations of teachings, that may be relied on

—Obviousness having regard to common general knowledge

3.21   *Add new paragraphs at end:*

The problems associated with objections based simply on the common general knowledge were explained by Birss J in *Accord Healthcare v Medac* [2016] EWHC 24 (Pat) at [119] onwards. The relevant common general knowledge must be that in the UK, see Arnold J in *Generics (UK) v Warner Lambert* [2015] EWHC 2548 (Pat) at [123]–[124]. The claimed subject-matter was obvious over one of the cited references, but for the following reasons not over the common general knowledge alone:

> "Many inventions involve a combination of known features. However, a combination of features, all of which individually were common general knowledge, can give rise to a valid patent claim if that combination is new and non-obvious. Patent trials are inevitably *ex post facto* and a key problem is to identify and avoid hindsight. Combinations of features can pose a particularly acute hindsight problem. The thing about concrete items of prior art, whether they are prior published documents or prior used products or processes, is that whatever combination of features that concrete prior art consists of, is not one which was created with hindsight knowledge of the invention.
>
> The problem with arguments over common general knowledge alone is that the combination of features relied on is always and necessarily one created with hindsight knowledge of the invention, and worse, is one which the person attacking validity has not been able to find as a pre-existing combination in the concrete prior art. If they had, they would have relied on that concrete prior art. Either the combination has not been made in the concrete prior art at all or it only appears with additional inconvenient details. If an invention is not obvious over the concrete prior art which is relied on, the court is entitled to be sceptical that an argument that it is nevertheless obvious over common general knowledge alone is correct.
>
> The problem is illustrated in this case... To invent as a starting point in the prior art an amalgam of the best bits of the two cited documents while leaving out the inconvenient aspects, which is in effect what the argument was, created a combination which did not hitherto exist."

The importance of proper pleading in relation to an objection based on common general knowledge alone was emphasized in *Meter-Tech Llc v British Gas Trading Ltd* [2016] EWHC 2278 (Pat) where it was not considered appropriate to base a decision on obviousness on this particular ground, where the grounds of invalidity had merely set out a disparate group of facts alleged to be part of the common general knowledge. It follows from *Ratiopharm GmbH v NAPP Pharmaceutical Holdings Ltd* [2008] EWHC 3070 (Pat), *Beloit Technologies Inc v Valmet Paper Machinery Inc* [1997] R.P.C. 489, *Accord Healthcare* and *Unwired Planet International Ltd v Huawei Technologies Co Ltd* [2016] EWHC 576 (Pat) at [233] that:

> "where a party is relying on obviousness over common general knowledge alone, it should set out in its statement of case, if ordered to provide one, not only what the common general knowledge is alleged to be but also how that differs from the invention of the patent and why such is said to render the claim in question obvious. That requires a pleading not of just the starting point but of the allegedly obvious route to the claimed invention so that the notional thinking of the skilled person can be seen and evaluated."

—Obviousness having regard to a single reference and common general knowledge

3.22   *To the end of the fourth paragraph (beginning "In Smith & Nephew Plc v Convatec Technologies Inc"), add:*

Note that the patent in issue in these proceedings was subsequently revoked in parallel

EPO opposition proceedings, see T 0449/13 *CONVATEC/Antimicrobial materials* of 21 November 2013 confirmed by T 0449/15 *CONVATEC/Antimicrobial material* of 25 February 2016.

Add new paragraph at end:

In *Unwired Planet International v Huawei* [2016] EWHC 576 (Pat) the court memorably observed at [232]: "I reject the obviousness case. A skilled person given this document at the priority date and reading it with interest would in all probability just put it to one side as a terrible idea. I doubt they would be motivated to go any further."

—Obviousness based on two or more references

Add new paragraph at the beginning: **3.23**

■ It was observed in *Unwired Planet v Huawei* [2017] EWCA Civ 266 at [122] that: "The fact that individual components of an invention can be identified with hindsight from the prior art and advantageously combined together does not amount to a case of obviousness."

Evaluation of the differences—additional evidence and arguments commonly adduced

—Allegedly trivial or arbitrary differences

To the end of the fourth paragraph (beginning "A feature may therefore be disregarded   **3.26**
if it is trivial or arbitrary"), add:

In *The Chamberlain Group, Inc's Application* BL O/596/15 the Hearing Officer relied on *Technip France SA's Patent* [2004] EWCA Civ 381 and *Glaxo Group Ltd's Patent* [2004] EWHC 477 (Pat) for the proposition that in cases involving multiple individual, apparently trivial, steps it was important to assess obviousness without the use of hindsight. Just because it was possible to set out from a document and take only obvious steps to arrive at the invention did not make it always obvious to do so. In the present case to go from a prior art reference to the invention required three steps. The first step was not obvious because the skilled person would not necessarily have realized that there was a problem over and above what was already inherent in the disclosure of that reference. The second step involved a purely arbitrary choice. The third step made complete sense with hindsight, but it nevertheless did involve an inventive step to choose to adopt it over and above the disclosure of the prior art reference.

Add new paragraph at end:

■ In the US, rejections based on "common sense" are often made to justify combinations of references or to supply a missing limitation. However, in *Arendi S.A.R.L. v Apple Inc.*, 832 F.3d 1355 (Fed. Cir. 2016) CAFC noted that "we do consider common sense, common wisdom, and common knowledge in analysing obviousness," but offered three caveats:

- "[C]ommon sense is typically invoked to provide a known motivation to combine, not to supply a missing claim limitation";
- "[I]n. . . . the only case Appellees identif[y] in which common sense was invoked to supply a limitation that was admittedly missing from the prior art, the limitation in question was unusually simple and the technology particularly straightforward"; and
- "[R]eferences to 'common sense'—whether to supply a motivation to combine or a missing limitation—cannot be used as a wholesale substitute for reasoned analysis and evidentiary support, especially when dealing with a limitation missing from the prior art references specified. Indeed, we stated that although there is no problem

with using common sense 'without any specific hint or suggestion in a particular reference,' the Board's 'utter failure to explain the 'common knowledge and common sense' on which it relied' is problematic."

—Obvious to try—reasonable expectation of success

3.30   *Add new paragraphs at end:*

Issues of alleged anticipation in relation to a press release were considered in *Hospira UK Ltd v Cubist Pharmaceuticals LLC* [2016] EWHC 1285 (Pat), see §2.09. In relation to obviousness, the issue was whether the skilled team would have considered that the proposed clinical trials would have a fair expectation of success in demonstrating efficacy. The patentees argued that this was mere speculation, but that argument was rejected firstly because the evidence was that the skilled reader would have assumed that the patentees had appropriate efficacy and safety data to justify the Phase III trial and that it was supported by Phase II work, and secondly because that reader would have been well aware that a company carrying out a Phase III trial would have thought that there would have been a very good prospect of success, otherwise they would not have invested the considerable amounts of money which such a trial would require. Accordingly, the claimed subject-matter lacked inventive step.

In *Actavis and Actelion v Teva and Generics* [2016] EWHC 1955 (Pat) in relation to how "obvious to try" arguments fit in a multi-step pharmaceutical development the court noted that some experiments undertaken without a particular expectation as to the result are obvious whereas others are not and once each step has been analysed individually it is still necessary to stand back and look overall [276]. It was further explained that:

"Patent law provides a clear answer to the rhetorical policy question posed by the claimants of whether a pharmaceutical originator is entitled to extend the practical monopoly they have enjoyed over a drug and its use in the treatment of a disease by obtaining a second patent. The answer is that the second patent must involve an inventive step (and otherwise comply with the law) and that the existence of an inventive step is a question of fact which is determined by the detailed technical arguments and evidence and the particular facts and circumstances. Wide generalisations do not assist either way. Patents exist to provide incentives for costly and uncertain research but not all costly and uncertain research will lead to patentable inventions.

When the invention derives from clinical and pre-clinical research it may be necessary to consider a stepwise series of tests which a skilled team might undertake. For an invention to be obvious it is necessary but not sufficient for all the individual steps to be obvious. Even if the steps all seem obvious it is still necessary to stand back and look at the facts as a whole because obviousness is ultimately a single question of fact. The risk of hindsight is significant when one is looking at a step-by-step analysis (*Technograph*) but not all step-by-step analysis is inappropriate. The skilled team's views about the likely prospects of success must always be taken into account both step-by-step and overall.

Pharmaceutical development work involves a number of rounds of routine testing which are costly and have an uncertain outcome. A good example is routine pre-clinical testing. A skilled team will carry out routine testing of that kind without any expectation as to what any particular result will be. That lack of expectation does not turn the results of truly routine testing into an invention.

The reason Phase I, Phase IIa and IIb, and Phase III studies are carried out is because they have uncertain outcomes. But they are routine tests and the fact their outcome is uncertain does not on its own turn their results into an invention. The fact one cannot say before pre-clinical and Phase I or IIa tests have been performed what particular doses would be tested in a Phase IIb dose-ranging study does not by itself make those doses inventive if some or all of them are found to work.

At each stage the skilled team will make value judgments about how to proceed based on whatever results are obtained. The fact the results are not predictable from the outset of the entire project does not necessarily make these decisions indicative of invention. An obvious goal is not turned into an invention by the existence of an unexpected bonus effect (*Hallen v Brabantia* [1991] RPC 195 at 216). On the other hand, the existence of surprising or unexpected properties can be indicative of an inventive step (*Schering-Plough v Norbrook* [2006] RPC 18 at para 34). If the case turns on whether a particular test is "obvious to try", which it may do especially when a skilled team is having to make value judgments about what to do next, then the skilled team's views about the likely prospects of success will be critical (*Teva v Leo*). A fair prospect of success will be required for that step to be obvious.

In the end the programme has to be considered as a whole. Even steps which are individually obvious in themselves need to be taken into account in deciding the overall question (*Gedeon Richter* paragraph 115)."

In the outcome a 5 mg daily dose of tadalafil as a treatment for erectile dysfunction was held to be not obvious over the cited prior art. That was for the following reasons articulated having regard to the factors identified above, based in part on *Lundbeck*:

"(i) In terms of motives to find a solution to the problem the patent addresses, the skilled team would be highly motivated by Daugan and the success of sildenafil to investigate tadalafil as a treatment for erectile dysfunction.

(ii) As for possible avenues of research, overall tadalafil would be obvious to investigate. In terms of doses however, 5 mg/day is a significantly lower dose than the 50 mg dose exemplified in the Daugan prior art and the marketed doses of sildenafil. It is also significantly lower than the 50 mg dose which would be chosen for the first test of efficacy at Phase IIa. It would not be chosen in the routine first dose-ranging study. The team would not have anticipated daily dosing as something to be studied from the outset but once the half-life was discovered it is likely that daily dosing would be included.

(iii) In terms of effort, overall the programme would involve very substantial resources of time, money and people but it would be pursued. However, by the time the idea of investigating lower doses presents itself, the team would have established safe, tolerable and effective doses of tadalafil at 25 mg on demand and 10 mg for daily dosing. At that stage the impetus to investigate lower doses would be reduced but not eliminated.

(iv) Expectations of success can be considered overall and in relation to particular studies. Overall the team would embark on the project with a reasonable expectation of success in establishing tadalafil as a safe, tolerable and effective treatment for tadalafil. However, the claimants failed to prove that efficacy at 5 mg tadalafil was predictable or worth considering by the skilled team based on the properties of tadalafil as compared to sildenafil. The team would know that in principle there would be a minimum effective dose for tadalafil but would also know that its definition depends on a value judgment made by the team. In relation to the dose-ranging studies, the team would conduct them hoping for a dose response. Following discovery of a plateau starting at 25 mg or 10 mg, there would very likely be a subsequent dose-ranging study which included 5 mg. The team would include a 5 mg dose in this study hoping to see a dose response but that does not mean they would have a reasonable expectation that 5 mg would produce a clinically relevant effect at all nor one with minimal side effects. Assuming a 5 mg/day dose of tadalafil was tested, it would not be tested with a reasonable expectation of success.

(v) Considering unexpected or surprising results, the position is as follows. The path to a 5 mg dose requires the discovery of new information such as the half-life and the IC50 vs PDE6. That information would inevitably be found in any clinical programme. The path includes an important result which is unexpected even if it is not actually surprising, i.e. the plateau in the dose response from 10 to 100 mg. There is also a surprising result: the existence of a useful effect with reduced side effects. The claimed 5 mg/day dose has that property.

(vi) A number of value judgments would be required of a skilled team in a programme which reaches the claimed invention. One is to define the level of clinical effect to be regarded as relevant. Another is to embark on investigating daily dosing. An important value judgment is what to do when an unexpected plateau in the dose response has been identified at the same time as a marketable dose."

■ In *Hospira v Genentech* [2016] EWCA Civ 780 the patents in issue concerned formulations of the important breast cancer drug Herceptin, the active ingredient in which is the monoclonal antibody trastuzumab. The invention concerned a lyophilised formulation using as excipients trehalose, histidine and polysorbate 20 as lyoprotectant, buffer and surfactant respectively. It was found at first instance that the formulation of large protein molecules was a more difficult and complex task than the formulation of small molecules and that finding a stable formulation was an essentially empirical exercise. Floyd LJ concluded that there the claimed formulations were not inventive, and his reasoning appears at [50], [51]:

"I have already explained why I do not accept that it is necessary in every case for the court to conclude that the skilled person acting only on the basis of the prior art and his common general knowledge *would* arrive without invention at the precise combination claimed. Given that the screening methods were part of the common general knowledge, that the tests involved were routine, that the excipients were common general knowledge excipients and that there was no a priori reason why a successful lyophilised formulation could not be made, it seems to me that it was beyond argument that the claimed combination in this case was one that could be made by the skilled team. The question is whether this is the type of case where it is necessary to go further and ask whether the skilled person would necessarily have made the precise combination claimed.

In an empirical field, it will seldom be possible to predict in advance that any individual experiment will work. In many cases, the fact that a routine screening exercise could be carried out will be inadequate to establish obviousness. Nevertheless, on the facts of an individual case such as the present, the team may have a reasonable degree of confidence that a series of experiments will produce some which will work. To impose a requirement that the skilled team must be able to predict in advance which would be the successful combinations is wholly unrealistic. It would lead to the grant of patents for a whole variety of combinations which in fact involved no inventive effort."

■ A further Herceptin case, *Hospira v Genentech* [2016] EWCA Civ 1185 involved a Swiss-form claim to the use of that antibody in combination with a taxane to give clinical effect as measured by time to disease progression in combination with reduced myocardial dysfunction. An issue before Arnold J [2015] EWHC 1796 (Pat) was whether the claimed subject-matter was obvious over an article mentioning a Phase III clinical trial involving a combination of the antibody and paclitaxel (taxol). In affirming the first-instance decision that the subject-matter was obvious the court declined to adopt the very high test in *Saint-Gobain Pam SA v Fusion Provida Ltd* [2005] EWCA Civ 177 at [35] that it must be "more-or-less self-evident that what is being tested ought to work". Instead, it held that there was no *lex specialis* for claims featuring a therapeutic effect or benefit. The test was flexible and was whether there was a fair prospect of success. In the present case, that expectation was founded on findings that combination therapy was common, and that these two drugs fitted the rationale for combination therapy, being directed at different targets and not having significantly overlapping toxicity. Genentech had put forward no convincing reason why the skilled person would have thought that the combination would not yield the relevant clinical benefit—there were no lions in the path. For a discussion of secondary evidence, see §3.32. A similar decision was handed down by the EPO in case T 1577/11 *ASTRAZENECA/Anastrozole*. Certainty of success is not required and it suffices if a skilled person would have followed the teaching of the prior art with a reasonable expectation of success, better than expected results being a bonus effect which cannot in itself establish an inventive step.

—Invention by way of selection from the prior art

3.31   *Add new paragraph at end:*
The importance of disclosing advantages relied on for patentability in the application as filed was emphasized in *Teva UK Ltd v Boehringer Ingelheim Pharma GmbH & Co KG* [2015] EWHC 2963 (Pat). The invention concerned capsules for a dry powder inhaler in which the capsule material was required to have a reduced moisture content. They would only exhibit an inventive step if the claimed moisture content levels were inventive. However, although the specification disclosed the general benefits of a reduction of moisture content in the capsule material, it did not disclose the benefit of the specific moisture levels claimed. Thus, the claimed moisture levels were held to be arbitrary and the claims were held to lack inventive step.

—Contemporaneous peer activities and peer reaction

3.32   *Add new paragraphs at end:*
In the US proceedings in *Apple v Samsung* the holding of the panel majority that the

invention was not obvious was supported by extensive secondary evidence that was not considered by the UK courts in the corresponding proceedings in *HTC v Apple*.

A video was shown of the iPhone launch, during which the crowd (including many representatives of the press) burst into cheers when Steve Jobs demonstrated its slide to unlock feature. The video was shown to the jury, and Apple's expert, an inventor, and Apple's Vice President of Marketing all referenced the video in their testimony. Numerous internal Samsung documents both praised Apple's slide to unlock feature and indicated that Samsung should modify its own phones to incorporate that feature. Five such documents were referred to in the opinion of the panel majority and were held to represent important admissions, acknowledging the merits of the patented advance over the then state of the art. There was therefore substantial evidence of praise in the industry that specifically related to features of the claimed invention. Further evidence was that Samsung copied the claimed iPhone features in its own products, which provided additional support to a finding that the claimed invention would not have been obvious.

■ In *Unwired Planet International v Huawei* [2017] EWCA Civ 266 the court observed at [105] that a statement that that secondary evidence must be kept in its place, see *Mölnlycke v Procter & Gamble* [1994] R.P.C. 49 at [113] and *Schlumberger Holdings Ltd v Electromagnetic Geoservices AS* [2010] EWCA Civ 819; [2010] R.P.C. 33 at [77], was not the same as stating that it was irrelevant. A surgical division of the evidence into "primary" and "secondary" was unreal on the facts of the present case, and the judge was entitled to turn to the secondary evidence to see what assistance it provided him with in reaching his conclusion.

■ Secondary evidence was not persuasive in *Hospira v Genentech* [2016] EWCA Civ 1185 discussed at §3.30. Results of a Phase II trial reported at a conference had attracted little attention, whereas 5,000 people had attended a subsequent presentation describing the Phase III results. The contrast in results was not persuasive of unobviousness, inter alia because the results presented were very striking whereas the claims extended to any increase in the time to disease progression, however small.

—Market reaction

Add new paragraph at end: **3.33**

In the US proceedings in *Apple v Samsung*, the plaintiffs established that the slide-to-unlock feature contributed to the commercial success of the iPhone. They presented survey evidence that customers would be less likely to purchase a portable device without the slide to unlock feature and would pay less for products without it. That feature would possibly be a customer's first experience of an iPhone in a retail environment when deciding whether to buy it, and this simple gesture gave an instant idea of how the touchscreen worked, showing that it did something simple and useful that it did not require a manual to figure out. It was held that this commercial success evidence further supported a finding that the claimed invention would not have been obvious.

The fourth question—evaluation of the evidence

—Technical invention or mere commercial idea?

Add new paragraph at end: **3.38**

In *Gareth Kevin Glass v Freyssinet Ltd* [2015] EWHC 2972 (IPEC) it was observed that higher cost is a commercial, not a technical, reason for preferring one alternative over another and therefore not relevant to inventive step, citing *Hallen Company v Brabantia (UK) Ltd* [1991] R.P.C. 195 at [213] (Slade LJ giving the judgment of the Court of Appeal).

Avoidance of hindsight

3.40   *Add new paragraphs at end:*
■ A paper by Warren D. Woessner, "Adjusting the Rearview Mirror II—Blocking Impermissible Hindsight Rejections", 2017 AIPLA Annual Meeting, available online at AIPLA, has many resonances for European practitioners. The need to avoid "siren hindsight" had been summarised by the US Supreme Court in *Diamond Rubber Co v Consolidated Rubber Tire Co*, 220 U.S. 428, 435 (1911) in language which is as compelling for the UK or the EPO as it is for the US:

> "Knowledge after the event is always easy, and problems once solved present no difficulties, indeed, may be represented as never having had any, and expert witnesses may be brought forward to show that the new thing which seemed to have eluded the search of the world was always ready at hand and easy to be seen by a merely skilful attention. But the law has other tests of the invention than subtle conjectures of what might have been seen and yet was not."

■ The paper explains that while it would seem that firm holdings by the courts would make it simple for the practitioner, the Examiner, or the courts to identify obviousness rejections or appellate decisions based on hindsight, unfortunately this is far from the case. Hindsight bias is insidious, as it can become a part of the resolution of the obviousness question very early in the process.

> "If I hand my three-year-old grandson a 'sunken puzzle' with an irregular border, he can fit in the pieces that have matching edges. It helps that a picture of the assembled puzzle is on the cover. If you hand an Examiner a claim with x elements, he/she can usually find the elements and arrange them to reproduce your claim if the he/she uses the claim as the picture on the cover. The difference is that while the Examiner can use the picture on the cover to find the pieces, he/she has to legally erase the picture from his/her mind before beginning to assemble the pieces. As stated *In re Carroll* 441 F.3d 977 (Fed. Cir. 2006) "In deciding obviousness, one must look at the prior art from the vantage point in time prior to when the invention was made; hindsight obviousness after the invention was made is not the test." It logically follows that the likelihood that the Examiner used the claims as a template by which to assemble the invention is directly proportional to (a) the number of prior art references required to provide all the claim elements and assembly instructions, and (b) the complexity of any individual reference, including the amount of extraneous or manifestly irrelevant material therein."

■ Apart from multiplicity per se, hindsight may well have been employed if an Examiner has extracted at least one element of the invention from a thicket of irrelevant material in a lengthy, complex publication or patent. The fact that a claimed product is within the broad field of the prior art and one might arrive at it by selecting specific items and conditions does not render the product obvious in the absence of some directions or reasons for making such selection. Where the prior art gives no indication of which parameters are critical and no direction as to which of many possible choices is likely to be successful, the fact that the claimed combination falls within the scope of possible combinations taught therein does not render it obvious. US cases on hindsight reconstruction include *Rolls-Royce, PLC, v United Technologies Corp*, 603 F.3d 1325 (Fed. Cir. 5 May 2010), *In re Chapman* 679 F.3d 1372 (Fed. Cir., 30 May 2012), *Neil Mintz v Dietz & Watson*, 679 F.3d 1372 (Fed. Cir., 30 May 2012; hindsight definition of the problem), *Otsuka Pharma v Sandoz*, 678 F.3d 1280 (Fed. Cir. 7 May 2012; selection of features from a "laundry list" of prior art compounds), *Grunenthal GMBH v Epic Pharma L.P.et al.*, 811 Fed. Cir. 1345 (Fed. Cir. 1 February 2016) and *Millennium Pharmaceuticals, Inc. v Sandoz Inc* (Fed. Cir., 17 July 2017).

Field of the invention

3.43   *Add new paragraph at end:*
■ As explained in the Woessner paper (see §3.40), the US has a "non-analogous art" test which also requires that a reference is either in the field of the applicant's endeavour or is reasonably pertinent to the problem with which the inventor was concerned, see *In re Kahn* 441 F.3d 977 (Fed. Cir. 2006).

Selection of the starting-point prior art

After the fifth paragraph (beginning "A generically different document does not **3.44**
qualify"), add new paragraphs:

In T 1841/11 *SHIN-ETSU/Manufacturing semiconductor substrate* it was held that even if prior art relating to the same purpose was available, a disclosure relating to a similar purpose could be a better, or at least an equally plausible, choice of closest prior art if a skilled reader could straightforwardly adapt what had been disclosed to the purpose of the invention using no more than common general knowledge. Where the starting point was a similar purpose disclosure, at least one claimed feature corresponding to the purpose of the invention would generally appear as a difference over that disclosure. However, that difference could not legitimately be invoked in support of inventive step because the problem-solution approach presupposes that a skilled person has a purpose in mind from the very beginning of the inventive process and within that conceptual framework it could not logically be argued that a skilled person would find no motivation to incorporate the difference. If incorporation of the difference was not straightforward, then that would indicate that the selected disclosure was not a promising starting point, but would not be an argument for inventive step. In the present case it was immediately apparent that by supplying both Si and Ge precursor gases in a CVD process, the result would be a SiGe film rather than a pure Ge film, so that a prior art document describing formation of a Ge film could be treated as the closest prior art for formation of a SiGe film.

■ It was explained in T 1742/12 *RAYTHEON/On-demand instantiation* that the choice of the closest prior art may not always be unambiguous and that, in such a case, the problem-solution approach may have to be repeated starting from other pieces of prior art, citing T 710/97 *FIFE/Non-contact detection*. If it was found that the skilled person had a choice of several workable routes, i.e. routes starting from different documents, which might lead to the invention, the problem-solution approach required that the invention be assessed relative to all these possible routes, before an inventive step could be acknowledged. Conversely, if the invention was obvious to the skilled person in respect of at least one of these routes, then an inventive step was lacking, citing T 967/97 *OVD Kinegram/Chipkarte* and T 21/08 *AKZO NOBEL/Separate application of resin and hardener*. A similar conclusion was reached in T 1570/13 *BRASKEM AMERICA/Polyolefin composition*.

Combining references—the EPC approach

—Advantages must be demonstrated

To the end of the fourth paragraph (beginning "As previously explained, a technical **3.49**
effort can only be relied upon"), add:

■ A further example is provided by *Merck Sharp and Dohme v Shionogi* [2016] EWHC 2989 (Pat) discussed at §14.29.

SECTION 4A [ADDED]—Methods of treatment or diagnosis

Add new paragraph 4A.00: **4A.00**

Contents

COMMENTARY ON SECTION 4A

Scope of the section

—The meaning of treatment of the human or animal body and diagnosis practised on the human or animal body

4A.04   *Add new paragraph at end:*

■ The prohibition in T 24/91 *THOMPSON/Cornea* was not applied in T 2420/13 *RODENSTOCK/lens* where it was held that using a spectacle lens to correct a glasses wearer's defective vision was not a method for treating the human body by therapy within the meaning of EPC art.53(c) since there was no direct effect on the eye of the spectacle wearer and no therapeutic effect achieved by action on the human body.

—The meaning of "therapy"

4A.05   *After the eleventh paragraph (beginning "The claimed subject-matter in Lalvani et al's Application"), add new paragraph:*

T 2451/13 *NUTRICIA/Sensoric imprinting* considered a claim to a non-therapeutic method for sensoric imprinting of different tastes in an infant by administration to the infant of certain food products. The patent explained that sensoric imprinting could prevent an infant from acquiring a dislike for the taste of different plant materials and that the resulting healthy lifestyle prevented later obesity and diabetes. It was held, applying T 1635/09 *SCHERING PHARMA/ Empfängnisverhütung*, that the non-therapeutic disclaimer did not change the therapeutic nature of the claimed method which was ineligible.

—Patents for the protection of the second (or further) medical indications

4A.09   *After the first paragraph, add new paragraph:*

■ The invention in T 943/13 *N.V. NUTRICIA/Composition comprising oligosaccharides as soluble dietary fibres for use against muscle wasting* is apparent from the title. Opponents cited a dietary composition in which the therapeutic benefit of preventing muscle wasting was obtained using whey, and alleged that the objective technical problem based on that reference was no more than the provision of an alternative composition. However, the Board held that for a further medical use claim it was the causal relationship between the substance or composition on the one hand and the effect achieved therewith on the other hand that constituted a functional feature of the claim. Inventive step hinged on whether this causal relationship, and not just the substance or composition as defined in the claim, was obvious. The objective technical problem was therefore not just the addition of a further arbitrary substance (fibre) to the prior art composition which already provided the therapeutic effect. Instead, it was the provision of this causal relationship, i.e. the achievement of the claimed therapeutic effect with different means, i.e. the specific fibres claimed. There was no indication in the cited document that this could be achieved using dietary fibres as now defined, and accordingly inventive step was established.

To the end of the ninth paragraph (beginning "In T 879/12 GENENTECH / APO-2 ligand"), add:

In T1673/11 *GENZYME/Treatment of Pompe's disease* granted "Swiss-type" claims which had been amended to EPC2000 format (purpose-limited product claims) during opposition were rejected as extending the protection conferred under art.123(3) EPC.

To the end of the tenth paragraph (beginning "In contrast, in T 1507/09 PROTISTA/ Alpha-ketoglutaric acid"), add:

The *MOPP* has been updated at 4A.28.3 to explain that in T 1099/09 *COLOPLAST/ Further medical indication* it was held that second medical use claims can only be used to protect the use of a known substance or composition as an active agent. The use of a known substance or composition as an inactive carrier or excipient for a therapeutic agent cannot therefore be protected by a second medical use claim.

To the end of the eleventh paragraph (beginning "A claim to the use of an implantable strip"), add:

Further, in T 2369/10 *CYBERONICS/Cranial nerve stimulation*, second medical use claims relating to a neurostimulator device for the treatment of substance addiction, which was known in the art to treat epilepsy, were not allowed. The Board referred to the Vienna Convention for the interpretation of treaties which required the wording of the EPC to be given its ordinary meaning but not to be extended to cover things that were not expressly provided for. Article 54(5) EPC allows for purpose-related product protection for a "substance or composition" but does not cover medical devices.

Add new paragraph at end:

■ The *EDWARDS* decision was not followed in T 773/10 *GAMBRO/Dialysis membrane* in which a Swiss-form claim was directed to a dialysis membrane for the treatment of multiple myeloma that allowed the passage of molecules of molecular weight up to 45 kDa in the presence of whole blood. The differences were that the membrane did not contain any "active" ingredient, was not a single-use product consumed during use, and therefore was not a "substance or composition" within art.54(5) EPC.

—"Swiss-form" second medical use claims

To the end of the sixteenth paragraph (beginning "Birss J. in Hospira UK Ltd v Genentech Inc"), add: **4A.10**

In *Actavis v Eli Lilly* [2015] EWHC 3294 (Pat), a case relating to a second medical use patent for treatment of ADHD using atomoxetine, Carr J held that "plausibility" is a threshold test that asks if the invention is "credible" based on the patent and common general knowledge. It is not to be equated with the fair expectation of success test for obviousness.

In the twenty-second paragraph (beginning "Finally, Pfizer was liable for making groundless threats"), after "Finally, Pfizer" add:

(as merged with *Warner-Lambert*)

To the end of the twenty-second paragraph (beginning "Finally, Pfizer was liable for making groundless threats"), add, before the full stop:

and a declaration of non-infringement was granted to Actavis and wholesalers who deal in the generic drug Lucaent, including doctors, pharmacists and patients. A useful discussion of this series of cases can be found in a paper by Alasdair Poore, "Warner-Lambert Update" [2015] 10 *CIPA* 24.

SECTION 5—Priority date

5.00   *Add new paragraph 5.00:*

Contents

COMMENTARY ON SECTION 5

The prima facie priority date (subs.(1)) and the onus of proof

5.15   ■ *In the first paragraph, after "Also, to establish this prima facie priority date, it is enough for the patentee to assert that the instructions in the priority document work to produce the results claimed in", replace "them" with "the application".*

Add new paragraph at end:

Birss J considered this in *Actavis Group PTC EHF v ICOS Corp & Eli Lilly and Co* [2016] EWHC 1955 (Pat) and held that in circumstances where it can be inferred that legal priority exists, the evidential burden of proof shifts to the patentee to rebut that inference.

The priority period and the necessity for a valid declaration (subss.(2) (both before and after amendment effective January 1, 2005), (2), (2B) and (2C))

—Person with right to make a declaration of priority

After the third paragraph (beginning "In Beloit v Valmet [1995] R.P.C. 705, the earlier patent-in-suit"), add new paragraphs: **5.20**

■ Although the Court of Appeal in *Idenix v Gilead* [2016] EWCA Civ 1089 found that it was not necessary for them to decide the issues arising on entitlement to claim priority, Kitchin LJ gave a brief indication of his views on those issues. In particular, he expressed the provisional view that the decisions in *KCI* and *HTC* on what amounts to a "successor in title" are correct, that the Paris Convention does not purport to identify the requirements for the effective transfer of title to an invention and that these matters are left to the relevant national law, referring to the decision of the Technical Board of Appeal in T 205/14 *TEVA/Ibandronate sodium, Form QQ* as support. He noted that "the notion that it is the transfer of the substantive right and title to the invention which is important makes eminently good sense", but left final determination of the issue to another case.

■ See also *Fujifilm Kyowa Kirin Biologics Co Ltd v Abbvie Biotechnology Ltd* [2017] EWHC 395 (Pat) where a late-filed PCT request including the signatures of all of the inventors did not suffice to transfer the right of priority to a Bermuda company, but it was established that the company was "successor in title" to the invention the subject of the priority application following detailed investigation of a complex chain of title under US and German law, AbbVie's evidence being credible and making commercial sense.

■ The EPO Appeal Board reviewed the applicable provisions of the PCT and the EPC, UK and German decisions and transfer of ownership with retroactive effect in Italian and Dutch law in T 577/11 *TENARIS CONNECTIONS/Entitlement to priority*. It acknowledged that the EPC does not establish a fully harmonised patent system and that the question of who can be a "successor in title" within art.87(1) EPC 1973 must, in the absence of EPC provisions governing this question, be answered on the basis of national law. In the present case, there had been a limited transfer of ownership which was contractual in nature and insufficient to prevail over the legal ownership. Accordingly, the priority claimed was not valid. Substantive requirements for a valid transfer of the right of priority—the successor in title with respect to the right to claim priority from a first application must prove that it owned (i) before the filing of the later application, (ii) the right of priority relating to the first application for the purpose of filing the later application claiming priority from it.

According multiple priorities or a partial priority

To the end of the eighth paragraph (beginning "In the July 17, 2015 decision in T 0557/13"), add: **5.22**

■ The Enlarged Board of Appeal issued its order in G 1/15 on 29 November 2016 followed by the full decision in February 2017. Given the diverging lines of case law that had developed at the EPO following G 2/98, and the potentially severe consequences of the so-called "poisonous divisionals" or "poison priority" problem referred to above, the referral had attracted a large number of amicus curiae submissions, most of which argued in favour of an approach that would effectively neutralise this problem. Given the significance of this decision, the order of the decision is set out:

"Under the EPC, entitlement to partial priority may not be refused for a claim encompassing alternative subject-matter by virtue of one or more generic expressions or otherwise (generic 'OR'-claim) provided that said alternative subject-matter has been disclosed for the first time, directly, or at least implicitly, unambiguously and in an enabling manner in the priority document. No other substantive conditions or limitations apply in this respect."

■ The Enlarged Board has, therefore, found that there are no other requirements for recognizing the right of priority beyond "the same invention", whether for single, multiple or partial priority, and that therefore the "limited number of clearly defined alternatives" test from G 2/98 "cannot be construed as implying a further limitation of the right of priority". The Enlarged Board set out a two-step test for assessing whether a generic "OR"-claim may enjoy partial priority:

1. Determine the subject-matter disclosed in the priority document that is relevant in respect of prior art disclosed in the priority interval (under the EPO's "direct and unambiguous" standard laid down in G 2/98 (see §5.27));
2. Examine whether this subject-matter is encompassed by the claim of the application or patent claiming said priority.

■ 3. If the answer to the second question is yes, the claim is de facto conceptually divided into two parts, the first corresponding to the invention disclosed directly and unambiguously in the priority document, the second being the remaining part of the subsequent generic "OR"-claim not enjoying this priority (but itself giving rise to a right to priority). In other words, the claim is entitled to partial priority.

■ The Enlarged Board did not directly consider the issue of "poisonous priority" or "poisonous divisionals" i.e. the decision does not directly address the question of whether a family member can form part of the relevant prior art. However, in endorsing a generous approach to partial priority based on a conceptual division of the claim, the problem should no longer arise. The subject-matter in the priority document or divisional application can no longer be "poisonous" because it shares the same priority as that subject-matter in the claim. In T 260/14 *3M INNOVATIVE PROPERTIES Polyether-based preparations* partial priority was acknowledged and parent/divisional conflict was avoided, citing G 2/08 and G 1/15 and T 1222/11 *KAO CORPORATION/Hair cosmetic composition* where it was observed at Reasons 11.8 that a decision on whether partial priority can be acknowledged for subject-matter disclosed in a priority document and encompassed by an "OR"-claim cannot depend on whether this subject-matter was expressly identified as a separate alternative in the claim.

■ Decisions of the Enlarged Board of Appeal are not binding on UK courts, although they are persuasive. It therefore remains to be seen whether the UK courts will follow G 1/15 or will continue to adopt the approach in *Nestec* above.

The nature of the test for priority (subs.(2))

—Test of "supported by matter disclosed" (subs.(2)(a))

5.24 *To the end of the seventh paragraph (beginning "See also Samsung Electronics Ltd v Apple Retail UK Ltd [2013] EWHC 467 (Pat)"), add:*

■ The latter decision was affirmed [2017] EWCA Civ 266, with the observation that although the law entitlement to priority shares with the law of novelty the common feature of assessing the disclosure of a document, it is important to recognise that that is where the analogy stops.

> "One does not assess priority, however, by asking whether everything which falls within the claim is clearly and unambiguously taught by the priority document. A test of that kind would make claiming priority impossibly hard. The exercise of determining priority involves asking whether the invention is directly and unambiguously derivable from the priority document, not whether every possible embodiment of the invention is so derivable."

After the eighth paragraph (beginning "It would therefore appear to follow that priority cannot be accorded"), add new paragraph:

In *Hospira UK Ltd v Cubist Pharmaceuticals LLC* [2016] EWHC 1285, Carr J carried out a detailed analysis of G 2/98 *PRESIDENT'S REFERENCE/Same invention* and applied the legal principles in the context of dosing ranges. He rejected the patentee's arguments that "same invention" is determined by asking whether "the same crux of the invention" or the "key concept" is disclosed in the priority document, and that when a dosage range is disclosed there is necessarily disclosure of a sub-range within that range. Birss J supported this conclusion in *Actavis Group PTC EHF v ICOS Corp & Eli Lilly and Co* [2016] EWHC 1955 (Pat), where he also considered dosing ranges, holding that "there is not a special law for priority concerning sub-ranges". Also in *Actavis Group* there is a lengthy discussion whether a compound named in the priority document is the compound tadalafil subsequently claimed or another compound of the same general structure but being a different stereoisomer and whether it is the same as a compound named in a table. In the outcome, although the named compound was held to be tadalafil, a clerical slip had been made in drafting the table, there were various options for interpreting the table and the skilled reader would understand that the relevant compound in the table might be tadalafil but would be left in real doubt. Although priority was maintained for relevant claims, the nomenclature and clerical error disputes took up some 57 paragraphs of a 490-paragraph judgment which shows, if such demonstration is needed, the importance of clarity in chemical nomenclature and structural formulae for relatively complex structures, especially where stereoisomers are involved.

—Test of "disclosed in the earlier relevant application" (subs.(2)(b))

Add new paragraph at end: **5.25**

■ In *Unwired Planet International Ltd v Huawei Technologies* [2017] EWCA Civ 266, the Court of Appeal considered the correct approach to determination of priority. Arnold J (sitting in the Court of Appeal) noted that, although the law of entitlement to priority shares with the law of novelty the common feature of assessing the disclosure of a document, it is important to recognise that that is where the analogy stops. For novelty, everything which falls within the claim must be novel. However, Arnold J said that priority is not assessed by asking whether everything which falls within the claim is clearly and unambiguously taught in the priority document: a test of that kind would make claiming priority impossibly hard. The exercise of determining priority involves asking whether the *invention* is directly and unambiguously derivable from the priority document, not whether every possible embodiment of the invention is so derivable. He also held that the priority document must not be read in a vacuum, but with the benefit of the common general knowledge which forms the factual matrix against which the technical disclosure is assessed. He commented that viewed with that knowledge, the disclosure may mean something different to the skilled person than it does to someone reading the document without that knowledge, particularly bearing in mind that one is concerned with both explicit and implicit disclosure.

—Test of "same invention" applied by the EPO (art.87(1))

Add new paragraph at end: **5.27**

■ See also §5.22 for a discussion of G 1/15, which consolidates the position following G 2/98, and T 0260/14 which applies G 1/15 in this context.

SECTION 6—Disclosure of matter, etc., between earlier and later applications

COMMENTARY ON SECTION 6

Relevant EPO decisions

Add new paragraph at end: **6.04**

■ A cautionary tale for all applicants and not just those in the life sciences field on the limited nature of "provisional protection" and the dangers of intervening publication is provided by case T 1213/05 *Breast and ovarian cancer/UNIVERSITY OF UTAH* discussed in §76A.18 of the Main Work. University inventors and others with incentives for early publication of research results are at particular risk of undue confidence in the protection given by an earlier-filed application and incautious publication of subsequent results or proposals.

Right to apply for and obtain a patent and be mentioned as inventor [Sections 7-13]

SECTION 7—Right to apply for and obtain a patent

7.00   *Add new paragraph 7.00:*

Contents

7.01   *Add new paragraph at end of Note:*

In the event that arrangements for the European patent with unitary effect come into force in the UK, the Patents (European Patent with Unitary Effect and Unified Patent Court) Order 2016/388, para.2(10) will ensure that, in s.7(2)(b), the reference to "the United Kingdom" will be a reference to "any of the Participating Member States".

COMMENTARY ON SECTION 7

Who may be granted a patent (subs.(2))

7.06   *To the end of the tenth paragraph (beginning "Consequently, s.7(2)(c) makes it possible to assign"), add:*

In *Wright Hassall LLP v George Shortland Horton Jr* [2015] EWHC 3716 (QB) it was held that an assignment of the s.7(2)(c) right to an invention (the right to apply for a patent) is not invalidated by an absence of consideration.

SECTION 12—Determination of questions about entitlement to foreign and convention patents, etc.

COMMENTARY ON SECTION 12

Application of section 12 in practice

After the third paragraph (beginning "In contrast, in Statoil v University of Southampton"), add new paragraph: **12.04**

In proceedings initiated by a reference pursuant to s.12, it is only in exceptional circumstances that a judge or Hearing Officer is entitled to resort to the burden of proof (alone) as the basis for decision: see *University of Warwick v Dr Geoffrey Graham Diamond* BL O/518/15 for an example of such exceptional circumstances in the context of a dispute under s.39, see also §39.07.

PRACTICE UNDER SECTION 12

After the first paragraph, add new paragraph: **12.06**

In *HAPSS Ltd* BL O/247/16, where a reference under s.12 was opposed, the opposition was deemed withdrawn under r.104(4)(c) after the opponent failed to provide an address for service within two months of having been directed by the Office to do so. By SI 2016/892 the Government has amended the Patents Rules 2007 to allow parties to request a two-month extension of time in which to provide an address for service, by removing the reference to r.104(2) from Pt 1 of Sch.4 and listing it instead under Pts 2 and Part 3 of that Schedule. Any request for an extension will need to be made on PF52 and accompanied by the relevant fee.

To the end of the second paragraph (beginning "While proceedings under s.12 are pending on an application"), add:

In joined cases J 2/14 and J 24/13 *ANHEUSER-BUSCH/Stay of proceedings*, the EPO Board of Appeal found that where grant proceedings had been stayed pursuant to r.14(1) EPC, the question whether the scope of the inventions claimed before the national court was identical to that conferred by the stayed patent applications lay within the exclusive competence of the court before which the entitlement action was brought. Only where it was clear that there was no identity could the EPO reject the request for a stay due to non-compliance with r.14(1). However, the EPO was competent to decide whether to lift the stay of grant proceedings under r.14(3), regardless of the stage reached in the national entitlement proceedings. In the circumstances of the case, where the entitlement proceedings had been started three and a half years previously and had not been actively pursued such that no substantive hearing had taken place, it was appropriate to lift the stay of the grant proceedings.

SECTION 13—Mention of inventor

COMMENTARY ON SECTION 13

Amendment of inventorship entities

After the fifth paragraph (beginning "Otherwise, correction may be effected under s.117 and r.105"), add new paragraph: **13.13**

New Rule 49(6)(b) (effective 1 October 2016, see §32.09) is intended to clarify that a name or address correction may arise from change of circumstances (rather than only by way of error).

Amendment of named inventors(s)

13.17   *In the fourth paragraph (beginning "The onus of proof is on the applicant"), replace the first sentence with:,*

■ The onus of proof is on the applicant who seeks addition or deletion of an inventorship entity, see *Bond Knittings Systems' Patent* BL O/125/87 and C/35/88; and *Mawzones' Patent* BL O/17/95, noted I.P.D. 18026, in each of which the application failed on its facts, and *Rose v Ability* BL O/247/11, which succeeded, and *Alan Neath v Peter Neath* BL O/407/16.

To the end of the fourth paragraph (beginning "The onus of proof is on the applicant"), add:

■ In *Alan Neath v Peter Neath*, Alan Neath succeeded in adding himself as inventor, but failed to have Peter Neath removed as inventor. The Hearing Officer noted that there was no burden of proof on Peter Neath in order for him to remain named as inventor.

Applications [Sections 14-16]

SECTION 14—Making of application

14.00   *Add new paragraph 14.00:*

Contents

RELEVANT RULES—RULES 12-14, SCHEDULE 2, AND RULES 15-16

Replace r.12 with: **14.02**

Rule 12—Applications for the grant of patents under sections 14 and 15

12.—(1) A request for the grant of a patent must be made on Patents Form 1.

(2) Where the documents filed at the Patent Office to initiate an application for a patent do not include the applicant's name and address, the comptroller shall notify the applicant that his name and address are required.

(3) Where the applicant has been so notified, he must, before the end of the period of two months beginning [with] immediately after the date of the notification, file his name and address; otherwise the comptroller may refuse his application.

(4) The specification mentioned in section 14(2)(b) must be preceded by the title of the invention and must be set out in the following order—

    (a) description;

    (b) the claim or claims; and

    (c) any drawing **or photograph** referred to in the description or any claim.

(5) But paragraph (4) does not apply where an application is delivered in electronic form or using electronic communications.

(6) The title of the invention must be short and indicate the matter to which the invention relates.

(6A) **The claim or claims must not rely in respect of the technical features of the invention on references to the description or any drawing or photograph unless the feature cannot otherwise be clearly and concisely defined in words, by a mathematical or chemical formula or by any other written means.**

(7) Where the specification includes drawings **or photographs**, the description must include a list of drawings **and photographs** briefly describing each of them.

(8) Where—

(a) the documents filed at the Patent Office to initiate an application for a patent include something which is or appears to be a description of the invention in a language other than English or Welsh; and

(b) the applicant has not filed a translation into English or Welsh of that thing, the comptroller shall notify the applicant that a translation is required.

(9) Where the applicant has been so notified, he must, before the end of the period of two months beginning with the date of the notification, file a translation; otherwise the comptroller may refuse his application.

Add new paragraph at end of Note:

Rule 12 has been amended (effective 1 October 2016) by para.3 of the Patents (Amendment) (No.2) Rules 2016 (SI 2016/892). The amended rule reads as set out above. The amendments are subject to the transitional provision that the amendment made by r.3(b) does not apply to an application for a patent in respect of which the compliance period expired before 6 April 2017.

Rule 14—Size and presentation of application

14.04   *Replace r.14(2)-(4) with:*

(2) The requirements for the documents contained in an application for a patent (other than drawings **and photographs**) are set out in Parts 1 and 2 of Schedule 2.

(3) The requirements for a drawing **and a photograph** contained in an application are set out in Parts 1 and 3 of that Schedule.

(4) All documents contained in an application (including drawings **and photographs**) must comply with the requirements set out in Part 4 of that Schedule.

Add new Note:

Note. Rule 14 has been amended (effective 1 October 2016) by para.4 of the Patents (Amendment) (No.2) Rules 2016 (SI 2016/892).

Replace heading to Part 2, all of Part 3, and para.21 to Part 4 as follows: **14.05**

Rule 14   **SCHEDULE 2**

Formal and other Requirements

PART 2

REQUIREMENTS: DOCUMENTS (OTHER THAN DRAWINGS AND PHOTOGRAPHS)

PART 3

REQUIREMENTS: DRAWINGS

11. There must be a margin around any drawing **or photograph** which must be at least—

(a) at the top and left side, 20mm;

(b) at the right side, 15mm; and

(c) at the bottom, 10mm.

12. All drawings **or photographs** must be numbered consecutively in a single series.

13. The drawings **or photographs** must begin on a new sheet of paper.

14. The pages containing the drawings or photographs must be numbered consecutively in a single series.

15. **Drawings must comprise black lines and may be shaded where the shading assists in representing the shape of a thing provided that it does not obscure other elements of the drawing.** *[Drawings must comprise black lines and must not be shaded.]*

16. Drawings may include cross-hatching to illustrate the cross-sections of a thing.

17. Any scale or other reference for making measurement must be represented diagrammatically.

18. Any drawing **or photograph** must be produced in such manner that it would still be clear if it were reduced by linear reduction to two thirds of its original size.

19. A drawing **or photograph** must not be included in the description, the claims, the abstract or the request for the grant of a patent.

20. The capital letters in any typeface or font used in any drawing **or photograph** must be more than 3mm high.

20A. **Photographs must be black and white, clear and capable of direct reproduction.**

PART 4

OTHER REQUIREMENTS

21. References must only be included in the drawing **or photograph** where they are mentioned in either the description or the claims.

Add new Note:

Note. Parts 2, 3 and 4 of Schedule 2 have been amended (effective 1 October 2016); para.15 of the Patents (Amendment) (No.2) Rules 2016 (SI 2016/892).

Rule 15—The abstract

14.07   *Replace r.15(4)-(6) with:*

(4) Where the specification contains more than one drawing **or photograph**, the abstract must include an indication of the drawing which should accompany the abstract when it is published.

(5) Where it appears to the comptroller that a drawing **or photograph** included in the specification better characterises the invention he shall publish it with the abstract.

(6) Where a feature of the invention included in the abstract is illustrated in a drawing **or photograph**, the feature must be followed by the reference for that feature used in that drawing or photograph.

Add new Note:

Note. Rule 15 has been amended (effective 1 October 2016) by para.5 of the Patents (Amendment) (No.2) Rules 2016 (SI 2016/892).

COMMENTARY ON SECTION 14

The Request (subs.(2)(a))

—Application fee

14.18   *Add new paragraph at end:*

■ A major change in application fees likely to come into effect on 6 April 2018 is reported in a Government response to a consultation in April-June 2017 and updated on 5 October 2017, downloadable from the UK IP Office website. The changes implement a policy objective of setting set fees at levels which can help shape customer behaviour and result in clearer, better defined applications whilst reducing the number of hopeless applications filed and will also benefit third parties who will better be able to see the nature of the invention and scope of protection. As a way of discouraging large numbers of unclear claims, the IPO is proposing to adopt a system used by many other patent offices (including the EPO) and introduce a fee for each individual claim which exceeds a threshold. As a way of encouraging clearly and succinctly defined applications, the IPO is proposing to introduce a fee for each page of description filed over a threshold. The current proposal envisages fees of £20 per claim for the 26th and subsequent claims payable as part of the search fee, which will affect the 25% of applications which at the time of search currently have more than this number of claims with 5% of applications containing 50 or more claims. A grant fee will be payable if the number of claims increases during prosecution. It is also proposed to introduce a fee of £10 for each additional page of description over the initial 35 pages, this fee being payable at the time of substantive examination. Other changes include an increase in basic application fees with a surcharge if the fee is not paid at the time of filing and increases in the search and substantive examination fees which are to be set at £150/180 and £100/130 for electronic and paper requests respectively.

The Specification (subs.(2)(b))

—The description

14.22   *Replace the eleventh paragraph (beginning "As discussed more fully in §14.35,") with:*

The amendments to Rule 12 now place limits on the use of "omnibus" claims as also discussed in §14.35. Such claims (being claims which are drafted in terms of the invention

42

"as described in" the description or drawings) are now only available in cases where the features of the invention cannot be clearly and concisely defined by other means.

—The drawings

Add new paragraphs at end: **14.23**
Effective 1 October 2016, the IPO relaxed requirements on formal drawings and photographs. See paras 3, 4, 5 and 15 of the Patents (Amendment) (No.2) Rules 2016 (SI 2016/892) reprinted at §14.02, §14.04, §14.05 and §14.07 respectively.

Despite these multitudinous amendments to add the word "photograph" after any reference in the rules to "drawing" s.14(2)(b) of the Act remains unchanged (since it cannot be changed by SI) referring only to "drawings". Nor has there been any change to s.125 defining the scope of protection by reference to drawings with no reference to photographs. There are various other sections of the Act which refer only to drawings. It is submitted that it is unhelpful to draw a distinction between drawings and photographs in the rules whilst the Act must require that drawings includes photographs.

In its Guidance of 1 September 2016, the IPO states the following:

> "[The IPO] will allow shading in drawings, providing the shading does not obscure other parts of the drawing. It will also be possible to include black and white photographs, providing they are clear and capable of reproduction. This will bring the legislation more clearly into line with current IPO practice, providing clarity and legal certainty for patent applicants. The IPO will continue to reject drawings and photographs if they are not suitable for publication."

Sufficiency of description (subs.(3))

—General requirements for sufficiency

Add new paragraph at end: **14.24**
In T 0809/12 *GUARDIAN/Matchable coated articles* the Board was of the opinion that the technical contribution does not normally reside in the fact that the problem is solved, but rather in the combination of features by which it is solved, i.e. by the essential features necessary to solve the technical problem underlying the application. The Board therefore concluded that, if an independent claim contains a feature defined by a result to be achieved which essentially corresponds to the problem underlying the application, to comply with art.84 EPC the remaining features of the claim must comprise all essential features necessary for achieving that result.

—References to other applications and documents

Add new paragraph at end: **14.26**
■ The *MOPP* explained at 14.93 that the allowability of a reference to another document needs to be considered in the context of the clear and complete disclosure requirement. A recently added note explains that on the other hand, a reference to a document containing information which is not essential for sufficiency need not be considered; such references are allowable.

—Classical insufficiency

After the first paragraph, add new paragraphs: **14.28**
■ In *Unwired v Huawei* [2016] EWHC 576 (Pat) at 149, Birss J summarised the situation thus:

> "Different kinds of insufficiency have been identified. One is sometimes called classical insufficiency. There the problem is that the skilled person just cannot make the invention work

either at all or without undue effort. Another type is sometimes called Biogen insufficiency. There the problem is that the claim is too wide and is not commensurate with the inventor's technical contribution. This case is concerned with a third type, ambiguity. Some forms of ambiguity pose no legal difficulty. An ambiguity in a descriptive passage in the specification which causes the skilled person to be unable to make anything at all is a kind of classical insufficiency which falls squarely within the section. However other cases are about ambiguity in the way the invention is defined in the claim."

A legally straightforward if scientifically complex example of classical insufficiency is found in *Regeneron Pharmaceuticals v Kymab Ltd* [2016] EWHC 87 (Pat) which concerned transgenic mice, a mouse variable gene being replaced with human variable genes to produce hybrid antibodies. It was found on the evidence that deletions and insertions of DNA on the necessary scale were not enabled by the disclosure in the patents. That finding was corroborated by the difficulties that the patentees had encountered when seeking to put the invention into practice and the ingenuity of the approach that led to eventual success. The difficulties did not relate to some hypothetical puzzle at the edge of the claim, but instead to the central disclosure of the specification, and the amounts of genetic sequence of which it contemplated the deletion and insertion. This outcome may be compared with the opposite conclusion reached by the EPO Appeal Board in case T 2220/14 *REGENERON/VelocImmune mouse*.

■ A recent example of classic insufficiency is *F Secure Corp* BL O/198/17, applying *Eli Lilly v Human Genome Sciences* [2008] EWHC 1903 (Pat); [2008] R.P.C. 29 at [239]. The specification did not enable the skilled addressee to select a malware processing method, a key step in the claim. The disclosure therefore did not satisfy the test in *Edison & Swan v Holland* (1889) 41 Ch. D 28; (1889) 6 R.P.C. 243 at 282 that if anything new has to be found out by a person of competent skill following the directions in the specification in order to succeed then the disclosure in the specification is insufficient.

■ Conversely in *Varian Medical Systems v Elekta* [2017] EWHC 712 (Pat) the disclosure was sufficient to produce a "workable prototype", notwithstanding it required "an awful lot of essentially routine work by a substantial team over a lengthy period, but involving challenges of a known kind and neither involving solution of new problems nor solution of old problems in a new way. In this field that is not an undue burden" [274]. An argument that if the patent was sufficient despite the paucity of the disclosure in the specification, it must follow that the invention was obvious, citing *Synthon BV v SmithKlineBecham Plc (No.2)* [2005] UKHL 59, was not followed because the position of the skilled person differed as between obviousness and insufficiency. However, the production of a combined machine as claimed was a desirable goal, and although it would have been difficult the skilled team would not have been deterred by the challenges facing them [310] and would have arrived at the invention, this not being a case like *Schlumberger* in which the invention brought two kinds of skilled people together [313].

After the eighth paragraph (beginning "In Idenix Pharmaceuticals Inc v Gilead Sciences Inc"), add new paragraphs:

In *Merck v Ono* [2015] EWHC 2973 (Pat) a submission was considered that *in vivo* data was required to make the invention there plausible. It was not accepted that there was any such principle and it was concluded at [139] that: "The principle applicable to purpose limited medical use claims must be that the material relied on to establish plausibility must be both sufficiently specific, and have a sufficient breadth of application, to fairly support the claim both in terms of the nature of the agent claimed to have an effect, and in terms of the effect claimed." That view was maintained in *Actavis and Actelion v Teva and Generics* [2016] EWHC 1955 (Pat) where it was explained [232] that the issue of enablement of a use claim (which involves plausibility) is a fact-sensitive question which cannot be summarised as a requirement for *in vivo* data. The fact the drug tested *in vivo* in patients in an example is not disclosed as the presently claimed compound did not necessarily rule out an enabling disclosure of the use claims.

■ In T 2059/13 *OTSUKA/ Aripiprazole against bipolar disorder* the specification disclosed agonism of the 5HT1A receptor, but the relationship between agonism of that receptor and utility in the treatment of bipolar disorder was held to be mere assertion unsupported by evidence or any conclusive line of argument. Plausibility was therefore held not to have been established and the minimum requirements for sufficiency set out in T 609/02 *SALT INSTITUTE/AP-1 complex* had not been met, see also e.g. T 1329/11 *ROCHE/Use of BNP-type peptides*.

—Insufficiency by breadth of claim

After the third paragraph (beginning "In Pharmacia v Merck [2002] R.P.C. 41"), add new paragraphs: **14.29**

■ One class of cases to which classical and arguably also *Biogen* insufficiency is applicable is chemical and pharmaceutical inventions for which activity is alleged for a genus of compounds defined as a Markush group, that principle being explained in T 488/16 *BRISTOL-MYERS SQUIBB/Dasatinib* discussed in §14.28.

■ In relation to inventions of this type, the objection that it is not plausible that the asserted technical effect is not exhibited by all members of the claimed group could be regarded as a substitute for experimental evidence that some members do not exhibit the effect. A classic example of experimentally demonstrated insufficiency is provided by *Monsanto v Merck* [2000] R.P.C. 77, affirmed sub nom *Pharmacia v Merck* [2001] EWCA Civ 1610; [2002] R.P.C. 41.

■ A further paradigm example is provided by *Merck Sharp and Dohme v Shionogi* [2016] EWHC 2989 (Pat) where the allegedly infringing antiviral agent raltegravir had not been disclosed as an individual compound in the patent in issue, but was alleged to fall within two generic Markush claims in Swiss form. There was experimental evidence that some of the claimed compound were ineffective. More significantly, on the issue of plausibility it was estimated that one of the relevant claims covered some 10^{39} compounds which exceeded the total number of unique chemical substances ever registered in the American Chemical Society CAS Registry by a factor of approximately 10^{31}. It was irrelevant that the claim was functionally limited to compounds that "worked". The specification taught the skilled team nothing about the relationship between the structures of the claimed compounds and their activity and they would appreciate that small changes in structures not merely could, but would be likely to, have an impact on the activity of the compounds. Plausibility was established only for a tiny fraction of the claimed compounds. Furthermore, the invention could not be performed across the scope of the claim without undue burden. Even assuming that compounds could be synthesised sufficiently quickly to enable a constant testing rate of 200 compounds/week, it would take 9.6×10^{30} years to assay just 0.01% of the claimed compounds, which is about 2×10^{21} times the age of the Earth. The upshot was that the patent presented the skilled team with a vast research project with a high likelihood of failure, but claims the results if they happen to succeed—even if (as in the case of raltegravir) such success had nothing to do with the teaching of the patent. As explained in the Main Work, this approach had been followed by Arnold J in *Idenix Pharmaceuticals Inc v Gilead Sciences Inc* [2014] EWHC 3916 (Pat), finding it implausible that all compounds covered by the claim had the alleged activity. That position has now been upheld by the Court of Appeal in a lead judgment by Kitchin LJ [2016] EWCA Civ 1089. Similar reasoning was applied by the UK IPO in *The Hong Kong University of Science and Technology's Application* BL O/326/17 in which a single compound had been isolated from the root of the herbal plant *Rhodiola Rosea* and was said to be useful in the management of pain and type 2 diabetes, but in which a genus of compounds had been defined by a Markush formula with substituents from R_1 to R_{11} some of which were defined by open-ended terms e.g. "alkyl" and "aryl". The Examiner identified from *Biogen Inc v Medeva Plc* [1997] R.P.C. 1 and *Pharmacia v Merck* [2001] EWCA Civ 1610; [2002] R.P.C. 41 three necessary conditions for sufficiency: (a) when a range of compounds is claimed the specification should contain sufficient information on how to make them, (b) the compounds covered by the claim must all have the advantage or avoid the disadvantage that characterizes the selected group and (c) sufficiency must be demonstrated at the date of filing. Disclosure of starting materials and synthetic routes was lacking, and the postulated structure-activity relationship (SAR) was not an inevitable consequence and necessarily predictable absent any evidence in the specification that there was clearly a SAR arising from the core scaffold structure provided in the Markush formula. In the outcome, the only amendment that might result in grant was restriction to the single novel compound that had been disclosed.

■ The EPO approach is similar. In T 488/16 *BRISTOL-MYERS SQUIBB/Dasatinib* a number of earlier decisions were reviewed and it was held that although experimental results are not always required, it is a *conditio sine qua non* that it is shown that the technical problem underlying the invention was at least plausibly solved at the filing date. If, as in the present case, the nature of the invention is such that it relies on a technical effect, which is neither self-evident nor predictable or based on a conclusive theoretical concept, at least some technical evidence is required to show that a technical problem has indeed been solved. It is not acceptable to draw up a generic formula, which covers millions of compounds, vaguely indicate an "activity" against a particular indication and leave it to the imagination of the skilled reader or to future investigations to establish which compound inhibits which enzyme and is therefore suitable to treat the respective diseases associated therewith. In the present case, the issue was not the absence of any *in vivo* data or clinical data, but rather the absence of any verifiable data with regard to the asserted technical effect.

■ A different outcome may be appropriate where prediction is possible, see *Element Six Technologies US Corporation's Application* BL O/001/17. Management of the heat generated in operation by electronic and optoelectronic devices is a critical design requirement, particular difficulties arising in devices made on a III-V semiconductor substrate e.g. gallium nitride (GaN), Polycrystalline diamond could be deposited on non-diamond substrates by CVD, and the invention concerned formation of an interface region of reduced thermal boundary resistance achieved by a nucleation layer which was more crystalline and less graphite-like, with the diamond crystals in that layer falling within a particular range of nucleation densities. Evidence in the specification showed that the quality of the diamond at the nucleation layer was linked with the thermal conductivity of this important interfacial region which was related to controlling the formation and size of diamond crystalline phase during nucleation. The product claim was held to be supported across its full breadth and to meet the fair entitlement requirement of *Schering Biotech Corp's Application, Re* [1993] R.P.C 249, 252-253 and *David Khan Inc v Conway Stewart & Co Ltd* [1972] F.S.R. 620; [1974] R.P.C 279 at pp.319-320 even though only a single embodiment had been disclosed.

To the end of the fourth paragraph (beginning "In relation to a claim for further medical uses"), add:

The above decision was affirmed sub nom. *Warner-Lambert Company LLC v Generics (UK) Ltd (t/a Mylan)* [2016] EWCA Civ 1006 where the court reaffirmed that plausibility is a low threshold test, and explained that:

"It is designed to prohibit speculative claiming, which would otherwise allow the armchair inventor a monopoly over a field of endeavour to which he has made no contribution. It is not designed to prohibit patents for good faith predictions which have some, albeit manifestly incomplete, basis. Such claims may turn out to be insufficient nonetheless if the prediction turns out to be untrue. A patent which accurately predicts that an invention will work is, however, not likely to be revoked on the ground that the prediction was based on the slimmest of evidence. Thus, the claims will easily be seen not to be speculative where the inventor provides a reasonably credible theory as to why the invention will or might work. The same is true where the data in the specification is such that the reader is encouraged to try the invention.

We heard argument as to whether the invention is only to be treated as plausible if the reader of the specification would be encouraged to try the invention with a reasonable prospect of success, thereby bringing the test for plausibility into line with that sometimes used in the context of obviousness. I do not accept that there is any reason to align the tests in this way. A test designed to prevent speculative claiming need go no further than requiring the patentee to show that the claim is not speculative: the specification does not need to provide the reader with any greater degree of confidence in the patentee's prediction than that."

It was accepted that there could be cases where an insufficiency attack focused on a contrived or artificial part of the claim, and where, as a consequence, the attack did not undermine the validity of the claim as a matter of substance. The present case was, however, a long way from such a case. Once it was accepted that there was a significant part of the claim which, although perhaps representing a minority of conditions, neverthe-less covered some important ones, there was no basis for saying that, as a matter of substance, that part of the claim could be ignored when considering whether it is plausible [121], [122].

The claims (subs.(5))

—Claims of a functional nature

After the third paragraph (beginning "In Mayne Pharma Pty Ltd v Debiopharm SA"), add new paragraphs: **14.34**

■ In *Acumen Design Associates Ltd* BL O/031/17, the claims related to a seating assembly for an aircraft cabin defined by the result that a passenger access path was produced between the seats. Although the Hearing Officer found that it was possible to define the invention without reference to the result to be achieved, it was considered that to define it in any other way would unduly restrict the scope of monopoly sought. In addition, it was determined that the claimed result could be easily verified by a person skilled in the art.

■ In *Element Six's Application* BL O/001/17 also discussed at § 14.29, the Hearing Officer was persuaded by evidence at a hearing that Raman spectroscopy was well known in the art as a method of characterizing a diamond material. Therefore, defining a device by reference to a Raman spectrum was not a definition by result to be achieved. However, in T 809/12 *GUARDIAN/Matchable coated articles* the Appeal Board noted that a particu-lar situation arises when a product is defined by the result to be achieved, the result corresponding in essence to the problem underlying the application. In T 573/03 *ASTRAZENECA/Azetidine-2-carboxylic acid* the independent process claim did not contain any physical process step and was defined only by the final result of the process, which final result corresponded to the problem underlying the application (see reasons 2, 3 and 7.3.3). The Board concluded that the requirements of art.84 EPC and r.29(1) EPC 1973 were not complied with (see reasons 2.5), similarly T 383/04 *MCALISTER/Operation of engines*, T 1787/08 *3M/Radio frequency identification tags* and T 2065/10 *HARRIS/Trellis decoder* where the claimed programmable decoder had been defined solely as a "black box" instead of its essential properties being specified. An independent claim must indicate all the essential features of the object of the invention in order to comply with the requirements of art.84 EPC 1973 (see G 2/88 *MOBIL OIL III/Friction reducing additive*, reasons 2.5 and G 1/04 *PRESIDENT'S REFERENCE/Diagnostic methods*). As explained in § 14.24 the Board was of the opinion that the technical contribution does not normally reside in the fact that the problem is solved, but rather in the combination of features by which it is solved, i.e. by the essential features necessary to solve the technical problem underlying the application. Therefore, if an independent claim contains a feature defined by a result to be achieved which essentially corresponds to the problem underlying the application, to comply with art.84 EPC 1973 the remaining features of the claim must comprise all essential features necessary for achieving that result.

—Claims of the "omnibus" type

Replace with: **14.35**

■ From 6 April 2017, the UK IPO will raise an objection to all applications bearing omnibus claims still pending on 6 April 2017 (unless the compliance period has already expired). See UK-IPO Guidance of 1 September 2016. This change is effected by the addition of sub-para.6A to r.12. See §14.02 for the text of this rule.

In justifying the change, the IPO Guidance states the following:

"Patent claims define the scope of the monopoly provided by the patent by setting out the technical features present in the invention. Sometimes claims are drafted in such manner as to refer generally to the description or drawings included in the patent application. Such claims do not state the technical features of the invention claimed and are known as "omnibus claims". Understanding these claims can be difficult and can lead to a lack of clarity about the scope of protection provided by the patent. This can make it difficult for businesses to know if they are likely to infringe a competitor's patent... Limiting the use of omnibus claims will increase legal certainty for businesses looking to determine whether they can operate in a particular technology area. It will bring UK requirements into line with the requirements of the European Patent Convention (EPC) and the international Patent Cooperation Treaty (PCT)."

The IPO has also stated that effective 6 April 2017 it is no longer possible to amend a granted patent to insert an omnibus claim.

During the consultation, the additional requirement of "concisely" was added to the text of the rule. It was observed that the text proposed seemed to go further than necessary only to outlaw omnibus claims and would potentially prohibit legitimate references to the description. The new text is therefore not intended to include scenarios such as those discussed in the *EPO Guidelines* at F-IV, 4.17. Those *Guidelines* give two examples of allowable references the first in which the invention involves some peculiar shape illustrated in the drawings but which cannot be readily defined either in words or by a simple mathematical formula; and the second of a chemical product some of whose features can be defined only by means of graphs or diagrams. A third example of a reference to the description permitted by the EPO is in relation to how a claimed parameter is to be measured in cases where it would be too long concisely to be recited in the claim. See the *Guidelines* at F-IV, 4.18.

As a matter of practice the EPO also appears to permit disclaimers of the form "except for Example X of EPXXXXXXX". Presumably such a form of disclaimer, until tested by EPO case law, should be permissible.

—Claims to be clear and concise (subs.(5)(b))

14.37   *After the second paragraph (beginning "The EPO Guideline F-IV, 4.1"), add new paragraphs:*

Additional fees are payable in the EPO for claims in excess of 15, and practitioners commonly combine claims to different embodiments using expressions such as "or", "optionally" or "preferably". The legitimacy of this practice was considered in T 1882/12 *HENKEL/Teeth polishing substances* (inexplicably classified as category D, no distribution despite the general importance of the issue raised) where the claim under consideration read in translation: "A mouth and tooth care and purification agent according to claim 1, characterized in that it contains 12 to 60 wt.-%, preferably 15 to 50 wt.-%, more preferably 17 to 40 wt.-% and particularly 20 to 35 wt.-% of sorbitol and/or glycerol and/or 1,2 propylene glycol." The Examining Division argued that this language contravened art.84 EPC and r.43(3) and (4). The Board held that neither of these rules precluded optional features, and that the issue was whether the clarity and conciseness requirements of art.84 EPC were complied with. The *Guidelines for Examination* at F-III 4.9 considered these expressions but expressed no rule that they were generally inadmissible. The Board confirmed this view provided that clarity is not compromised. The Board also rejected the Examining Division's argument that thus-formulated claims are not concise, since they arguably contained superfluous, non-limiting features. The Board recognised that from the applicant's perspective such optional preferred features served the purpose of providing fall-back positions in the further proceedings or later in opposition proceedings. It held that it was conceivable that there could be instances where convoluted pyramid-like claims might be less clear and easy to understand than several dependent claims avoiding optional features. However, it was of the view that in the present case the use of optional preferred features was reasonably confined, that the understandability of the claims was not compromised thereby and that the effort required to analyse the claims was not unduly increased by the presence of these preferable features. The practice is further discussed by Yanin Robin, "An Ambiguous Relationship, Optional Features, Article 84 EPC and Rule 137(5) EPC" [2016] 10 *CIPA* 46.

■ Clarity of the expression "consisting essentially of" was considered in T 2027/13 *LUPIN/Controlled release pharmaceutical compositions of pregabalin*. The term is normally used in the context of the whole composition claimed, and is inappropriate when used for a single ingredient of a multi-ingredient composition, especially where that composition is defined by an open formulation (in view of the word "comprising"), permitting additional components and impurities.

■ Use of optional language in claims and its relationship to art.84 EPC is discussed by Yanin Robin, "An Ambiguous Relationship, Optional Features, Article 84 EPC and Rule 137(5) EPC" [2016] 10 *CIPA* 46-48.

To the end of the seventeenth paragraph (beginning "In Fruehauf's Application BL O/185/83"), add:

■ More recently the practice has been modified, and where trade marks relate to internationally agreed standards which specify the technologies identified by those trade marks, for example Bluetooth and WiFi, these trade marks may be allowable.

Add new paragraphs at end:

In *Unwired Planet International v Huawei* [2016] EWHC 576 (Pat) the court considered *Plimpton v Malcolmson* (1876) 3 Ch.D. 531, *British Thomson-Houston v Corona* (1921) 39 R.P.C. 49, *Biogen v Medeva* [1997] R.P.C. 1 and *Scanvaegt v Pelcombe* [1998] F.S.R. 786, but ultimately concluded that an objection of insufficiency was not established because the present case differed from *Kirin-Amgen v Hoechst Marion Roussel* [2004] UKHL 46 on its facts, observing that:

"In *Kirin-Amgen* the claim required an SDS-PAGE test to be applied to two proteins in order to decide which had the higher molecular weight. The fact that the test was understood did not remove the ambiguity, namely knowing which uEPO should be used in the test. The defendants submitted that the position was the same here. I do not agree. The claim in this case is different from the one in *Kirin-Amgen*. This claim does not set its scope based on the outcome of a particular run of a comparison test. It is concerned with a conversion to allow the skilled person to carry out a direct comparison test in accordance with whatever comparison scheme the skilled person has chosen. What the outcome of the individual instances of undertaking the comparison actually is does not matter as far as the claim scope is concerned. The fact that a network operator who converts values to make them directly comparable will produce a scheme which differs in its outcome for a given case from a scheme implemented by another operator is not relevant, nor is the fact that the operators have the facility to alter the way the comparison works."

Insufficiency on the basis of ambiguity was an issue in *Actavis v Eli Lilly* [2016] EWHC 1955 where the claim in issue required a particle size less than 40 microns. It was argued that the skilled person would understand that either a volume distribution or a number distribution could be used, but these two distributions produced radically different answers so that the claim was truly ambiguous. However, this objection was dismissed, the evidence being that the skilled formulator's common general knowledge was that a volume distribution wouldbe what he or she would wish to use.

—Claims to be supported by description (subs.(5)(c))

14.38   *Add new paragraph at end:*
■ The *MOPP* advises that the use of a compact style of consistory clause, which imports a reference to one or more claims into the statement of invention, is strongly encouraged instead of including counterparts for the claims.

After the fifteenth paragraph (beginning "The EPO has also held, though before these decisions, that the absence"), add new paragraph:
■ The *MOPP* explains at 14.139.2 and 14.144 that amendments will be needed to remove any serious inconsistency between the claims and the description e.g. as regards features said to be essential but not included in the main claim, embodiments not falling within the claims and general statements which suggest that the scope of protection is broader than the claims.

Abstract (subss.(2)(c) and (7) and r.15)

14.41   *Add new paragraph at end:*
Under the text of r.15 effective 1 October 2016, the abstract may now, at least in theory, be published with a photograph. See §14.07.

PRACTICE UNDER SECTION 14

Formal and Other Requirements

—Drawings

14.48   *Add new paragraphs at end:*
Photographs were not usually objected to under current practice provided that they were clear and reproducible. As noted in §14.05 and §14.23, there is a change to Sch.2 to the rules to include explicit reference to photographs as well as drawings to bring the Schedule in line with actual practice. The formal requirements for drawings are now generally applicable for photographs. See rr.12, 14, 15 and Sch.2 as amended by paras 3, 4, 5 and 15 of the Patents (Amendment) (No.2) Rules 2016 (SI 2016/892) reprinted at §14.02, §14.04, §14.07 and §14.05 respectively.
Under amended para.15 of Sch.2 shading may now be added to drawings insofar as it assists in representing shape.

SECTION 15—Date of filing application

15.00   *Add new paragraph 15.00:*

Contents

RELEVANT RULES—RULES 17-22

Replace r.19 with: **15.04**

Rule 19—New applications filed as mentioned in section 15(9)

19.—(1) For the purposes of section 15(9)(a) a new application may only be filed in accordance with this rule.

(2) A new application may be filed as mentioned in section 15(9) if—

(a) the earlier application has not been terminated or withdrawn; and

(b) the period ending three months before the compliance date of the earlier application has not expired.

(3) A new application must include a statement that it is filed as mentioned in section 15(9).

Replace Note with:

Note. Rule 19 has been substituted by the above (effective 1 October 2016; para.6 of the Patents (Amendment) (No.2) Rules 2016 (SI 2016/892)).

COMMENTARY ON SECTION 15

Time limits set by subsection (10) and rule 22

—Time limits set by other rules for application prosecution

15.16   *Replace Rule 32 with:*

Rule 32:   This rule has been amended so as to change the time limit for requesting reinstatement. See §§20A.02 and 20A.04.

Divisional and replacements applications (subs.(9))

—Time for filing divisional application

15.20   *Replace with:*

A divisional application may be initiated by compliance with the requirements of subs.(1) (as described in §15.10), with the facility for filing the other required documents at a later date.

Where the parent application is an international application (UK), a divisional application thereof filed after the application has entered the UK national phase will be an application under the Act governed by r.66 (beginning of national phase) and r.68 (altered prescribed periods). These matters are discussed in the commentaries on ss.89A and 89B.

The time within which a divisional application may be filed is governed by r.19 (see §15.04). As noted in §15.04 this rule is being changed so that a two-month period for filing divisional applications based on a communication under s.18(4) is no longer provided for. Instead, an advance notice of intention to grant will be provided by the UK-IPO, as is done at the EPO, so as to make clear the final date on which a divisional application may be filed (that is, the day before grant). The Government's consultation response document proposed 4 weeks or one month's advance notice of grant. The new rule will apply to existing applications.

Rule 19(2) prohibits the filing of a divisional application after the earlier application has been terminated or withdrawn which includes the position where a patent has already been granted on the application because this then no longer exists.

It also provides that the period for filing a divisional application expires three months before the "compliance date", which is the date on which an application fails if not then in condition for acceptance as required by ss.18(4) and 20(1), this period being defined in r.30 (reprinted in §18.04 and discussed in §18.11) and often described as the "rule 30 period". This is the period permitted by that rule for placing the application in compliance with the Act and Rules, including any extension of it under r.108. The compliance date is four and a half years from the earliest declared priority date if any, or otherwise from the date of filing, but with the proviso of a minimum period of 12 months after the date of the first substantive examination report issued under s.18, and three months from the filing of third party observations (see r.30(2)(b) and (4) discussed in §18.11).

It may still be advisable to indicate any intention to file a divisional application when responding to an examination report. In *Luk Lamellan's Application* [1997] R.P.C. 104, it was indicated that, where an applicant has indicated an intention to file a divisional application and the application is otherwise in order for grant, it is the practice of the UK-IPO to postpone grant for one month pending clarification of that indicated intention (see also *MOPP* 15.46).

—Late filing of divisional applications

Add new paragraph at end: **15.21**
Presumably the principles of *Fieldturf's Application* BL O/371/04 remain applicable to the period under r.19(2)(b).

PRACTICE UNDER SECTION 15

Divisional applications

—Deadline for filing

Add new paragraph at end: **15.38**
Note change to r.19 re filing of divisional applications (see §§15.04 and 15.20).

Examination and search [Sections 17-21]

SECTION 18—Substantive examination and grant or refusal of patent

Add new paragraph 18.00: **18.00**

Contents

COMMENTARY ON SECTION 18

Grant of the patent (subs.(4))

Add new paragraph at end: **18.10**
From 1 October 2016, the IPO has changed the procedure surrounding grant from that

described in the Main Work. The s.18(4) report now includes a notification of intention to grant. Subsequent to the issue of this report (and contrary to previous practice) an applicant may now make voluntary amendments to its application and/or file a divisional application (in respect of the latter see §§15.04 and 15.20).

PRACTICE UNDER SECTION 18

Plurality of invention

18.14   *Add new paragraph at end:*
See §18.10 for the new practice from 1 October 2016 and §§15.04 and 15.20 concerning the period for filing divisionals. The second paragraph of this section in the Main Work is therefore no longer applicable.

SECTION 19—General power to amend application before grant

19.00   *Add new paragraph 19.00:*

Contents

RELEVANT RULE—RULE 31

Rule 31—Amendment of application before grant

19.02   *Replace r.31(3) with:*
(3) **Subject to rule 66A** the applicant may amend his application only within the period beginning with the date on which the applicant is informed of the examiner's report under section 17(5) and ending with the date on which the comptroller sends him the first substantive examination report.

Add new paragraph at end of Note:
Rule 31 has been amended (effective 1 October 2016) by para.7 of the Patents (Amendment) (No.2) Rules 2016 (SI 2016/892).

COMMENTARY ON SECTION 19

Scope of the section

19.03   *Add new paragraph at end:*
For the effect of the change in r.31(3), see §89A.36.

54

SECTION 20A [ADDED]—Reinstatement of applications

■ *Add new paragraph 20A.00:*   **20A.00**

Contents

20A.01   Statute
20A.02   Rule 32—Reinstatement of applications under section 20A
20A.03   Scope of section
20A.04   Time period for making reinstatement request
20A.05   The meaning of "unintentional"

Relevant Rules—Rule 32

Rule 32—Reinstatement of applications under section 20A

Replace r.32(2) with: **20A.02**
(2) For this purpose the relevant period is **twelve months beginning immediately after the date on which the application was terminated.** *[is—*

(a) *two months beginning [with] immediately after the date on which the removal of the cause of non-compliance occurred; or*

(b) *if it expires earlier, the period of twelve months beginning [with] immediately after the date on which the application was terminated.]*

Replace r.32(8) with:
(8) The applicant may, before the end of the period of one month beginning [*with*] **immediately after** the date of that notification, request to be heard by the comptroller.

Replace Note with:
Note. Rule 32 was amended as from 1 October 2011 by the Patents (Amendment) Rules 2011 (2011/2052) and (effective 1 October 2016) by para.8 of the Patents (Amendment) (No.2) Rules 2016 (SI 2016/892).

Commentary on Section 20A

Time period for making reinstatement request

Replace with: **20A.04**
The amended r.32 (effective 1 October 2016) sets a single time limit for reinstatement of applications, namely 12 months following the date of termination. This amendment is to be applauded in that it removes the previous additional requirement of the application being within two months of the "cause of non-compliance" and with it the both sizeable and intellectually questionable body of EPO case law on the comparable provision.

Note that the transitional provisions (or lack of them) are such that certain application which would have fallen outside the two-month period as at 1 October 2016 will now be eligible for reinstatement. The IPO Guidance of 1 September 2016 makes clear that this is intentional.

The meaning of "unintentional"

20A.05   *Add new paragraph at end:*

■ In *Hurley's reinstatement application* BL O 514/15 the IP Office had notified the applicant that a form and fee for substantive examination had been submitted too late, and that an extension was needed. When requesting a search, the applicant, who had moved, wrote his new address on a Form FS2 and received official receipts directed to his new address. However, he never received any of the official correspondence regarding substantive examination which was sent to his old address. He therefore argued that there had been an irregularity in procedure justifying an extension of the time for applying for reinstatement. It was held that the cause of non-compliance was the applicant's ignorance of the fact that his address for service was still recorded as the original address, but r.107 could not be invoked to extend the time for seeking restoration because the new address written on Form FS1 could not be equated with a request on Form 20 to change the address for service in accordance with r.49 and accordingly there had been no irregularity of procedure within the Office. Given that on a broader view the equities favoured the applicant it is difficult to see how the public interest was served by such cold-hearted inflexibility. Similarly, in *Cypress Semiconductor Corp's Application* BL O/326/16 an application for reinstatement was allowed following failure to respond to an office action, and a period of two months was prescribed for the response, but no new compliance period was specified in the reinstatement order. Accordingly the application was terminated for failure to provide an adequate response to the outstanding examination report in the period specified in the order for reinstatement, and for failure to bring the application into compliance within the period specified under s.20.

Provisions as to patents after grant [Sections 24-29]

SECTION 25—Terms of Patent

25.00   *Add new paragraph 25.00:*

Contents

Rule 39—Renewal notice

Replace r.39(3) with: **25.05**

(3) The comptroller must send the renewal notice to—

    (a) the **last** address specified by the proprietor on payment of a [*the last*] renewal fee (or to another address that has since been notified to him for that purpose by the proprietor); or

    (b) where such an address has not been so specified or notified, the address for service entered in the register.

Add new Note:

Note. Amended by para.9 of the Patents (Amendment) (No.2) Rules 2016 (SI 2016/892).

SECTION 27—General power to amend specification after grant

Add new paragraph 27.00:   **27.00**

Contents

Grounds of opposition

Add new paragraph at end: **27.12**

■ In *MWUK Ltd v Fashion at Work Ltd* BL O/531/16 it was held that an examiner can rely on the prior art cited in the course of pre-grant proceedings and on his own background knowledge in deciding whether to exercise comptroller's discretion to amend the patent. However, an opponent cannot advance arguments which challenge the validity of the patent in any way beyond that suggested by the patentee.

SECTION 28—Restoration of lapsed patents

28.00   *Add new paragraph 28.00:*

Contents

COMMENTARY ON SECTION 28

Term for filing the application for restoration

28.06   *After the sixth paragraph (beginning "The period for filing an application for restoration"), add new paragraph:*
    ■ It may also be possible to extend the restoration period under r.111 (delays in communication (i.e. postal service)) as to which see §123.79.

Property in patents and applications, and registration [Sections 30-38]

SECTION 32 [SUBSTITUTED]—Register of patents etc.

32.00   *Add new paragraph 32.00:*

Contents

RELEVANT RULES—RULES 103 AND 104 AND 44-50

Rule 44—Entries in the register

Add new Note: **32.04**

Note. The Patents (Amendment) Rules 2016 (SI 2016/517), r.2(2), if and when in force, will add "other than in relation to a European patent with unitary effect," at the end of r.44(5)a) of the Patents Rules 2007 (SI 2007/3291). Paragraph 2(1) of SI 2016/517 provides that it will come into force on the date of entry into force of the Agreement on a Unified Patent Court. The treaty record for the UPC agreement can be found at *http://treaties.fco.gov.uk/treaties/treatyrecord.htm?tid=14651.*

Replace title with: **32.09**

Rule 49—Correction of name or address; correction of address for service

Replace r.49(6) with:

(6) For the purposes of this rule a request for a correction includes

   (a) a correction made for the purposes of section 117**; and**

   (b) **a change to any of the matters listed in paragraph (1)(a) or (b) in** respect of an entry recorded in the register or made to any application or other document filed at the Patent Office.

Add new Note:
Note. Rule 49 has been amended (effective 1 October 2016) by para.10 of the Patents (Amendment) (No.2) Rules 2016 (SI 2016/892).

COMMENTARY ON SECTION 32

Scope of section

32.13   *Add new paragraph at end:*
■ Readers in the licensing field may be aware of the so-called Lambert Toolkit which provides a range of model agreements between universities and other research organizations and industry which now provides seven model collaboration agreements, four model consortium agreements, two model heads of terms and two model variation agreements including a new split ownership agreement and a fast track model agreement. Details may be found on the UK IPO website.

Correction of errors

32.21   *Add new paragraph at end:*
Rule 49 has been amended to clarify that it applies to both corrections and changes, and that a request for a correction in relation to a name or address in the register or any application or document may be made where there has been any change in those matters.

PRACTICE UNDER SECTION 32

Furnishing address for service

32.23   *Add new paragraph at end:*
From 1 October 2016 applicants may request a two-month extension to the period for providing an address for service (previously non-extendable). See §123.26.

Alteration of address for service

32.24   *Add new paragraph at end:*
Under new r.49(6)(b) (effective 1 October 2016, see §32.09) correction of an address for service may arise from change of circumstances (rather than only by way of error).

Alteration of name and address of proprietor

32.25   *Add new paragraph at beginning:*
Under new r.49(6)(b) a name or address correction may arise from change of circumstances (rather than only by way of error).

SECTION 37—Determination of right to patent after grant

37.00   *Add new paragraph 37.00:*

Contents
37.01   Statute
37.02   CPC Article 23—Claiming the right to the Community Patent

COMMENTARY ON SECTION 37

Powers of the Comptroller and court to determine entitlement disputes

After the fourth paragraph (beginning "In Innovia Films BL O/461/11 a reference was made"), add new paragraph: **37.08**

In *NGPOD Global Ltd v Aspirate N Go Ltd* BL O/431/16, after filing a counter-statement, the defendant asked the Comptroller to decline to deal with the references because of the importance of the patents to the defendant, the nature of the issues in dispute, the procedural complexity, and the different costs regimes in proceedings before the Comptroller and before the High Court. Bearing in mind in particular the overriding objectives of saving expense and dealing with the case in ways that are proportionate to the amount of money involved, the Hearing Officer did not accept that the issues in these proceedings would more properly be determined by the court, and therefore he did not decline to deal. Regarding the complexity of the factual issues and the non-patent law issues in the case, the Hearing Officer observed that in the end, the successful party is usually the one that succeeds in making these issues look easiest.

Time bar for orders under section 37 (subss.(5) and (9))

After the eleventh paragraph (beginning "In Duncan Riach & Anthony Brown v Fulcrum Systems Ltd"), add new paragraphs: **37.11**

An application for revocation inter alia under s.72(1)(b) was made to the court in *Angle Ring Company Ltd v ASD Westok Ltd* [2015] EWHC 2779 (IPEC). The application was more than two years after grant of the patent so that s.72(2)(b) applied, which requires the registered proprietor to have had subjective knowledge of non-entitlement at the time of grant. It was held that Angle Ring's failure to make an application in the IP Office did not prevent them from running the argument that the court has inherent jurisdiction, so that the ground of revocation would not be struck out. On subjective knowledge, the court pointed out that:

> "In any circumstances where a court must decide on the subjective knowledge of an individual, plainly the court cannot literally probe into his mind. Far less is that possible when the relevant date for such probing is in the past. So what the court must always do is look at all the surrounding circumstances and come to a conclusion, on the balance of probabilities, whether those circumstances point to a conclusion that the individual had the requisite subjective knowledge or not. Putting this, I think, colloquially, what the court is having to decide, on all the relevant evidence, is whether the individual in question must have known the relevant facts. Mr. Austen sought to suggest that there is a distinction between (a) proving that the patentee knew that he was not entitled to the patent and (b) proving that he must have known that he was not entitled to the patent. That, it seems to me, is a false distinction. In practice, they amount to the same thing. The latter in reality is what the court will decide at trial in order to reach a conclusion as to the former."

At the stage the proceedings had reached, the court declined to go through all of the evidence in the form of a mini-trial and concluded that the case had been pleaded sufficiently so that it should go forward to trial in the usual way.

Employees' inventions [Sections 39-43]

SECTION 39—Right to employees' inventions

39.00   *Add new paragraph 39.00:*

Contents

COMMENTARY ON SECTION 39

Ownership of employee inventions by an employer

—The basic rule

39.07   *After the thirteenth paragraph (beginning "The inventor in Szewczyk's Application"), add new paragraph:*

There was in *University of Warwick v Dr Geoffrey Graham Diamond* BL O/518/15 a paucity of evidence on the issue whether Dr Diamond's contribution was made within or outside the duties he had for the university which made it extremely difficult to make a finding of fact on that point. An exceptional situation was needed before a judge or Hearing Officer was entitled to resort to the burden of proof, see *Andrew Cooke v Watermist Ltd* [2014] EWHC 125 (Pat) discussed in the Main Work at §7.11, but this was such a case. The onus was on the claimant to show that the invention had been made in the course of Dr Diamond's normal duties as a Research Fellow of the University and this they had not done so that the claim failed.

SECTION 40—Compensation of employees for certain inventions

COMMENTARY ON SECTION 40

Scope of the section

■ *In the second paragraph (beginning "This section is concerned with an employee-inventor making a claim"), delete the second occurence of "of outstanding benefit to the employer".* **40.04**

Invention belonging to the employer (subs.(1))

—Meaning of "outstanding benefit"

To the end of the fourth paragraph (beginning "However, the case law discussed below arises"), add: **40.12**
■ Care should be taken when reading the Court of Appeal's decision in *Shanks v Unilever* [2017] EWCA Civ 2, as the main judgment refers to the "benefit of the invention", when the court should have been referring to the "benefit of the patent", because the relevant wording of the Act was that which prevailed before the amendments brought about by the 2005 Act came into force.

After the fifth paragraph (beginning "In Memco-Med's Patent [1992] R.P.C. 403"), add new paragraph:
■ In *Shanks v Unilever* [2017] EWCA Civ 2, the court reflected on the intention behind the section and the circumstances in which compensation would be available. Although s.40 redressed a balance between employees and employers "it does not follow from this that s.40 was intended to provide some universal measure of compensation and it is clear from the statutory language that it was not. Awards of compensation are limited to cases where the invention *[sic—in this case, the judge should have referred to the patent, because it was granted before the 2005 Act came into force]* confers on the employer what is described as an outstanding benefit in money or money's worth measured against all relevant factors including the size and nature of the employer's undertaking. On any view these will be exceptional cases but the difficulty, as ever, is to specify with a sufficient degree of certainty where the line is to be drawn which is, of course, a threshold question prior to any consideration of fair share." (see para.12). See also at para.23, where the court held "Outstanding is an ordinary English word with a readily understood meaning and was doubtless chosen by Parliament to identify the exceptional nature of the benefit that must exist.", and where the Court of Appeal also went on to remark that the focus was "on the benefit to the employer and not the degree of inventiveness of the employee" (further disapproving aspects of *British Steel Patent* (infra).

In the ninth paragraph (beginning "The issues of "outstanding benefit" was also discussed in Shanks v Unliver), after "reduced on appeal to £17 million", add:
■, and restored to £24 million by the Court of Appeal

At the end of the ninth paragraph, replace "It is understood that permission for a further appeal to the Court of Appeal has been given, and that the appeal is likely to be heard during 2016." with:
■ The Court of Appeal's judgment in *Shanks v Unilever* [2017] EWCA Civ 2 upheld the Hearing Officer's decision and the court declined to interfere. "It is only if it can be shown to be based on a misdirection as to the relevant statutory test or, for example, on some misapprehension as to the material facts that it would be open to this Court to set the Hearing Officer's decision aside and to re-make it" (para.44). The Court of Appeal found

that the Hearing Officer had addressed all the benefits put forward and the weighting of those was up to him.

■ There were two other factors which were considered in calculating the benefit. One was the time value of money and the second was whether corporation tax should reduce the calculation of the sum to be considered as the "outstanding benefit". Briggs LJ commented, at para.74, that the time at which money is received may be relevant to the consideration of "outstanding benefit", as the size of the employer's undertaking may also vary with time. But this does not mean that the time value of money (which can be quantified) should be added to the benefit actually received to determine if a benefit which might have been substantial would then be outstanding (see para.36). On the other hand, it was wrong to deduct the corporation tax which Unilever had to pay on the receipts to the calculation of the benefit received (see para.43).

—Meaning of employer's undertaking

40.13   *Add new paragraph at the beginning:*

■ The Court of Appeal discussed the meaning of the phrase in *Shanks v Unilever* [2017] EWCA Civ 231. At para.31, Patton LJ stated: "There is no definition of 'undertaking' in the 1977 Act nor, in my view, is one really necessary. As a matter of language, the word can describe the company or other entity which employs the inventor either in terms of its organisational structure or simply as an economic unit." (There is a definition of that word in the Companies Act 2006 s.1161, meaning either a body corporate or partnership, or an unincorporated association carrying on a trade or business, with or without a view to forfeit.)

In the fourth paragraph (beginning "In Shanks v Unilever [2011] R.P.C. 12"), after the first sentence, add:

■ Note the comments of Patten LJ in the Court of Appeal [2017] EWCA Civ 231 at para.21, that the Jacobs LJ comments were "Delphic".

Add new paragraphs at end:

■ This was upheld by the Court of Appeal, see para.34 [2017] EWCA Civ 231.

■ Permission has been given for an appeal to the UK Supreme Court. An amicus submission has suggested that the term "undertaking" has been given too expansive a meaning by the Court of Appeal and that the Parliamentary intention was that it should, by analogy with cases on inventive step, be more closely tied to the field of endeavour within which the employee was working. That this should apply even in the case of a single central institution researching for a group of companies, which in appropriate cases should be treated not as a single entity but as a collocation of discrete entities. For example, research on detergents carried out for one member of a group of companies would have no foreseeable effect on the quality, production or sales of ice cream produced by a different member of the group. It was submitted that if this approach were to be followed the impact of "too big to pay" would be reduced.

SECTION 41—Amount of compensation

Notes

41.01   *Add at end:*

■ 6. Prospective insertion, substitution and deletion as follows:

In section 41(3) (assignment of right in patent)—

(a) after "Where the Crown" insert ", United Kingdom Research and Innovation",

(b) for "or, as the case may be, Research Council" substitute ", United Kingdom Research and Innovation or the Research Council (as the case may be)", and

(c) omit the words from "or the Arts" to the end.

■ The prospective insertion is not yet in force (as at 1 October 2017). Words prospectively inserted by Higher Education and Research Act 2017 Sch.12 para.13(a). The erroneous identification of the purport of the relevant section of the Patents Act appears in the amending Act.

COMMENTARY ON SECTION 41

Connected persons

In the fourth paragraph (beginning "Decisions in Shanks v Unilever BL O/259/13"), after "[2010]EWCA Civ 1283", add: **41.04**

■, [2017] EWCA Civ 231

SECTION 43—Supplementary

COMMENTARY ON SECTION 43

Meaning of "benefit" (subs.(7))

To the end of the second paragraph (beginning "In Shanks v Unilever BL O/259/13"), add: **43.09**

■ The Court of Appeal agreed that the time value of the money Unilever has received should not be added in to the calculation of "benefit", but disagreed with Arnold J that the "gross benefit" should be reduced by the corporation tax paid. "The incidence of tax is unconnected to the financial benefit which the patent produced for the employer. Its deduction is no more part of the calculation of what constitutes the benefit than the time value of the money received. Both are consequences of the benefit rather than part of it." So the Hearing Officer's valuation of £24.5 million was restored.

Use of patented inventions for services of the Crown [Sections 55-59]

SECTION 58—References of disputes as to Crown use

Notes

Add to end of note 7:   **58.01**

■ The statutory instrument has been published as the Patents (European Patent with Unitary Effect and Unified Patent Court) Order 2016 (SI 2016/388) (not yet in force).

Add at end:

8. ■ Section 58(6) is prospectively amended by para.2(2) of the Patents (European Patent with Unitary Effect and Unified Patent Court) Order 2016 (SI 2016/388) to come into force on the date of entry into force of the Agreement on a Unified Patent Court. Equivalent provision was made for the Isle of Man by the Patents (Isle of Man) (Amendment) Order 2017 (SI 2017/162).

Infringement [Sections 60-71]

SECTION 60—Meaning of infringement

60.00   *Add new paragraph 60.00:*

Notes

60.01   *Add at end:*

11. ■ Section 60 is prospectively amended as follows:
    In subsection (5), after paragraph (i) insert—

    (j) it consists of a use referred to in Article 27(c) of the Agreement on a Unified Patent Court;

    (k) subject to subsection (6H), it consists of an act or use referred to in Article 27(k) of the Agreement on a Unified Patent Court.

After subsection (6G), insert—

(6H) Subsection 5(k) applies to an act or use in relation to a European patent (UK) or a European patent with unitary effect, but does not apply to an act or use in relation to a patent granted by the comptroller.

Words prospectively inserted by Patents (European Patent with Unitary Effect and Unified Patent Court) Order 2016 (SI 2016/388) and coming into force on the date of entry into force of the Agreement on a Unified Patent Court signed at Brussels on 19 February 2013, cm 8653.

COMMENTARY ON SECTION 60

Direct (or substantive) infringement (subs.(1))

—Infringement of product invention (subs.(1)(a))

Add new paragraph at end: **60.05**
A party who approaches potential customers individually or by advertisement saying it is willing to supply a machine, terms to be agreed, is offering it or putting it on the market, see *Gerber Garment v Lectra Systems* [1995] R.P.C. 383. However, mere supply of brochures or data sheets without the flavour of a negotiation about the supply of a product as in *Gareth Kevin Glass v Freyssinet Ltd* [2015] EWHC 2972 (IPEC) does not amount to an offer to dispose of the product within s.60(1)(a) and does not amount to direct infringement.

Indirect (or contributory) infringement under subs.(2)

—Scope of subs.(2)

To the end of the final paragraph, add: **60.09**
On appeal sub nom. *Warner-Lambert Company LLC v Generics (UK) Ltd (t/a Mylan)* [2016] EWCA Civ 1006 the court noted in relation to direct infringement under s.60(1) that the judge had considered the state of mind of the three participants in the process, namely the prescribing doctor, the pharmacist, and the patient. So far as the doctor was concerned, the judge concluded that the necessary intention was not present because he would not know whether the pharmacist would dispense the patented or the generic product. The pharmacist would simply dispense the drug which was on the prescription but would lack information which the doctor had, namely the indication for which the drug was prescribed. The patient merely intended to take whatever drug the doctor had prescribed for whatever condition the doctor had prescribed it for. On appeal it was held that the judge fell into error in seeking to dissect the requirement for intentional treatment of pain in this way. Because claims in this form relied for their novelty on the purpose of the use of the drug, it was only essential that the manufacturer was able to foresee that there would be intentional use for the new medical indication as opposed to a different indication. The issue which the judge was called upon to decide was whether the defendants knew or could have foreseen that at least some of the prescriptions written generically for the relevant drug to treat the relevant indication would in fact be fulfilled with their generic product. Had the patentees succeeded in upholding valid claims, it would then have been necessary to decide whether that test of knowledge or foresight was satisfied. If so the judge should have gone on to consider whether the defendants had taken all reasonable steps in their power to prevent their generic product from being used to treat the patented indication. On indirect infringement under s.60(2) there was a danger in implying a requirement for a "downstream act of manufacture". What was required is that means were provided which were for putting the invention into effect. As the example of labelling by a pharmacist showed, that process was not completed when the drug had been

formulated into a pharmaceutical composition by a manufacturer. The process of preparing the composition could continue through any packaging step performed by the manufacturer and included the labelling step performed by the pharmacist. The court of appeal disagreed with the conclusion of the judge that there was no relevant act of preparation by pharmacists, nor any prospect of such an act.

Acts exempted from infringement (subs.(5))

—Acts done for experimental purposes (subs.(5)(b))

60.15   *Add new paragraphs at end:*
The experimental use defence was considered in *Meter-Tech LLC v British Gas Trading Ltd* [2016] EWHC 2278 (Pat) in relation to earlier decisions in *Monsanto Co v Stauffer Chemical Co* [1985] R.P.C. 515, *Corevalve Inc v Edwards Lifesciences AG* [2009] EWHC 6 (Pat), *Klinische Versuche (Clinical Trials) II (Case X ZR 68/94)* [1998] R.P.C. 423 and *SK&F v Evans Medical* [1989] 1 F.S.R. 513 at [523]). The court observed that:

> "Although it is tempting to place a gloss on the statutory wording, in my judgment that would not be appropriate. The evaluation in each case involves consideration of a range of factors of which the following are some:
> (a) Whether the acts in question are properly characterized as trials and whether those trials can be described as undertaking scientific or development research;
> (b) Whether the trials were carried out in order to discover something technically unknown or to test a technical hypothesis or whether they were carried out to discover whether the product was commercially acceptable to the market;
> (c) Whether the trials were intended to find out whether something which was known to work in specific conditions would work in different conditions and, in the case of a system intended to operate on a large scale, whether it was capable of operating on such a scale;
> (d) Whether the trials were carried out mainly in order to demonstrate or collect information to demonstrate to a third party customer or regulator that a product works – which points away;
> (e) Whether the purpose of the trial was mainly directly or indirectly to generate revenue as a result of the use of the invention in the trial itself – which points away.
> It is, in my judgment, impossible to allocate a precise ranking to the importance of these factors and the evaluation must take an overall view. Moreover, the court must take into account the extent to which the acts undertaken were reasonably necessary to determine the facts sought to be determined. A small-scale trial of a product may be treated as involving acts done for experimental purposes whereas the supply of a product in quantities far beyond that required to find out how it worked in certain conditions may not do so."

On the facts, the court held [271] that although the boundary between a large-scale pilot designed to test acceptability and a demonstration of acceptability was not a very clear one, the use in question was for experimental purposes. However, there was no technical documentation exhibited showing communication with the designer/manufacturer of the relevant meters, and the use appeared to have been a test primarily of the suitability of the meters and metering system for the defendants' purposes rather than the conduct of genuine research relating to the development of improvements in metering. A sufficiently direct link had not been established between the purposes for which the products/systems were used and the subject-matter of the claim. Accordingly, the defence of experimental use relating to the subject-matter of the invention was not made out.

—Extemporaneous pharmaceutical preparations (subs.(5)(c))

60.16   *Add new paragraph at end:*
In *Actavis v Eli Lilly* [2016] EWHC 234 (Pat), there was some discussion about the meaning of subs.5(c) concerning extemporaneous preparation of medicine in a pharmacy, but the court did not reach any conclusion about whether it should be interpreted narrowly

(i.e. covering only pharmacists preparing a medicine for an individual following its prescription) or widely (i.e. covering hospitals as well as pharmacists and covering the general preparation of medicine, not just for specific patients).

Terms of full licence to work the invention

Add new paragraph at end: **60.26**

In *Koninklijke Philips v Asustek Computer* [2016] EWHC 867 (Pat), the court ordered the trial of a preliminary issue regarding a potential defence under a third-party licence: a finding regarding the extent of the licence would have the potential to narrow the issues between the parties considerably, reducing costs.

Joint tortfeasance by acting in a "common design"

Add new paragraph at end: **60.28**

In *Magnesium Elektron v Molycorp Chemicals* [2015] EWHC 3596 (Pat), the court considered an application for permission to serve proceedings against the second defendant, a sister company to the first defendant based in China. The proceedings alleged infringement under subs.1(c) by the importation into the United Kingdom of the product of a process claim by the first or the second defendant, the product having been manufactured in China. The Court decided that there was a good arguable case that the nexus between the defendants was sufficient for an argument of joint tortfeasance and that there was serious issue to be tried regarding the manufacture and importation of the allegedly infringing product.

SECTION 61—Proceedings for infringement of patent

Add new paragraph 61.00: **61.00**

Contents

COMMENTARY ON SECTION 61

Interim injunctions

—The principles upon which pre-trial relief is granted

Add new paragraph at end: **61.08**

■ In *Warner-Lambert v Sandoz* [2016] EWHC 3317 (Pat), Arnold J continued an interim injunction, notwithstanding the failure of the appellant to overturn an underlying substantive decision in the Court of Appeal. The judge noted that not only might the appellant succeed on appeal to the Supreme Court but that the defendants had made it clear that they intended the drug to be used for a use that would infringe claims that had been held to be valid. In those circumstances, the injunction should be continued. In reaching this conclusion, he made it clear that he was taking into account the fact that the appellant was no longer relying on one of the claims relied upon when seeking the original interim injunction but that, notwithstanding that change in circumstances, the balance lay in favour of continuing the injunction.

—The claimant's cross-undertaking

Add new paragraph at end: **61.10**

In *AstraZeneca v KRKA* [2014] EWHC 84 (Pat) the proceedings concerned a pharmaceutical called esomeprazole for which the UK market while the patent remained in force amounted to some £65 million. AstraZeneca learned of KRKA's intention to enter the UK market, instituted proceedings and applied for an interim injunction to which KRKA submitted subject to a cross-undertaking in damages. Another generic company with a similar product obtained a declaration of non-infringement, see *Ranbaxy v AstraZeneca* [2011] EWHC 1831 (Pat); [2011] F.S.R. 45, after which the injunction against KRKA was lifted. They had planned to launch their product at a price 25% less than that charged by AstraZeneca and claimed damages primarily for loss of the opportunity to enjoy almost a year as the only generic available to the market which they described as the loss of the "first mover" and argued was basis for a damages claim in excess of £32 million. AstraZeneca pointed to the relatively small market share subsequently achieved by KRKA in the face of other generic competition, and said that they had suffered modest losses of £3-6 million. Sales J concluded that severe cost pressures and the relative simplicity of promoting a switch in prescribing behaviour in favour of the KRKA product would, but for the injunction, have led to a high level of switching, broadly in line with estimates given by KRKA, and also that this would have created a market which the KRKA would have been better able to protect against the later launch by other companies of generic products. Nevertheless, he applied a 20% uncertainty discount in reaching his award of £27 million. On appeal, [2015] EWCA Civ 484, it was held that a liberal and fair assessment of the loss was supported by the patentees' evidence in support of their application for an interim injunction that the KRKA was substitutable for the AstraZeneca product, that over 90% of the market would be accessible to KRKA, and that there would be loss of market share or a downward price spiral. The judge had made findings which were properly supported by the detailed evidence before him, and there was no benchmark for the uncertainty discount which depended on the facts in each case and was not subject to criticism by comparison with discounts that had been applied in other cases.

—Maintaining the status quo

61.13   *Add new paragraph at end:*
In *Warner-Lambert v Sandoz* [2015] EWHC 3153 (Pat), the court granted an application to continue an interim injunction where doing so would maintain the status quo (i.e. it would keep a full label generic product off the market pending resolution of the underlying claim).

—The adequacy of damages as a remedy

61.15   *Add new paragraphs at end:*
In *Epoch v Character Options* [2015] EWHC 3436 (IPEC), the court refused to grant an interim injunction where doing so would cause irreparable harm to the defendant and where damages could be easily calculated and would be an adequate remedy.
In *Stretchline v H&M* [2016] EWHC 162 (Pat), the court refused to grant a final injunction, deeming it unnecessary where future infringement was covered by contractual terms in a settlement agreement.

Relief by post-trial injunction (subs.(1)(a))

61.21   *To the end of the fifth paragraph (beginning "In Huawei Technologies Co Ltd"), add:*
The background to this decision and its conclusions are discussed by Antony Graggs, "Abuse or not abuse?" [2015] 8-9 *CIPA* 16.

After the fifth paragraph, add new paragraph:
■ In further proceedings before Birss J [2017] EWHC 711 (Pat) the court expressed doubt that the FRAND undertaking could be specifically enforced in such a way that either party could legally be compelled to enter into a contract against their will, but went on to explain that even if a patentee cannot be compelled to enter into a contract by specific performance of the FRAND undertaking, that undertaking can still have substantive legal

effect. FRAND is an objective standard. Courts concerned with patent cases in countries around the world had set FRAND rates and this court would do so also. If a patentee refused to enter into a licence which a court has determined was FRAND then, subject to the *Vringo* problem (whether there could be a FRAND range as opposed to a FRAND rate, see *Vringo v ZTE* [2013] EWHC 1591 (Pat) and [2015] EWHC 214 (Pat)) a court could and normally should refuse to grant relief for patent infringement. The converse applied to an implementer who refused to accept a FRAND licence, where the normal relief for patent infringement should normally follow. There was no need for contract law to go as far as creating a power to compel parties to enter into FRAND licences against their will because patent law already had the tools available to give legal effect to the FRAND undertaking. In the present case, since Unwired Planet had established that Huawei had infringed two valid EP (UK) patents, since Huawei had not been prepared to take a licence on the terms the court had found to be FRAND, and since Unwired Planet were not in breach of competition law, a final injunction to restrain infringement of these two patents by Huawei should be granted. However, the injunction should be considered at a hearing in a few weeks' time once Unwired Planet had drawn up a full set of the terms of the worldwide licence incorporating the decisions made in the present judgment. Any damages awarded would be at the same rate as the appropriate FRAND rate. At that further hearing [2017] EWHC 1304 (Pat), a FRAND injunction was granted, which would be discharged if the defendant entered into a settled FRAND licence annexed to the decision, the injunction being stayed pending appeal for which permission was granted.

Relief by damages (subs.(1)(c))

—Basis for assessment

Add new paragraphs at end: **61.24**

In *AP Racing v Alcon Components* [2016] EWHC 116 (IPEC), the broad principles governing the enquiry were said to be those set out in *SDL Hair Ltd v Next Row Ltd* [2014] EWHC 2084 (IPEC) at [16] and as regards damages on the "user principle" *Henderson v All Around The World Recordings Ltd* [2014] EWHC 3087 (IPEC). As regards so-called "convoyed sales", the court applied *Alfrank and OOO Abbott v Design & Display Ltd* [2014] EWHC 2924 (IPEC). Such sales were relevant provided that there was a causative link in the mind of the purchaser between his or her purchase of the infringing product and their purchase of one or more other specific products. Only then would the sale of the infringing product have caused the sale of those other products (within the legal sense of causation)—as opposed to the latter sales being merely statistically linked as a matter of probability. If causation was proved, subject to unusual facts being raised by the defendant, losses related to the latter sales would be expected to satisfy the requirements of the law on remoteness generally.

In the related case of *AP Racing v Alcon Components* [2016] EWHC 815 (Ch), on appeal from the IPEC, the court held that it was not an abuse of process to bring a second claim for additional infringements where such infringements had not been identified until after the original finding of liability and could have been included in the assessment of damages but had not been included because the defendant had objected to their inclusion.

—Interest on damages

In the first paragraph, after "see Hunt v Douglas [1990] 1 A.C. 398 HL.", add: **61.25**

In *AP Racing v Alcon Components* [2016] EWHC 116 (IPEC), the court reached its own view on the appropriate level of interest to award, in the absence of any evidence from the parties.

Relief by account of profits (subs.(1)(d))

61.28   *Replace the last paragraph with:*
For recent decisions in IPEC see *Ifejika v Ifejika* [2014] EWHC 2625 (IPEC) (designs) and *OOO Abbott v Design and Display* [2014] EWHC 2924 (IPEC).

■ The latter decision was appealed to the Court of Appeal, see [2016] EWCA Civ 95. It concerned a slotted display panel having a snap-in protective and deformable insert, the shape and structure of the insert being the characterising features of the claim. It was held [12] that the judgment of Birss J on liability at [2013] EWPCC 27 was concerned with whether the claimed subject-matter was obvious over the prior art, and not with the different issue of identification of the inventive concept for the purposes of assessing damages or an account of profits. If the inventive concept was the inserts, then sale of the panels was sale of "convoyed goods" and it was incorrect to conclude that because the sales went together, the sale of inserts caused the sale of the panels and that the whole of the profit earned on the composite item was derived from the invention [36]. The judge should have apportioned the overall profit, see the extensive review of *Meters Ltd v Metropolitan Gas Meters Ltd* (1910) 27 R.P.C. 721; (1911) 28 R.P.C. 157 where the infringing mechanism was the very essence of the meter, *Celanese International Corp v BP Chemicals Ltd* [1999] R.P.C. 203 at [43], [47] and [51], *Gerber Garment Technology Inc v Lectra Systems Ltd* [1997] R.P.C. 443 (on causation), *Environment Agency v Empress Car Co (Abertillery) Ltd* [1999] 2 A.C. 22 at [29] (also on causation), *Dart Industries Inc v Decor Corp Pty Ltd* [1994] F.S.R. 567, *Hollister Inc v Medik Ostomy Supplies Ltd* [2012] EWCA Civ 1419 and *Colbeam Palmer Ltd v Stock Affiliates Pty Ltd* [1972] R.P.C. at 315. General overheads were only deductible, following *Woolley v UP Global Sourcing* [2014] EWHC 493 in two circumstances: (a) if an overhead was increased by the acts of infringement (i.e. the increase would not have occurred but for the acts of infringement); and (b) if the defendant was running to maximum capacity such that the infringing business displaced an alternative business which otherwise would have been conducted. Allowing the appeal, it was held that it was not possible to assess the profits to which the patentee was entitled on the basis of the facts already found, and the case was remitted to IPEC. *OOO Abbott v Design and Display* returned to IPEC [2017] EWHC 932 (IPEC) for a decision against the first defendant as to (a) what proportion of sales of slatted panel sold together with infringing inserts should be included within the appellant's account of profits, and (b) what deductions (if any) for general overheads may the appellant make in its account of profits. In the outcome, it was found that 10% of the defendant's customers wanted the infringing panel and no substitute, and that the defendant should pay the whole of the profit made on the relevant inserts plus 10% of the profit made on the panel, general overheads, rent and delivery charges being deductible from its profits on the infringing business, but not payments to directors.

In *Stretchline v H&M* [2016] EWHC 162 (Pat), the court refused to order an account of profits where the claim was of breach of contract. It confirmed that such a remedy was only available in such claims in exceptional circumstances.

Costs

—The principles for award and assessment of costs

61.34   *After the fifth paragraph (beginning "Under the new costs budgeting regime,"), add new paragraphs:*
■ Following the decision in *Sony Communications International AB v SSH Communications Security Corp* [2016] EWHC 2584 (Pat) the case returned to the Patents Court for determination of the order for costs consistent with a Costs Management Order dated 21 December 2015. It followed from *Henry v News Group Newspapers Ltd* [2013] EWCA Civ 19 that the budget was not a cap but was a guideline, but that the court would depart from the budget only where there was good reason to do so. On expert reports Sony had

spent £580,906 when the budget was £215,425. It was held that there were arguments on both sides since Sony had clearly failed in its duty to seek to vary its cost budget when it became aware of the overspend, but SSH had not been taken by surprise that there was an overspend since their budget for the same phase was also higher. There was good reason to depart from the budget since the case involved scrutiny by experts of a larger number of documents than anticipated. Sony's budget should be increased to £323,270 which is what SSH had estimated at the budget phase. Costs in the trial preparation and trial phases were also considered. The overall award of costs to Sony was £876,347.

■ Remedies following a main judgment [2017] EWHC 705 (Pat) in the so-called "non-technical" trial were considered by Birss J in *Unwired Planet v Huawei* [2017] EWHC 1304 (Pat). Unwired Planet's actual costs of the non-technical trial were about £12.4 million and Huawei's costs were about £7 million. Arguments about the appropriate FRAND rate were argued to be more like a tariff-setting exercise in the Copyright Tribunal, where Mummery J held in *AEI Rediffusion v PPL* [1999] 1 W.L.R. 1507, 1518 that when the tribunal found that both side's proposed terms were unreasonable and arrived at a result somewhere in the middle, it was not correct to proceed on the basis that the outcome must produce a winner and a loser. Since Unwired Planet's rates were further from FRAND than those proposed by Huawei, the correct thing to do was to deprive Unwired Planet of these costs but to go no further. With other deductions the appropriate payment that Huawei should make was £2.9 million. Further issues are discussed at §D27.

■ The court concluded in *Napp Pharmaceutical v Dr Reddy's Laboratories (UK)* [2017] EWHC 1433 (Pat) that cost budgeting at early stages should not be imposed and observed that estimates given before trial can operate as a practical constraint on a payment on account of costs.

To the end of the seventh paragraph (beginning "Costs in the Intellectual Property Enterprise Court are governed"), add:

The Court of Justice of the European Union has confirmed that cost caps, like those in the Intellectual Property Enterprise Court, are compliant with art.14 of Directive 2004/48/EC (the Enforcement Directive) as long as they ensure that a significant and appropriate proportion of the costs of the successful party are borne by the unsuccessful party.

Add new paragraphs at end:

In relation to proceedings before IPEC, Claire O'Brien and Alasdair Poore, "Breaking the seal on costs" [2015] 6 *CIPA* 50 argue that where there has been an abuse of process or unreasonable conduct it is important to maintain a balance of interests and guard against the lack of any real sanction for such behaviour, and that the cost caps in IPEC provide very limited tools to do this in an effective manner.

In *AP Racing v Alcon* [2015] EWHC 1371 (IPEC) the claimant had succeeded in proceedings for infringement in respect of certain articles and wished to raise a further allegation of infringement of the same patent in relation to other articles. In considering whether there was abuse of process it was relevant to consider how long it would take to resolve further arguments on infringement and whether additional evidence would be needed. It was unlikely that further evidence would be admitted, and any further argument would last about one hour. The issues could also have been dealt with in the enquiry as to damages in the first case, so that it was not apparent that there could be unjust oppression or harassment. The decision was affirmed by the Patents Court on appeal, see *AP Racing v Alcon* [2016] EWHC 815 (Ch) in which it was held that *Unilin Beheer BV v Berry Floor NV* [2007] EWCA Civ 364; [2007] F.S.R. 25 applied in IPEC and that the practice of allowing further infringements to be considered at the damages enquiry once infringement is established is in accordance with the aims of IPEC. It would not be appropriate to replace a broad, merits-based enquiry concerned with whether the defendant has suffered oppression with a test whether res judicata applies to prevent consideration of further infringements. The general complaint was about the costs and inconvenience of the second action and whether the second action was oppressive. It was held not to be, and the fact that the further products were included in the new proceedings was a result of Alcon's objection to including them in the damages inquiry in the first action, as would have been possible.

Merck Sharp & Dohme v Ono Pharmaceutical [2015] EWHC 3973 (Pat) concerned the validity of two patents: one was amended and a declaration of non-infringement was made, by consent; the other was found valid and infringed. It was relatively straightforward to attribute costs following the agreement to amend the first patent but the court was required to make an order in respect of costs prior to that agreement. The Court found that the claimant was the overall loser and, as such, was required to pay all costs prior to the agreement, unless it could fairly show that they were attributable to the amended patent.

See *Wobben v Siemens* [2015] EWHC 2863 (Pat) for an attempt by the court to apportion costs on an issue by issue basis where, although one party was successful overall, it had lost or dropped certain arguments along the way.

The circumstances in which a successful claimant should be denied its costs in respect of certain issues and possibly be required to pay the defendants' costs were considered in *Hospira v Cubist* [2016] EWHC 2661 (Pat) having regard to the White Book at 44.2.7, p.1254, *Monsanto v Cargill No.2* [2007] EWHC 3113; [2008] F.S.R. 16, *MMI v Cellxion* [2012] EWCA Civ 139, *F&C Alternative Investment (Holdings) Ltd v Barthelmy (No.3)* [2012] EWCA Civ 843; [2013] 1 W.L.R. 548, per Davis LJ at [47]-[49] and *Hospira UK Ltd v Novartis AG* [2013] EWHC 886. Henry Carr J commented that:

> "... it will be seen that there is a tension between the requirement of a suitably exceptional case before costs are ordered in a patent case against a successful party; *Monsanto v Cargill No.2*; and the express rejection of this requirement in *F&C Alternative Investment (Holdings) Ltd and Barthelmy*. This raises the question of whether the approach to awards of costs in patent cases differs from that adopted in other types of litigation. In my judgment it does not. Patent litigation is very expensive, and it is important that parties should be encouraged only to pursue their best points, and to be aware of the cost implications of failing to do so.
>
> In my view, this apparent dichotomy may be resolved by a proper understanding of the phrase "suitably exceptional". It is intended to indicate that if the unsuccessful party succeeds on a particular issue, that is not, on its own, sufficient to award costs against the successful party. There must be something which makes it appropriate and just to order not only that the successful party does not recover his costs, but also that it should pay the costs of the relevant issue. On the other hand, it is not intended to imply that such awards of costs will be extremely rare. Where there is a discrete issue, which required substantial expenditure of costs, it may be just in all the circumstances to order payment of costs."

In the outcome there were a number of issues on which it was considered both appropriate and just that the successful claimant should not recover its costs and should pay the defendant's costs, reasons including in one instance maintaining an objection of insufficiency which was an obviously bad point but needed a great deal of evidence to resolve, Permission to appeal was refused.

■ For review articles, see Andrew Clay, "Cost control in IPEC" [2017] 1 *CIPA* 11, and also Alasdair Poore, "Car Crash derails IPEC" [2017] 3 *CIPA* 38.

—*Costs of interim proceedings*

61.36   *Add new paragraphs at end:*

■ In *Varian Medical Systems v Elektra* [2016] EWHC 2679 (Pat) which was an application for disclosure, costs of the partially successful applicant were not treated as costs in the case. The fair way of reflecting the outcome, reflecting a measure of success achieved by the claimant, but also rewarding the defendants for cooperating in the course of this hearing and coming up with a pragmatic way forward, was to make an order that half the claimant's assessed costs of the application be summarily assessed and paid by the defendant. Their overall costs of £66,000 were in line with the costs incurred by the defendant, and half of those costs were ordered to be paid.

■ In *Warner-Lambert v Sandoz* [2017] EWHC 216 (Pat) a summary assessment of costs was made following dismissal of an application by Sandoz to vary an interim injunction which had been granted against Sandoz by order dated 17 November 2015, see [2016] EWHC 3317 (Pat). It was held that this was not a case where costs should be reserved to the trial judge even though there had been a change in material circumstances, i.e. claims to the broadly defined indications of pain generically and neuropathic pain generically had been declared invalid but claims to more specific types of neuropathic pain remained. However, the balance of risk of injustice was unaffected and Sandoz were properly to be regarded as having been unsuccessful in their application. Warner-Lambert's statement of costs claimed £145,775, but Sandoz criticised hourly rates charged by Warner-Lambert's solicitors, the use of two partners, the failure to delegate work from a senior associate to more junior staff and certain elements of counsel's fees. It was considered that that each of those criticisms had force. The claimed total was high, so that a reasonable and proportionate assessed sum was £100,000.

PRACTICE UNDER SECTION 61

The differing roles of the Patents Court and the Intellectual Property Enterprise Court

Add new paragraphs at end: **61.42**

On 7 December 2015 Arnold J issued a practice statement regarding the listing of cases for trial in the Patents Court. The text of the statement is as follows:

"The Patents Court endeavours bring patent cases on for trial where possible within 12 months of the claim being issued. To this end, the following procedure will be adopted.

1. The parties will be expected (a) to start to consider potential trial dates as soon as is reasonable practicable after the service of the proceedings and (b) to discuss and attempt to agree trial dates with each other when seeking to agree directions for trial.

2. The starting point for listing trials is the current applicable Trial Window advertised by the Chancery List Office. Patent cases will be listed on the basis that the Trial Windows are divided as follows: estimated hearing time (excluding pre-reading and preparation of closing submissions) up to 5 days; estimated hearing time (excluding pre-reading and preparation of closing submissions) 6 to 10 days; and estimated hearing (excluding pre-reading and preparation of closing submissions) over 10 days.

3. Where it will enable a case to be tried within 12 months, or shortly thereafter, the Court may list a trial up to one month earlier than the applicable Trial Window without the need for any application for expedition.

4. The Court will use its case management powers in a more active manner than hitherto, with a view to dealing with cases justly and at proportionate cost in accordance with CPR rule 1.1. This may have the effect of setting limits on hearing times that enable cases to be listed promptly. For example, the Court may direct that a case estimated at 6 days will be heard in 5 days, and may allocate time between the parties in a manner which enables that to be achieved.

5. Where it makes a significant difference to the time which cases must wait to be listed for trial and it will not cause significant prejudice to any party, cases may be listed without reference to the availability of counsel instructed by the parties.

These steps do not exclude the possibility of cases being expedited where expedition is warranted. Nor do they exclude the possibility of the parties opting to use the streamlined procedure or the Shorter Trial pilot scheme or the Flexible Trial pilot scheme.

This Practice Statement is issued with the concurrence of the Chancellor of the High Court. It supersedes the Practice Statement issued on 28 January 2015."

A pilot for what is known as the Shorter Trials Scheme commenced on 1 October 2015. It provides for a streamlined procedure inter alia in the Patents Court, akin to that offered by the Intellectual Property Enterprise Court but without the associated costs caps. Cases in the Shorter Trials Scheme can last no longer than four days including reading time, although it has been indicated that a day off may be permitted during the trial for the drafting of closing submissions. Cases in the scheme will be allocated to a designated judge at the case management conference (which may or may not be the judge presiding at the case management conference).

Claims may be transferred into or out of the scheme, either on the application of the parties or at the suggestion of the court. Practice Direction 51N sets out details for pleadings and timescales for cases in the scheme. Selected paragraphs of the Practice Direction are reproduced below:

1.5 Where a case is agreed or ordered to be suitable for the Shorter Trials Scheme, the court expects the parties and their representatives to cooperate with, and assist, the court in ensuring the proceeding is conducted in accordance with the Scheme so that the real issues in dispute are identified as early as possible and are dealt with in the most efficient way possible.

2.3 The Shorter Trials Scheme will not normally be suitable for—

    (a) cases including an allegation of fraud or dishonesty;

    (b) cases which are likely to require extensive disclosure and/or reliance upon extensive witness or expert evidence;

    (c) cases involving multiple issues and multiple parties, save for Part 20 counterclaims for revocation of an intellectual property right;

    (d) cases in the Intellectual Property Enterprise Court...

2.16 The procedure set out in this paragraph shall be substituted for any applicable pre-action protocols.

2.17 Save where there is good reason not to do so, as in a case of urgency, a letter of claim should be sent giving succinct but sufficient details of the claim to enable the potential defendant to understand and to investigate the allegations.

2.18 The letter of claim shall notify the proposed defendant of the intention to adopt the Shorter Trials Scheme procedure.

2.19 The proposed defendant shall respond within 14 days stating whether it agrees to or opposes that procedure, or whether it has insufficient information to commit itself either way.

2.20 Particulars of claim must be served with the claim form.

2.21 In addition to the requirements of rule 16.4, the particulars of claim should include

    (a) a brief summary of the dispute and identification of the anticipated issues;

    (b) a full statement of all relief or remedies claimed;

    (c) detailed calculations of any sums claimed.

2.22 The particulars of claim should be no more than 20 pages in length. The court will only exceptionally give permission for a longer statement of case to be served for use in the Shorter Trials Scheme and will do so only where a party shows good reasons.

2.23 The particulars of claim should be accompanied by a bundle of core documents.

2.24 The claim form and particulars of claim shall be served promptly following—

    (a) the 14 day period allowed for the defendant's response to the letter of claim; or

    (b) the defendant's response, if a longer period for response is agreed between the parties.

2.25 The claimant shall, promptly after serving the claim form and particulars of claim, take steps to fix a CMC for a date approximately (but not less than) twelve weeks after the defendant is due to acknowledge service of the claim form.

2.26 The defendant shall be required to file an acknowledgment of service within the time periods prescribed by the rules.

2.29 The defence and any counterclaim must be served within 28 days of acknowledgment of service of the claim form.

2.30 The defence should include—

    (a) a statement indicating whether it is agreed that the case is appropriate for the Shorter Trials Scheme and, if not, why not;

    (b) a summary of the dispute and identification of the anticipated issues (if different to that of the claimant).

2.31 The defence and counterclaim should be no more than 20 pages in length. The court will only exceptionally give permission for a longer statement of case to be served for use in the Shorter Trials Scheme and will do so only where a party shows good reasons.

2.32 The defence should be accompanied by a bundle of any additional core documents on which the defendant intends to rely.

2.35 If the suitability of the Shorter Trials Scheme procedure is disputed then that issue will be determined at the first CMC, if not before, and further directions given in the light of that determination.

2.36 The legal representatives for the claimant will be responsible for producing and filing a list of issues, and where appropriate for revising it.

2.37 The claimant's legal representatives shall provide a draft list of issues to the defendant's solicitors in sufficient time to enable the parties to use their best endeavours to discuss and agree the contents thereof prior to filing the CMC bundle at court.

2.38 At the CMC the court will—

    (a) review the issues;

    (b) approve a list of issues;

    (c) consider ADR;

    (d) give directions for trial;

    (e) fix a trial date (or window), which should be not more than 8 months after the CMC and with a trial length of not more than 4 days (including reading time);

    (f) fix a date for a Pre-Trial Review.

2.40 If and insofar as any party wishes to seek disclosure from another party of particular documents or classes of documents or of documents relating to a particular issue, they must write to the other party to make such requests not less than 14 days in advance of the CMC and, absent an agreement regarding the extent of the disclosure to be given, raise such requests at the CMC.

2.41 Where there is a dispute as to whether requested disclosure should be provided, in deciding whether it is necessary so to order the court will have regard to how narrow and specific the request is, whether the requested documents are likely to be of significant probative value and the reasonableness and proportionality of any related search required, having regard to the factors set out in rule 31.7(2).

2.44 Unless otherwise ordered, witness statements will stand as the evidence in chief of the witness at trial. No witness statements should without good reason be more than 25 pages in length.

2.45 The court will consider at the CMC whether to order that witness evidence shall be limited to identified issues or to identified topics.

2.46 Expert evidence at trial will be given by written reports and oral evidence shall be limited to identified issues, as directed at the CMC or as subsequently agreed by the parties or directed by the court.

2.53 The court will manage the trial to ensure that, save in exceptional circumstances, the trial estimate is adhered to. Cross-examination will be strictly controlled by the court.

2.54 The trial will be conducted on the basis that it is only necessary for a party to put the principal parts of its case to a witness, unless the court directs otherwise.

2.55 The court will endeavour to hand down judgment within six weeks of the trial or (if later) final written submissions.

There is no requirement for cost budgets but the parties are required to exchange and file costs schedules within 21 days of the trial to enable the court to summarily assess costs at the same time as judgment.

Practice Direction 51N also introduces a Flexible Trials Scheme but, as this is of less relevance to intellectual property disputes, it is not described in any detail here.

Commencing a claim

Add new paragraphs at end: **61.53**

In *Medical Research Council v Celltech R&D* [2015] EWHC 2139 (Ch), the court refused to transfer proceedings to the Patents Court where the dispute appeared to relate to licensing and contractual construction rather than construction of the underlying patents.

In *Stretchline v H&M* [2015] EWHC 3298 (Pat), a settlement agreement prevented the defendant from running arguments of invalidity in its defence to a claim of infringement.

Particulars of claim

To the end of the third paragraph (beginning "In general in the Patents Court the   **61.54** *claimant"), add:*

In *Glass v Freyssinet* [2015] EWHC 2972 (IPEC), the court acknowledged that parties were generally not permitted to run unpleaded arguments at trial. It found, however, that arguments about the construction of patent claims fell into a special category that remained open up to and during trial, unless such arguments had either been concealed or caused significant prejudice.

Split trial

61.55   *Add new paragraph at end:*
In *Celltrion v Biogen* [2016] EWHC 188 (Pat), the court took the relatively unusual step of ordering a split liability trial, with a first trial to deal with two patents and a second trial dealing with a third related but significantly different patent.

Acknowledgement of service and defence

61.56   *Add new paragraph at end:*
■ In patent infringement proceedings, defendants sought at the case management conference to introduce what was described as a non-technical defence based on competition law issues, see *Illumina Inc v Premaithia Health Plc* [2016] EWHC 1726 (Pat). At that conference, it was ordered that the application to introduce that defence should be adjourned to a separate hearing. It now emerged that the technical trial which involved alleged infringement of at least ten claims might have various outcomes, that the non-technical defence would fall away if the defendant was wholly successful on the technical issues, or if there was infringement of only some of the claims the shape of the non-technical defence might be significantly altered. The appropriate way forward was therefore to adjourn this application, to be restored on the handing down of judgment in the technical trial and then to be heard as directed by the trial judge, who might direct that the non-technical issues should be heard by a judge with experience in competition law.

Case management: the case management conference

61.59   *Add new paragraph at end:*
In *Unwired Planet v Huawei and Samsung* [2016] EWHC 958 (Pat) proceedings whose overall cost was estimated at about £50 million had been split into a set of distinct trials. Four technical trials, three of which had been completed and a fourth was due to start the following week related to patent validity and infringement/essentiality to standards and there was a fifth technical trial scheduled for July. The present proceedings were non-technical and related to competition law issues and licensing of the patents under FRAND terms. In these proceedings, the defendants Samsung contended that the competition law aspects of the case should be transferred to the Competition Appeal Tribunal (the CAT), see *Sainsbury's v Mastercard* [2015] EWHC 3472 (Ch). However, transferring the competition law aspects of the claim to the CAT would leave the interrelated contract claims in the High Court. To split the issues in this way would create a division in the handling and decision-making process, and the application for transfer was refused.

Case management: strike-out pursuant to CPR 3.4(2)(b): abuse of process

61.63   *To the end of the second paragraph (beginning "An extended civil restraint order (CRO) was granted"), add:*
■ A further general civil restraint order ("GCRO") for a period of two years was granted against the claimant in *Perry v FH Brundle* [2017] EWHC 678 (IPEC).

Case management: hearing of a preliminary issue

61.65   *Add new paragraphs at end:*
In *Napp v Dr Reddy's* [2016] EWHC 493 (Pat), the court refused an application for a

trial of a preliminary issue where the defendants had failed to give adequate notice and where they were seeking to avoid a final decision being made in respect of a parallel interim injunction application.

In *Generics v Warner-Lambert* [2015] EWHC 3370 (Pat), the court found, as a preliminary issue, that a post-trial application to amend a patent was an abuse of process. The patent had been found invalid for insufficiency; the amendment could have been put forward earlier; and if the amendment were allowed, it would necessitate a retrial of the original dispute.

Case management: application to stay proceedings

Add new paragraph at end: **61.66**

In *Eli Lilly v Janssen Sciences* [2016] EWHC 313 (Pat) the guidelines on whether to stay proceedings as set out in *IPCom GmbH & Co KG v HTC Europe Co Ltd* [2013] EWCA Civ 1496 were considered, see §74.07. The Court refused an application to stay a claim to revoke a divisional pharmaceutical patent and for a declaration of non-infringement. The Court deemed that the claimant's interest in knowing whether it infringed and whether the defendant would be able to obtain an SPC outweighed arguments in favour of a stay.

Disclosure: general rules

Add new paragraph at end: **61.67**

The discretion available to US district courts to grant US discovery requests for use in foreign proceedings was considered by Anthony Tridico et al., "A way around the EPO wall" [2016] 1 *CIPA* 20 and explained that although there is no mechanism for adversarial discovery in EPO opposition proceedings, 28 USC 1782 provides a mechanism for parties in an EPO opposition to seek discovery in the US without any parallel substantive proceeding in the US by analogy with the US Supreme Court decision in *Intel Corp v Advanced Micro Devices, Inc,* 542 U.S. 241 (2004) where AMD had filed a complaint against Intel with the European Commission, alleging that Intel was using its size unfairly to dominate the computer microprocessor market.

Disclosure: product and process descriptions

Add new paragraphs at end: **61.71**

In *Stretchline v H&M* [2015] EWHC 3298 (Pat), the court emphasised the requirement for a product and process description to contain true information and for that information to be sufficient to enable all issues to be determined by the court.

The court held in *Teva v ICOS* [2016] EWHC 1259 (Pat) that, where a party puts forward a new claim construction not covered by a previously provided product and process description, the party providing the product and process description should be required to provide information or samples dealing with that revised claim construction.

Disclosure: obviousness and secondary evidence

Add new paragraph at end: **61.72**

In *Positec Power Tools v Husqvarna* [2016] EWHC 1061 (Pat), the court refused an application for disclosure of the inventor's documents given the difficulty of attempting to compare the actual inventor with the skilled person and the likely associated costs. The likely costs of obviousness disclosure were assessed by the court as about £90,000, which in context were neither substantial nor trivial. Cross-examination using the inventor's documents was unlikely to be probative either at all or without opening up a further costly and uncertain dispute about the personal qualities of the inventor. The court was aware that refusing this disclosure ran counter to the Court of Appeal in *Nichia v Argos*. However, the change in CPR r.31.5(7) meant that *Nichia* was not a binding authority. Experience in

IPEC showed that the obligation to disclose documents which may be adverse to a party's case can be preserved as a critical aspect of a fair trial at common law within an issue by issue-based disclosure regime in which disclosure on some issues, such as obviousness, is not ordered because the likely probative value of what is produced is not worth the cost. Applying what was perceived to be the right approach under the current Civil Procedure Rules, the court was not satisfied that an order for standard disclosure, or an order for issue-based disclosure including the issue of obviousness, would be in accordance with the overriding objective in this case. This was an ordinary obviousness case with no special features which might make such disclosure worth the cost.

Experiments

61.75   *Add new paragraph at end:*
In *Electromagnetic Geoservices v Petroleum Geo-Services* [2016] EWHC 27 (Pat), the court held that notices of experiments *must* explain the role of the experiments in the proceedings (i.e. to state the facts which the experiments seek to prove), see CPR PD63 7.1. In the outcome, the court was satisfied that the experiments had a proper role in the proceedings.

Expert evidence

61.77   *After the sixth paragraph (beginning "The principle that an expert should not adopt a partisan approach"), add new paragraphs:*
■ Objections to the objectivity of the evidence of an expert witness in *Fujifilm Kyowa Kirin Biologics Co Ltd v Abbvie Biotechnology Ltd* [2017] EWHC 395 (Pat) were based on her earlier involvement with parallel proceedings in the EPO, the USPTO and in the Canadian Patent Appeal Board and her close involvement with the claimant's legal teams from around the world for a number of years, which it was argued lead her to try to defend extreme propositions, and to avoid direct answers to direct questions. Carr J commented at [116], [117] that:

> "I approach this submission with caution. The Patents Court is privileged to be educated in technical issues by leading experts, and generally such evidence is of great value. If an expert does not agree with the case advanced by the client, he or she will not be instructed. If an expert concedes a point in cross-examination, that concession will be seized upon by the opposite party, either as evidence of inconsistency, or as conceding a key point in the case. There is nothing wrong in instructing the same expert in several jurisdictions, who may thereby gain a greater awareness of the weaknesses, as well as the strengths, of the case which he/she is supporting.
>
> On the other hand, it is vital that experts comply with the duty to be objective, to point out weaknesses in the case that they support, and to recognise that their first duty is not to their client, but to the Court... Furthermore, if, during cross-examination, it becomes clear that some part of the expert report is mistaken, it is necessary to say so, rather than doggedly to adhere to the party line."

■ In the same case, another expert during cross-examination gave an estimate of a parameter which it was objected was made "on the hoof" and not a considered response which could be relied on as accurate, pointing out an observation of Birss J in *Actavis v Lilly* [2016] EWHC 1955 (Pat) at [304]:

> "I will also add this. One of the vices of raising a point like this in cross-examination when it is not foreshadowed in the expert evidence is that it can become a test of how quickly people can think. That is not helpful."

■ In the outcome, the estimate was held to be an assumption rather than a hard and fast value on which reliance could be placed.

Scientific advisers or assessors

61.78   *Add new paragraphs at end:*
Birss J held, in *Electromagnetic Geoservices v Petroleum Geo-Services* [2016] EWHC

27 (Pat), that, given the technical nature of the subject-matter of the patent, the court should have the benefit of a non-controversial introductory course from a scientific adviser in advance of the trial and that attendance at such course would remove the need for a scientific adviser to attend the whole trial. Birss J stressed that it was helpful for the instructions to the scientific adviser to be settled by the court and for transparency, for the written materials provided to the judge to be provided to the parties after the introductory course. Finally, although in the instant case the instructions had not touched on the nature of the claim, Birss J noted that in some cases it might not be necessary to avoid the nature of the claim in the instructions to the scientific adviser. On difficulty, the present case was at the top end of category 5, those categories being explained at [29]:

> "The Patents Court operates a technical rating system for allocating patent cases to the appropriate type of judge. The technical category runs from 1 to 5. Cat 5 is the most complex. The complexity is technical complexity, not legal complexity and not commercial importance. A case about simple mechanics may be in Cat 1 or 2 whereas cases about biotechnology and some areas of telecommunications may be in Cat 4 or 5. The system does not and is not there to allocate cases to individual judges, it exists because the Patents Court has the benefit of judges with different kinds of experience and seeks to make most efficient use of the available judicial resources. Some of the judges of the Patents Court came from the patent bar and have experience of litigating patents for many years. They may have science degrees too. They are sometimes referred to as Cat 4/5 judges. Currently Arnold J, Henry Carr J and myself are the Cat 4/5 judges. Other designated judges of the Patents Court did not get involved in patent actions before going on the bench. They may also have a science degree but are less likely to have made heavy use of their scientific training in the intervening years. These other patents judges, while fully capable of dealing with patent cases which involve less complex science, do not profess to be comfortable handling technically difficult cases with the sort of expenditure of time and effort which a Cat 4/5 judge would require."

Although the matter settled, in *Electromagnetic Geoservices v Petroleum Geo-Services* [2016] EWHC 881 (Pat), Birss J went on to state the benefit he had obtained from the introductory course and the ability to have a candid conversation with the scientific adviser.

Trial

Add new paragraph at end: **61.79**

In *Regeneron v Kymab* [2016] EWHC 87 (Pat), the court made general observations about post-judgment submissions that had been made following circulation of the draft judgment but before it was handed down. The Court confirmed that counsel had an obligation to raise any perceived omissions in the judgment but stressed that they should not use this obligation as an opportunity to reargue points. The Court also noted that, even in trials of complex matters, the provision of a list of issues in advance should avoid the problem of omissions.

SECTION 63—Relief for infringement of partially valid patent

Commentary on Section 63

Scope of the section

Add new paragraph at end: **63.02**

■ In *Sandoz Ltd v GD Searle LLC* [2017] EWHC 987 (Pat), s.63 was cited as one of the provisions of the Patents Act that provided implicit support for a presumption of validity.

SECTION 64 [SUBSTITUTED]—Right to continue use begun before priority date

Add new paragraph at end of Note: **64.01**

In the event that arrangements for the European patent with unitary effect come into force in the UK, the Patents (European Patent with Unitary Effect and Unified Patent Court) Order 2016 (SI 2016/388), para.2(10) will apply s.64 to these patents.

SECTION 65—Certificate of contested validity of patent

PRACTICE UNDER SECTION 65

65.05 *Add new paragraph at end:*
■ In *Sandoz Ltd v GD Searle LLC* [2017] EWHC 987 (Pat) at [36], a case on the validity and scope of a Supplementary Protection Certificate and Markush practice, s.65 was cited as one of the provisions of the Patents Act that provided implicit support for a presumption of validity.

SECTION 69——Infringement of rights conferred by publication of application

COMMENTARY ON SECTION 69

Scope of the section

69.04 *Add new paragraph at end:*
The nature of the rights under s.69 was considered by Arnold J in *Global Flood Defence Systems Ltd v Johan Van Den Noort Beheer BV* [2016] EWHC 1851 (Pat). HHJ Hacon had adjourned trial of a threats action when it became apparent that a European Patent would imminently be granted: [2016] EWHC 99 (IPEC). Reading s.60 with s.69(1), Arnold J dismissed the claimants' appeal; "the reference in section 70(2A) to acts which 'constitute... an infringement of a patent' are capable of being understood as extending to infringement of the rights conferred by a patent pursuant to section 69": [2016] EWHC 1851 (Pat) at [38].

Rights conferred by the section (subs.(1))

69.06 *Add new paragraph at end:*
In *Global Flood Defence Systems Ltd v Johan Van Den Noort Beheer BV*, the decision noted in the Main Work was followed by a decision of HHJ Hacon to adjourn trial of the threats action [2016] EWHC 99 (IPEC) and an unsuccessful appeal against this procedural decision [2016] EWHC 1851 (Pat).

Limitation of the section 69 right (subss.(2) and (3))

69.07 *After the third paragraph (beginning "A literal construction of subs.(2)(b) would be absurd"), add new paragraph:*
In *AP Racing Ltd v Alcon Components Ltd* [2016] EWHC 116 (IPEC) defendants argued that s.69(3) concerns the reasonable expectation of skilled person who is deemed to have read both the patent application, and anything else which would reasonably be consulted, including here the UK and EPO searches. Based on that information it would not have been expected that the relevant claims would have been granted. However, the court was not convinced that merely because prior art has been cited against a claim of the patent application, the conclusion should follow that a skilled person would not reasonably expect a patent to be granted containing that claim. In any event, the issue threatened to give rise to a costly and time-consuming investigation into the skilled person's reasonable expectations in all the relevant circumstances, resulting in little likely benefit to the defendants. It did not satisfy the cost/benefit test applying to all issues before IPEC under CPR 63PD, 29.2(2).

SECTION 70—Unjustified threats

Add new paragraph 70.00:   **70.00**

Contents

Replace paragraph 70.01 with:

Threats of infringement proceedings

70.—(1) A communication contains a "threat of infringement proceedings" if a   **70.01**
reasonable person in the position of a recipient would understand from the
communication that—

(a) a patent exists, and

(b) a person intends to bring proceedings (whether in a court in the United
Kingdom or elsewhere) against another person for infringement of the
patent by—

(i) an act done in the United Kingdom, or

(ii) an act which, if done, would be done in the United Kingdom

(2) References in this section and in section 70C to "a recipient" include, in
the case of a communication directed to the public or a section of the public,
references to a person to whom the communication is directed.

Actionable threats

70A.—(1) Subject to subsections (2) to (5), a threat of infringement proceedings made by any person is actionable by any person aggrieved by the threat.

(2) A threat of infringement proceedings is not actionable if the infringement
is alleged to consist of—

(a) where the invention is a product, making a product for disposal or
importing a product for disposal, or

(b) where the invention is a process, using a process.

(3) A threat of infringement proceedings is not actionable if the infringement
is alleged to consist of an act which, if done, would constitute an infringement of
a kind mentioned in subsection (2)(a) or (b).

(4) A threat of infringement proceedings is not actionable if the threat—

(a) is made to a person who has done, or intends to do, an act mentioned in
subsection (2)(a) or (b) in relation to a product or process, and

(b) is a threat of proceedings for an infringement alleged to consist of doing
anything else in relation to that product or process.

85

(5) A threat of infringement proceedings which is not an express threat is not actionable if it is contained in a permitted communication.

(6) In sections 70C and 70D "an actionable threat" means a threat of infringement proceedings that is actionable in accordance with this section.

Permitted communications

70B.—(1) For the purposes of section 70A(5), a communication containing a threat of infringement proceedings is a "permitted communication" if—

    (a) the communication, so far as it contains information that relates to the threat, is made for a permitted purpose,

    (b) all of the information that relates to the threat is information that—

        (i) is necessary for that purpose (see subsection (5)(a) to (c) for some examples of necessary information), and

        (ii) the person making the communication reasonably believes is true.

(2) Each of the following is a "permitted purpose"—

    (a) giving notice that a patent exists;

    (b) discovering whether, or by whom, a patent has been infringed by an act mentioned in section 70A(2)(a) or (b);

    (c) giving notice that a person has a right in or under a patent, where another person's awareness of the right is relevant to any proceedings that may be brought in respect of the patent.

(3) The court may, having regard to the nature of the purposes listed in subsection (2)(a) to (c), treat any other purpose as a "permitted purpose" if it considers that it is in the interests of justice to do so.

(4) But the following may not be treated as a "permitted purpose"—

    (a) requesting a person to cease doing, for commercial purposes, anything in relation to a product or process,

    (b) requesting a person to deliver up or destroy a product, or

    (c) requesting a person to give an undertaking relating to a product or process.

(5) If any of the following information is included in a communication made for a permitted purpose, it is information that is "necessary for that purpose" (see subsection (1)(b)(i))—

    (a) a statement that a patent exists and is in force or that an application for a patent has been made;

    (b) details of the patent, or of a right in or under the patent, which—

        (i) are accurate in all material respects, and

        (ii) are not misleading in any material respect; and

    (c) information enabling the identification of the products or processes in respect of which it is alleged that acts infringing the patent have been carried out.

Remedies and defences

70C.—(1) Proceedings in respect of an actionable threat may be brought against the person who made the threat for—

    (a) a declaration that the threat is unjustified;

    (b) an injunction against the continuance of the threat;

    (c) damages in respect of any loss sustained by the aggrieved person by reason of the threat.

(2) In the application of subsection (1) to Scotland—

  (a) "declaration" means "declarator", and

  (b) "injunction" means "interdict".

(3) It is a defence for the person who made the threat to show that the act in respect of which proceedings were threatened constitutes (or if done would constitute) an infringement of the patent.

(4) It is a defence for the person who made the threat to show—

  (a) that, despite having taken reasonable steps, the person has not identified anyone who has done an act mentioned in section 70A(2)(a) or (b) in relation to the product or the use of a process which is the subject of the threat, and

  (b) that the person notified the recipient, before or at the time of making the threat, of the steps taken.

Professional advisers

70D.—(1) Proceedings in respect of an actionable threat may not be brought against a professional adviser (or any person vicariously liable for the actions of that professional adviser) if the conditions in subsection (3) are met.

(2) In this section "professional adviser" means a person who, in relation to the making of the communication containing the threat—

  (a) is acting in a professional capacity in providing legal services or the services of a trade mark attorney or a patent attorney; and

  (b) is regulated in the provision of legal services, or the services of a trade mark attorney or a patent attorney, by one or more regulatory bodies (whether through membership of a regulatory body, the issue of a licence to practise or any other means).

(3) The conditions are that—

  (a) in making the communication the professional adviser is acting on the instructions of another person; and

  (b) when the communication is made the professional adviser identifies the person on whose instructions the adviser is acting.

(4) This section does not affect any liability of the person on whose instructions the professional adviser is acting.

(5) It is for a person asserting that subsection (1) applies to prove (if required) that at the material time—

  (a) the person concerned was acting as a professional adviser, and

  (b) the conditions in subsection (3) were met.

Supplementary: pending registration

70E.—(1) In sections 70 and 70B references to a patent include references to an application for a patent that has been published under section 16.

(2) Where the threat of infringement proceedings is made after an application has been published (but before grant) the reference in section 70C(3) to "the patent" is to be treated as a reference to the patent as granted in pursuance of that application.

Supplementary: proceedings for delivery up etc.

70F.— In section 70(1)(b) the reference to proceedings for infringement of a patent includes a reference to proceedings for an order under section 61(1)(b) (order to deliver up or destroy patented products etc.) and proceedings in the Unified Patent Court for an order for delivery up made in accordance with articles 32(1)(c) and 62(3) of the Agreement on a Unified Patent Court.

Notes.

1. Section 70 is substituted and ss.74, 78 and 106 are amended by the provisions of the Intellectual Property (Unjustified Threats) Act 2017 which are brought into force by reg.2 of the Intellectual Property (Unjustified Threats) Act 2017 (Commencement and Transitional Provisions) Regulations 2017 (SI 2017/771).

2. Section 70 was previously amended by ss.12 and 16 of and by paras 1 and 17 of Sch.2 to the Patents Act 2004; s.74 by para.3 of the Schedule to the Intellectual Property Act 2014, para.10 of Sch.5 to the Copyright, Designs and Patents Act 1988 and s.13 of the Patents Act 2004; s.78 by SI 2004/2357, para.22 of Sch.5 to the Copyright, Designs and Patents Act 1988, and paras 1 and 3 of Sch.1 to the Patents Act 2004; s.106 by s.14 of and Sch.3 to the Patents Act 2004 and by s.59 of and para.23 of Pt 4 of Sch.11 to the Constitutional Reform Act 2005. However, the provisions in force prior to 1 October 2017 continue to apply to threats made before that date.

3. The Law Commission and the IPO have worked up examples as to how they expect the new provisions to work and so the commentary at *https://www.gov.uk/ government/uploads/system/uploads/attachment_data/file/633353/unjustified- threats-act-guidance-for-business.pdf* makes invaluable reading.

COMMENTARY ON SECTION 70

Scope of the section

70.02   *Replace with:*

■ Sections 70 and 70A–F replace the former Section 70 with effect from 1 October 2017.

■ Section 3 of the Intellectual Property (Unjustified Threats) Act 2017 (Commencement and Transitional Provisions) Regulations 2017 (SI 2017/771) provides that where proceedings are brought in respect of an alleged threat made before the appointed day the proceedings in respect of that alleged threat are to be determined in accordance with the law in force at the time the alleged threat was made. Section 70, which therefore continues to apply to communications made before that date, provided for relief in certain circumstances against threats of action for patent infringement. Such threats were actionable against whomsoever made them, it not being necessary that the person making the threat be the patent proprietor or a licensee. As noted above, the former s.70 was extensively amended with a view to limiting the grounds for bringing a successful action in respect of threats of infringement and so in relation to alleged threats to which s.70 continues to apply pre-2005 and pre-2017 case law (as the case may be) should be considered with this in mind.

■ The 2017 Act also contains provisions in relation to threats of infringement of registered trade marks, Community trade marks, registered designs, design rights and Community designs. There is, however, no corresponding provision in respect of threats for infringement of other intellectual property rights, e.g. infringement of a copyright or in respect of a common law tort, such as an alleged "passing off". The absence of similar provisions in other statutes has been held to be deliberate so that threats of litigation of other unregistered intellectual property rights are not actionable, even if presented as an action for wrongful interference with contractual relations (*Granby v Interlego* [1984] R.P.C. 209). Threats of litigation in respect of other intellectual property rights which can be made with impunity may nevertheless become actionable if coupled with notification of the existence of an intellectual property right, such as a patent. This is despite such notification by itself being a permitted communication, see the design case of *Jaybeam v Abru Aluminium* [1976] R.P.C. 308 discussed in §70.06.

■ The revised provisions were introduced following a review requested in 2012 by the Department for Business, Innovation and Skills (BIS) and the Intellectual Property Office (IPO) which resulted in a report of the Law Commission, "Patents Trade Marks and Design Rights: Groundless Threats", Law Commission Report No.346 (2014), Cm 8851.

■ A classic case of misuse of threats identified in that report is *Halsey v Brotherhood* (1881) 19 Ch. D. 386 in which both parties manufactured steam engines but only Mr Brotherhood had a flourishing business based in part on his habit of "systematically threatening" to sue Mr Halsey's customers for infringing his patents. He never did sue: threats were enough. When the customers received threats, they stopped buying Mr Halsey's engines. Mr Halsey sought an injunction against Mr Brotherhood to stop him making threats, but the courts held that the common law provided no protection unless it was shown that Mr Brotherhood acted with malice. In 1883, Parliament intervened and provided a statutory remedy for those aggrieved by groundless threats of patent litigation. Under the 1883 legislation, a proprietor could avoid liability if he commenced and pursued patent infringement proceedings with due diligence. Thus under that legislation, a patentee could still utter as blood-curdling threats as he liked as long as he followed them through. The legislation was subsequently changed so that was no longer a defence to follow up the threats with proceedings. A threat was actionable even if the proprietor had every intention of commencing and pursuing the infringement proceedings and did so. The Law Commission report identified a continuing need for threats provisions as exemplified by *SDL Hair Ltd v Next Row Ltd* [2013] EWPCC 31 where threats against a product proposed to be exhibited at a trade fair were made against an alleged primary infringer and its distributions with damaging effects, but the product was ultimately found to be non-infringing, see also the explanation by Pumfrey J in *Quads 4 Kids v Campbell* [2006] EWHC 2482 (Ch) at [23], [24].

■ The groundless threats provisions had been, however, criticised by Laddie J in *Reckitt Benckiser UK v Home Pairfum Ltd* [2004] EWHC 302 (Ch); [2004] F.S.R. 37 at [17] where he said: "There is then an obvious tension between the sensible 'talk first' policy of the CPR and the 'sue first' policy encouraged by the legislation." The Law Commission recognised that there had been difficulties in distinguishing between primary and secondary acts of infringement, and that there were cases where a rights holder had good reason to write to a secondary infringer. However, it was easy to go inadvertently beyond what might safely be said and risk incurring liability as in *Cavity Trays Ltd v RMC Panel Products Ltd* [1996] R.P.C. 361 where RMC's lawyers wrote to an alleged primary infringer threatening infringement proceedings in respect of acts of manufacture, promotion and marketing, and the Court of Appeal held that only threats regarding manufacturing were protected by s.70(4) and other threats were not protected even if made to the same alleged primary infringer. It was observed that the line between an allegation and a threat was a difficult one to draw, with the result that the groundless threats provisions were driving cases to court. The report noted that legal advisers had been granted immunity in Australia in 1990, and recommended that professional advisers should not be personally liable when they act in a professional capacity and on instructions from their clients. It concluded with the following summary of the problems flowing from the previous groundless threats provisions:

(1) advisers must devise complex strategies about how to communicate with the alleged infringer. As the IP Working Party, CLLS and IPLA put it, they must decide "whether to write pre-action correspondence at all and how to frame any such letter, on whose headed notepaper". It takes time (and cost) to explain these strategies to clients.

(2) Pre-action letters may not set out the case clearly, making disputes less easy to resolve.

(3) In some cases, rights holders may sue first, without any pre-action communication. This may "entrench animosity" between the parties and therefore prolong disputes.

(4) Legal advisers may ask rights holders for indemnities against the possibility that the advisor may be sued personally; these take time (and cost) to explain.

(5) Small rights holders who cannot provide indemnities may end up writing letters in their own name. This disadvantages them as their letters are less likely to be taken seriously.

(6) In extreme cases, the threats provisions can be used aggressively to rack up costs, which impacts disproportionately on smaller business.

(7) Where legal advisers are sued, they may not be able to continue to act for their clients.

■ A new statutory definition of a communication containing a threat of infringement proceedings is introduced by s.70, see §70.03. Both actionable and non-actionable threats are now defined in s.70A. As previously, the claimant must be "a person aggrieved", see §70.04. As previously, non-actionable threats are those against primary infringers for making or importing a product for disposal or using a process, re-enacting the provisions of the former s.70(4), but the definition has been expanded to cover other acts which if done would constitute an infringement and to cover intended future acts. Significantly, non-actionable threats against primary infringers now cover related acts, so that the risk of liability identified in *Cavity Trays* is no longer so acute and the tight language of the 2005 Act, which referred to things done, and did not cover future acts, has also been extended.

■ A new statutory class of permitted communications is introduced by s.70A(5), these being communications which may be made to both primary and secondary infringers, not containing an express threat, and being for a "permitted purpose" as defined in s.70B. Significantly, s.70B(3) provides that a court may treat other purposes as permitted purposes if it considers that it is in the interests of justice to do so. It is therefore likely in accordance with the Law Commission Report that at least some pre-action correspondence will fall into the "permitted communication" safe harbour. Thus a court may be reluctant to grant relief in respect of an actionable threat made in the course of "without prejudice" settlement discussions, because such should not be inhibited by litigation arising from what was said during such discussions, see *Unilever v Procter & Gamble* [1999] F.S.R. 849, upheld on appeal [2000] F.S.R. 344 CA. In this way, it seems that the requirements of the CPR, that parties must make efforts to settle disputes before commencing litigation can be met without fear that the attempts to settle would be regarded as an actionable threat.

■ Section 70C(1) and (2) specify that the specified relief is a declaration (in Scotland: declarator) that the threats are unjustifiable, an injunction (in Scotland: interdict) against continuance of the threats and damages in respect of any loss suffered by the claimant/threatened person.

■ Again, as previously, the threat must be groundless (i.e. unjustifiable). New s.70C(3) preserves the defence of the former s.70(2A) that that the act in respect of which proceedings were threatened constitutes (or if done would constitute) an infringement of the patent. It omits the express reference of former s.70(2A)(a) to proof by a claimant of invalidity in a relevant respect, but the right to put validity of the patent in issue in respect of an actionable threat is continued under s.74(1)(b) by reference to s.70A substituted for s.70 by the 2017 Act. In *Icon Health v Precise Exercise Equipment* BL C/29/01, noted I.P.D. 24054, relief for unjustified threats was ordered, the patent being held not to be infringed and it therefore not being necessary to consider the validity of the patent. New s.70C(4) preserves in relation to secondary infringers the defence that the person making the threat had notified the recipient of the reasonable steps taken before or at the time of making the threat to discover the identity of a primary infringer, and that the person threatened had not identified any such person.

■ In accordance with the recommendations of the Law Commission Report, new s.70D exempts professional advisers or those vicariously liable for the actions of such advisers (e.g. law firms employing associate solicitors) from threats proceedings in respect of communications made on the instructions of another person who is identified in such a communication. These provisions are not limited to UK or even EU-based professional advisers—see the new definition in s.70D(2)—over the need for there to be some form of regulation and legal advice, patent attorney or trade mark attorney advice.

■ The consequence of threats action is usually that the defendant contends that the threat was justified because there is an infringement of the patent, with the defendant counterclaiming for infringement (if the defendant is the proprietor or exclusive licensee under the patent in issue and if the claimant, being the person threatened, is alleged to be an actual infringer); and the claimant then counterclaiming that, even if he is an infringer, the patent is not valid in relation to the alleged infringing activities. An advantage of bringing a threats action under the section is that an interim injunction may be available despite an allegation of justification, see the Main Work at §70.06. Also, the person threatened can seize the initiative. As claimant, that person will enjoy the right to open the oral argument and normally to have the final speech as well. The claimant can also, at least initially, choose the forum in which the proceedings should be heard. This is a potent factor now that proceedings for threats, infringement and validity can all be brought before the Intellectual Property Enterprise Court as an alternative to the general list in the High Court, not forgetting the possibility of proceedings in Scotland or Northern Ireland.

■ In *Kenburn Waste Management v Bergmann* [2002] F.S.R. 44 the parties had previously settled a threats action by means of undertakings by the German defendant that it would not utter further threats. On the defendant being alleged to have breached the undertakings, questions arose as to the proper forum for adjudication of this further dispute. The defendant argued that because he was domiciled in Germany and operated his business from there, the proper forum for the dispute was Germany. The court considered the relevant provisions of the Brussels Convention (now Regulation 44/2001) and held that because the object of the contract was to achieve results in the UK (fulfilment of the negative obligation not to make threats) and because the contract was concerned with the purely English right of action under the former s.70, the contract was strongly connected with the UK and therefore the matter was actionable there. The judgment was upheld on appeal ([2002] EWCA Civ 98 at [41]).

Threats of infringement proceedings

Change heading to "Threats of infringement proceedings" and replace text with:　　**70.03**

■ The new s.70 (which was introduced as an amendment to the original Bill) provides a statutory definition of a threat, referring to a communication directed to a reasonable recipient, the existence of a patent, and the necessary communicated intent, and being subject to s.70(A) as to whether it is actionable. When introduced it was said by the Law Commission to follow current case law.

■ The newly defined communication/recipient threat pathway replaces the reference in former s.70 to "circulars, advertisements or otherwise", but preserves the position that the person making the threat need not be the patent proprietor or a licensee. An actionable threat may be made by mass communication but must still be addressed to some person, and not merely be a general warning not addressed to any particular person. Likewise, in *Alpi v Wright* [1972] R.P.C. 125, where an advertisement announced that an infringement action had been started, it was held that an actionable threat must point a warning finger at the products of a specific person, though an actionable threat need not be made directly to the actual infringer. For example, in *Bristol-Myers v Manon* [1973] R.P.C. 836, there was an actionable threat when a retailer was informed that a claim would be made against the manufacturer, though not against the retailer, of the alleged infringing goods. There was also an actionable threat when a manufacturer was informed that claims might be made against its customers, see *Sudarshan v Clariant* [2012] EWHC 1569 (Ch) since if a manufacturer knows that its customers are going to be harassed by patent infringement claims it will be wary of supplying those customers, for fear of damaging its business relationships with them.

■ To be actionable under the section there must be a "threat" to bring proceedings for some infringement of a patent, whether past, present or future, but a threat merely of legal proceedings without reference to a patent is not enough, see *Easycare v Bryan Lawrence* [1995] F.S.R. 597. By s.70E, the reference to the existence of a patent includes reference to a patent application published under s.16. Where a threat is made in respect of a published application the reference in s.70C(3) to "the patent" is treated as a reference to the patent as subsequently granted. The section is applied to granted European patents (UK) by s.77(1)(b), is applied to international applications for patents (UK) by s.89(1), and is now also applied to applications for European patents (UK) by s.6 of the 2017 Act which inserts a reference to new ss.70-70F into s.78(2).

■ The definition requires a reference to intent to bring proceedings, implying that the recipient of a communication would understand from that communication that the originator has a plan to bring proceedings and is resolved or determined to do so. It has been held under the former law that such a test is objective, see *Luna Advertising Co Ltd v Burnham & Co* (1928) 45 R.P.C. 258 and that the initial impression that a communication would have on a reasonable addressee is particularly important: see *Brain v Ingledew Brown (No.3)* [1997] F.S.R. 511, 521, *C&P Development v Sisabro* (1953) 70 R.P.C. 277 CA, *Continental Linen v Kenpet [South Africa]* [1986] 4 SA 703(t), noted [1987] E.I.P.R. D–87 and the design case of *Quads 4 Kids v Campbell* [2006] EWHC 2482 (Ch) in relation to an application for interim injunction. See also the trade mark case of *L'Oréal v Johnson & Johnson* [2000] F.S.R. 686 where a letter, the "work of a master of Delphic utterances", was held to be a veiled threat muffled by protestations of a continuing state of uncertainty but sufficient to be an intimation to a reasonable person of an intention to enforce rights, it being irrelevant that the letter was sent in response to an enquiry from the party threatened. In *Bowden Controls v Acco Cable Controls* [1990] R.P.C. 427, a letter addressed to a supplier to car manufacturers, which referred to a German court decision, stated that the patentee had corresponding patents in most other European countries, and stated that he intended to enforce his rights. This was held to be a threat of infringement proceedings, even though the patentee argued that it would be commercial suicide to sue a potential customer in view of the established practice in the industry of requiring dual sourcing of car components. Aldous J commented at p.432: "... I believe that the purpose of the letter was to give [the recipient] information and a warning. That requires the answer: a warning as to what?" In *FNM Corp v Drammock* [2009] EWHC 1294 (Pat), an e-mail was sent to a third-party customer of the defendant, informing the customer that a dispute existed between the defendant and the patentee. Although this contained no direct allegation against the customer, it was held nonetheless to amount to an actionable threat when viewed from the point of view of the ordinary reader in the position of the actual recipient, who clearly understood this as a threat. Another case in which the question of what constitutes a threat was broadly construed was *Zeno v BSM-Bionic Solutions* [2009] EWHC 1829 (Pat) where a letter sent to a retailer seeking an explanation of why the device in issue did not infringe was held to amount to an actionable threat. In *Best Buy v Worldwide Sales* [2011] EWCA Civ 618, reversing the judge at first instance on this issue at [2010] EWHC 1666 (Ch), the Court of Appeal held that a letter made an actionable threat of trade mark infringement proceedings even though it included an offer to negotiate a settlement and thus might have been thought to attract the privilege accorded to "without prejudice" communications. The offer to settle did not contain any concession or admission and looking at the letter as a whole, the Court of Appeal held that it was unrealistic to treat the offer as amounting to the sort of settlement proposal which should be treated as privileged from use in court, on the grounds of public policy.

■ A relevant threat must be addressed to some person, now defined as a reasonable person in the position of the recipient, and not merely a general warning not addressed to any particular person. In *Alpi v Wright* [1972] R.P.C. 125, where an advertisement announced that an infringement action had been commenced, it was held that a threat must point a warning finger at the products of a specific person, though it need not be made directly to the actual infringer. On similar reasoning, in *Bristol-Myers v Manon* [1973] R.P.C. 836, there was a threat when a retailer was informed that a claim would be made against the manufacturer, though not against the retailer, of the alleged infringing goods. There was also a threat when a manufacturer was informed that claims might be made against its customers, see [2012] EWHC 1569 (Ch).

■ The amended section now provides statutory basis for the position that a threat can be in respect of a projected, rather than existing, act of alleged infringement, see *Therm-a-Stor v Weatherseal* [1981] F.S.R. 579 CA.

■ To be actionable, the new section now specifically provides that the threat should be one made within, or reaching, the United Kingdom: otherwise, the Act would have extra-territorial effect contrary to general jurisprudence. This is also made in contemplation of the UPC and the fact that, when that comes into force, infringement proceedings for EP granted patents may be brought there. Threats of litigation in relation to EP patents may have no connection to the UK and are not intended to be globally caught by the UK threats provisions. In *Samsung v Apple* [2012] EWHC 889 (Ch), the court found that although parallel proceedings in the Netherlands and Germany indicated an intention to sue throughout the European Union, there had been no specific threat in the United Kingdom. A failure by the defendant to respond to a letter seeking agreement that there was no infringement could not be construed, in and of itself, as a threat. See also the Community trade mark decision in *Best Buy Co Inc v Worldwide Sales Corp España SL* [2011] EWCA Civ 618.

■ If a letter is deemed to be a threat, the individual who signs the letter may be personally liable for the threat, along with any company who he/she represents, see *SDL Hair v Next Row* [2013] EWPCC 31 and *Cassie Creations v Simon Blackmore and Mirrorkool Ltd* [2014] EWHC 2941 (Ch) at [37], citing a review by Barling J in *Twentieth Century Fox Film Corp v Harris* [2014] EWHC 1568 (Ch) at [135] to [137]. In *Sudarshan v Clariant* [2013] EWCA Civ 919, the defendant attempted, unsuccessfully, to separate the knowledge of the inventor from that of the individual responsible for the letter. The court concluded that the controlling mind of the company must be deemed to include the knowledge of both individuals and an internal breakdown in communication was thus no defence. (However, note the exemption for professional advisers discussed above and below.)

■ The section can, apparently, be avoided by issuing a claim form before issuing the threat, even if this form has not been served at the time of the threat. This is because there can scarcely be a threat of infringement proceedings if they are already in being. However, the courts have been prepared to grant relief in cases where the commencement of legal proceedings can be seen as harassment rather than legitimate, especially if allegations of infringement have been insufficiently particularised (*Landi den Hartog v Sea Bird* [1976] F.S.R. 489); or if separate complaints have been issued against customers of an existing defendant without adding the defendant as a party (*Jacey v Norton & Wright* [1977] F.S.R. 475).

■ Because remarks may so easily be construed as an implied threat (even under the newly introduced provisions), there is frequently a need to give a warning to lay persons, particularly salespersons, not to refer to patents, and in particular not to refer to pending applications except in terms which have previously been approved by a solicitor or patent attorney. Lay persons also need to be told that advertisements may lead to action being taken for unjustifiable threats under the section. See also the warnings in §70.04 of the Main Work in respect of references to pending litigation and the danger of committing a contempt of court or uttering a malicious falsehood if reports of litigation are not entirely accurate and free from contrary innuendo.

Malicious Falsehood and Contempt of Court

■ See §70.04 of the Main Work.   70.04

Actionable threats

Change heading to "Actionable threats" and replace text with: 70.05

■ New s.70A provides three conditions for a threat to be actionable: (a) there must have been a threat as defined in new s.70, (b) a person must be aggrieved by the threat, and (c) the threat is not to a primary infringer or in a permitted communication and hence protected by subss.(2)–(5).

■ As in previous s.70, new s.70A(1) provides that proceeding can only be instituted by a person aggrieved. In *Brain v Ingledew Brown (No.3)* [1997] F.S.R. 511, some of the threats complained of were directed to a company owned and operated solely by the claimant, but these were not seen to be directed at the claimant personally and were therefore not actionable by him, the company having been struck off the register. However, another letter written to a third party was likely to be understood by that party as applying to the claimant in a personal capacity and was therefore actionable. It was (unsuccessfully) argued that, unless threats were made directly to the claimant, he/she must prove that he/she has suffered actual damage before it can be held that he/she is "a person aggrieved". It was held sufficient that the claimant shows: "that his commercial interests are or are likely to be adversely affected in a real as opposed to a fanciful or minimal way". In *Dimplex v De'Longhi* [1996] F.S.R. 622, threatening letters had been sent to many major retailers of the claimants' goods. It was unsuccessfully contended that, because the patent had been abandoned, the claimant was not a "person aggrieved".

■ For intended or actual making of products, using of processes and importation of products for disposal, subss.70A(2), (3) and (4) substantially re-enact the protection of communications to primary infringers of previous s.70(4)(a) and (b). The section may absolve threats against persons who, as indirect infringers under s.60(2), supply others with products for use in making the claimed products (*Therm-a-Stor v Weatherseal* [1981] F.S.R. 579 CA). The reference in s.70A(4)(b) to "doing anything else" apparently removes the anomaly that arose in *Cavity Trays*, see §70.02 further exemplified by *FNM Corp v Drammock* [2009] EWHC 1294. In that case, a letter that specifically referred only to manufacture was held not to entitle the patentee to the protection of previous s.70(4) as it had to be read in conjunction with the associated form of undertakings which referred also to supply. Therefore, although the threat was protected in respect of manufacture by previous s.70(4)(a), it was not protected in respect of supply by previous s.70(4)(b), as that only protected a threat to a person "who had made... a product" and did not protect a threat to a person who is wrongly alleged to have made a product—which was the case here as the defendant was not the manufacturer. An opposite conclusion would have apparently been reached under the current legislation. It should be noted that the reference in subs.(5) is to doing anything else in respect of the relevant product or process, so that threats in relation to other products or processes, e.g. an equivalent product of another manufacturer will not be protected.

■ Threats contained in permitted communications are also non-actionable provided that they are not express threats, see §76.06.

Permitted communications

70.06 *Change heading to "Permitted communications" and replace text with:*

■ The provisions of previous subss.(4)–(6) have been largely incorporated into s.70B.

■ A communication in the newly permitted class is not actionable if it is not an express threat, see s.70A(5). Section 70B(4) defines a range of requests that cannot be treated as permitted purposes: to cease doing, for commercial purposes, anything in relation to a product or process, to deliver up or destroy a product or to give an undertaking in relation to a product or process.

■ All information in a permitted communication must be both necessary for a permitted purpose and reasonably believed true. The court has under s.70B(3) an over-riding discretion to treat any purpose as permitted if it is in the interests of justice to do so, but the purposes specifically mentioned as permitted are giving notice of the existence of a patent, discovering the identity of a primary infringer or whether primary acts of infringement have occurred and where relevant to any proceedings that might be instituted giving notice that a person has rights in or under the patent. Necessary information includes notice that a patent exists and is in force or that an application for a patent has been made, accurate and non-misleading details of the patent, and information enabling allegedly infringing products or processes to be identified. It is apparently envisaged (as was the case for previous s.70(5)) that, as a result of these changes, an enquirer will be able to make assertions regarding an alleged primary infringement, as part of an attempt to trace the primary infringer, but that assertions regarding an alleged secondary infringement will not necessarily be excluded from the definition of a "threat". By s.70C(4)(b) communications (e.g. to a retailer or stockist) attempting to discover the identity of a primary infringer should only be after other reasonable steps to discover that identity have been taken and should include information about those steps.

■ Under the previous legislation the exemption for a mere notification was construed strictly. For example, in *Jaybeam Ltd v Abru Aluminium* [1975] F.S.R. 334 the relevant letter threatened proceedings for infringement of copyright and ended with the words "... and as a separate matter we would also drew your attention to the fact that Abru are registered proprietors of registered design no. 940 140"). It was held that given the context, this additional sentence went beyond the protection of former s.26(3) of the Registered Designs Act 1949 and that any businessman receiving it would think he was being threatened in respect of everything, including the registered design. Similarly, in *Reynes-Cole v Elite Hosiery (No.2)* [1964] R.P.C. 255; and [1965] R.P.C. 102 CA, a letter notifying the existence of patents also stated that a number of firms were infringing and that action was being taken against some of them, and this was held to be an actionable threat. It is difficult to see, if considered under s.70C, how the latter statements would qualify as necessary for a permitted purpose.

Remedies and defences (s.70C)

Change heading to "Remedies and defences (s.70C)" and replace text with: **70.07**

■ The relief available is similar to that under previous s.70(3) for which see the Main Work at §70.06. The defence of justification is now provided by s.70C(3) and a further defence is provided by s.70C(4) for attempts to trace primary infringers.

■ Under the amendments introduced by the 2004 Patents Act, it was a defence to show that the patent would have been infringed, if the grounds on which the patent was found to be invalid had not been known to the patentee. That has now been abolished. If the patent is invalid for any reason, then the justification defence will fall away, even if the patent would have been infringed had it been valid.

■ Under the previous legislation, in *Global Flood Defence Systems v Johann Van Den Noort* [2016] EWHC 99 (IPEC) proceedings for groundless threats were adjourned. This was to allow the defendant the opportunity to defend the allegations, following the grant of its European patent. The decision was upheld on appeal ([2016] EWHC 1851 (Pat)) and the assessment of costs in relation to separate issues that had been resolved was adjourned pending resolution of the claim for groundless threats ([2016] EWHC 189 (IPEC)).

Professional advisers

Change heading to "Professional advisers" and replace text with: **70.08**

■ Section 70(D) which is largely self-explanatory now provides that an actionable threat may not be brought against a professional advisor, defined as a person who is acting in a professional capacity in providing legal services, or the services of a patent (or trade mark) attorney, and is regulated by one or more regulatory bodies, e.g. the Solicitors Regulation Authority (SRA) or the Intellectual Property Regulation Board (IPReg). But note, this is specifically not limited to UK or even to EU-based legal advisers. It will be interesting to see how the case law develops in relation to what is needed to satisfy the regulatory hurdle. The new safe harbour applies only when the professional advisor is acting on the instructions of a principal and the relevant communication identifies the principal on behalf of whom the professional advisor is acting. The exemption for professional advisers does not alter any liability of the principal on whose behalf the advisor is acting.

■ An indication of policy is provided by *Reckitt Banister v Home Parfum* [2004] EWHC 302 (Pat) which was a trade marks case. The legislation then in force exempted threats relating to the application of a mark to goods or their packaging or the importation of goods or their packaging to which the mark had been applied, but proceedings were being maintained for other acts on the then applicable *Cavity Trays* principle. It was argued that proceedings against the claimant's solicitors would be abusive. The defendants responded that they were entitled to select who they wanted to enforce a damages judgment against and that there was insufficient to suggest any motive other than a desire to pursue their legal rights. Laddie J commented that although retaliation was unobjectionable, a desire to make relations between the claimants and their solicitors uncomfortable was an illegitimate purpose and was an issue on which it would be appropriate to exercise proportionate case management powers, so that an application to join the solicitors in the then existing proceedings failed [44].

PRACTICE UNDER SECTIONS 70—70F

70.09   *Add new paragraph at end:*
■ In order to ensure benefit of the s.70D safe harbour, a professional advisor would be well advised to keep file notes recording the instructions received from a client regarding any third-party communication containing a potential threat and/or record them in correspondence with the client and to check before sending the communication that the principal on behalf of whom the advisor is acting is identified.

SECTION 71——Declaration or declarator as to non-infringement

71.00   *Add new paragraph 71.00:*

Contents

COMMENTARY ON SECTION 71

Requirements for seeking a declaration (subs.(1))

71.05   *After the eighth paragraph (beginning "In deciding a question of non-infringement"), add new paragraph:*
In *Actavis v Eli Lilly* [2016] EWHC 234 (Pat), the court granted declarations of non-infringement to the claimant in respect of the UK, French, Italian and Spanish designations of the patent. The court gave the defendant leave to apply, notwithstanding the declarations, in the event that a change of circumstances during the life of the patent led to an alternative, infringing preparation being made using the claimant's product (see also [2015] EWHC 3302 (Pat)).

Required description of the alleged non-infringement

71.06   *Add new paragraph at end:*
■ An application to the Comptroller for a declaration of non-infringement to be struck

out on the basis that the applicant had failed to comply with its obligations under s.71 failed in *The BVG Airflo Group Ltd v Dyson Technologies Ltd* BL O/077/17. The Comptroller concluded that the applicant for the declaration had filed sufficient information to demonstrate how its device would fall outside the claims and, therefore, that the application should proceed.

Revocation of patents [Sections 72-73]

SECTION 72—Power to revoke patents on application

Add new paragraph 72.00:   **72.00**

Contents

COMMENTARY ON SECTION 72

Scope of the section

Add new paragraph at end: **72.09**

The extent of discovery appropriate for validity proceedings was considered by Birss J in *Positec Power Tools (Europe) Ltd v Husqvarna AB* [2016] EWHC 1061 (Pat); [2016] W.L.R. (D) 244 (10 May 2016). After reviewing the cases, the importance of the overriding objective in limiting disclosure (including the established practice of limiting in time to a four-year window around the priority date), and the need to obviate sharp practice, Birss J held that *Nichia v Argos* [2007] EWCA Civ 741 was no longer binding authority in view of post-Jackson changes to CPR r.31.5(7). The application was refused. See further §62.71.

Forum for revocation

72.10   *Add new paragraph at end:*

Jurisdiction in the light of Brussels art.22(4) was further considered in *Anan Kasei Co, Ltd Rhodia Opérations SAS v Molycorp Chemicals & Oxides (Europe) Ltd* [2016] EWHC 1722 (Pat) (14 July 2016). Arnold J held that the court did not have jurisdiction to hear the infringement claim of German designation owing to art.24(4): *Coin Controls Ltd v Suzo International (UK) Ltd* [1999] Ch. 33, *Fort Dodge Animal Health Ltd v Akzo Nobel NV* [1998] F.S.R. 222, *Prudential Assurance Co Ltd v Prudential Insurance Co of America* [2003] EWCA Civ 327; [2003] 1 W.L.R. 2295; *GAT v LuK* discussed. The Court of Justice had implicitly endorsed Laddie J's reasoning in *Coin Controls v Suzo International* [1999] Ch. 33 at 43 (*Anan Kasei* at [23]). The Court did not have jurisdiction to order samples in aid of German proceedings, either. But if it had jurisdiction, it would have been expedient to grant the application for samples.

Grounds of revocation

—Insufficient description (subs.(1)(c))

72.14   *Add new paragraphs at end:*

"Biogen insufficiency" is also referred to as "excessive claim breadth", as noted at [340] in *Generics (UK) Ltd v Warner-Lambert Company LLC* [2015] EWHC 2548 (Pat). In that case, Arnold J applied the principles for assessment of sufficiency listed by Jacob LJ in *Eli Lilly & Co v Human Genome Sciences Inc* [2012] EWCA Civ 1185; [2013] R.P.C. 22 at [11], approving Kitchin J [2008] EWHC 1903 (Pat); [2008] R.P.C. 29 at [239]. These cases are discussed in detail at §14.29 of the Main Work. In *Generics v Warner-Lambert*, Arnold J held that although the specification referred to likely effectiveness of the patented product in treating inflammatory pain, there was nothing that made it plausible that the drug would be effective for neuropathic or other forms of pain. See Alasdair Poore, "Warner-Lambert update" [2015] 10 *CIPA* 24.

The requirement of plausibility of disclosure, as discussed in *Generics v Warner-Lambert*, applying *Human Genome Sciences Inc v Eli Lilly & Co* [2011] UKSC 51; [2012] R.P.C. 6, is a useful threshold test for sufficiency. A plausible disclosure may nonetheless be insufficient: *Accord Healthcare Ltd v Medac Gesellschaft Für Klinische Spezialpräparate mbH* [2016] EWHC 24 (Pat) (13 January 2016). The disclosure must make the claim credible, rather than speculative: *Actavis v Eli Lilly* [2015] EWHC 3294 (Pat) at [173]-[178]; [2016] EWHC 1955 (Pat) 10 August 2016 at [233]; to suppose that the invention will work across the breadth of the claim: *GlaxoSmithKline v Wyeth* [2016] EWHC 1045 (Pat).

For a view from Singapore, see Uma Baskaran and Ian Rodney Mirandah, "Obviously insufficient" [2015] 12 *CIPA* 30, commenting on *Lonza Biologics Tuas Pte Ltd v Genpharm International Inc* [2015] SGIPOS 13.

Regeneron v Genentech, Sandvik v Kennametal [2011] EWHC 3311; [2012] R.P.C. 23 at [106]-[124] and other cases cited in this paragraph were applied in *Regeneron Pharmaceuticals Inc v Kymab Ltd* [2016] EWHC 87 (Pat). Here, Henry Carr J held the patent invalid where the "whole subject-matter defined in the claim... was not capable of being performed at the priority date without undue burden and without invention" [257].

—Impermissible amendments (subs.(1)(d) and (e))

After the third paragraph (beginning "To avoid added matter there must be clear and ambitious initial disclosure"), add new paragraph: **72.15**

■ Synthon's appeal from Birss J's judgment was dismissed in *Synthon BV v Teva Pharmaceutical Industries Ltd* [2017] EWCA Civ 148 (Floyd LJ, Briggs and Kitchin LLJ concurring). The principles for assessing added matter were not in dispute—that "the matter in question must be disclosed directly and unambiguously, although this does not exclude an implicit disclosure". However, in the present case the judge had not erred in holding that a general teaching to minimise the levels of impurity was not equivalent to a disclosure specifically low levels.

Add new paragraphs at end:

■ In *Warner-Lambert Company LLC v Novartis (Singapore) Pte Ltd* [2016] SGHC 106, George Wei J considered an application for revocation on the grounds of added matter and extension of scope under the Singapore Patents Act (which is close the UK Act in this regard). He held that that amending the form of a claim from method-of-treatment to Swiss claim did not add matter. No technical information was added; the person skilled in the art would understand the reason and understand that manufacturing of the medicament was implicitly disclosed. However, adding a manufacturing step did enlarge scope. The decision is thought to be under appeal but contains useful discussion of UK and EPO case law.

In *Hospira UK Ltd v Cubist Pharmaceuticals LLC* [2016] EWHC 1285 (Pat) (daptomycin) at [189] and [309] Henry Carr J reviewed the principles for assessment of added matter, both in relation to claims in suit and proposals to amend, a once-daily dosage regimen of daptomycin minimising skeletal muscle toxicity as compared to shorter dosing intervals, and this being taught as a generally applicable feature and not one which was only of significance in a specific context. In relation to amendment of a second patent an added matter attack was rejected because the objection was based on form and not substance, and failed to have regard to the technical disclosure of the application when read as a whole [318]. The *Hospira* decision demonstrates how amendments proposed to restore validity may be assessed not only for added matter, but also for clarity, a dependent claim in the first patent not enabling a skilled reader to know where the claimed range started.

Statement of case

Add new paragraph at end: **72.23**

American Science & Engineering Inc v Rapiscan Systems Inc BL O/119/16 concerned an application for revocation on the ground of lack of inventive step, citing several documents. Following the initial statement of grounds, no further evidence was filed and no witnesses were called by either party. The claimant filed skeleton arguments shortly before the hearing in which an argument relating to the invention being a collocation of two of the documents appeared for the first time. It was held this was in effect a late request by the claimants to amend their statement of case via their skeleton arguments and that the factors needing to be considered were the substance and the timeliness of the amendment, the diligence of the claimant, the extent to which the amendment might disadvantage or prejudice the defendant, and the more general question of public interest. The collocation argument did not fall into a special category that remained open up to and throughout trial as in *Glass v Freyssinet Ltd* [2015] EWHC 2972. It could not be decided without giving the defendants the opportunity to file submissions and appropriate evidence, and accordingly it should be set aside.

Amendment of patent during revocation proceedings

72.26   *Add new paragraph at end:*
For comment on amendment practice in *Monkey Tower Ltd v Ability International Ltd* [2014] EWHC 18 (Pat); [2014] Bus. L.R. 291, see §75.06.

SECTION 73—Comptroller's power to revoke patents on his own initiative

73.00   *Add new paragraph 73.00:*

Contents

COMMENTARY ON SECTION 73

Revocation for double patenting in corresponding European patent (UK) (subss.(2)–(4))

73.06   *Add new paragraph at end:*
In *Xtera Communication's Patent* BL O/507/15, a UK patent claimed feature A, while a corresponding EP(UK) patent claimed a combination of features A+B. The proprietor argued that B was added to address an inventive step objection, resulting in a different invention being claimed. Feature B, however, was found to add nothing of inventive merit and the patents therefore related to the same invention, resulting in revocation of the UK patent.

PRACTICE UNDER SECTION 73

73.08   *Replace the third paragraph with:*
The new provisions of subss.(1A) and (1B) provide for a limited extension of the Comptroller's existing powers to initiate revocation under ss.73(1) and 73(2). Currently around 50-60 patents a year are revoked using the powers under subss.(1) and (2). As of August 2016, 13 opinions have issued finding a lack of novelty or inventive step out of a total of 42 requests since commencement of the new provisions, 25 of which related to validity. Of these, only two (opinions 04/15 and 14/15) have resulted in revocation, and in each case the proprietor did not contest the examiner's finding. Three other opinions resulted in the Office deciding either not to initiate or not to proceed with revocation proceedings based on the patent as granted, one of which (opinion 10/15) was the subject of a review under s.74B that upheld the examiner's finding of invalidity. The reasons behind the Office's decisions are unclear, as no reasons are provided in the final decision. Based on the limited sample to date, however, these reasons could include: relevant prior art documents not being available in English (opinion 23/14); a strong defence by the patentee being made following initiation of revocation proceedings (opinion 05/15); and the issues surrounding the examiner's finding of invalidity being complex and

multi-faceted (opinion 10/15, which found a claim for a dosage regime to lack inventive step). Two other opinions (15/05 and 07/15) resulted in the proprietor submitting amendments that the Office decided were sufficient to remove the need to revoke the patent. Such amendments may be made under s.27 or, in the case of an EP(UK) patent, via central limitation under art.105a EPC.

Putting validity in issue [Section 74]

SECTION 74—Proceedings in which validity of patent may be put in issue

Add new paragraph 74.00: **74.00**

Contents

■ **74.**—(1) Subject to the following provisions of this section, the validity of a   **74.01**
patent may be put in issue—

(a) by way of defence, in proceedings for infringement of the patent under section 61 above or proceedings under section 69 above for infringement of rights conferred by the publication of an application;

(b) in proceedings **in respect of an actionable threat under section 70A** above;

(c) in proceedings in which a declaration in relation to the patent is sought under section 71 above;

(d) in proceedings before the court or the comptroller under section 72 above for the revocation of the patent;

(e) in proceedings under section 58 above.

Add at end:

■ 3. Subsection (1)(b) was amended by s.1(5) of the Intellectual Property (Unjustified Threats) Act 2017, with effect from 1 October 2017.

COMMENTARY ON SECTION 74

Proceedings in which validity may be put in issue (subss.(1)–(3) and (8))

After the second paragraph, add new paragraphs: **74.03**
■ The problem in *Arrow Generics* recurred in *Fujifilm Kyowa Biologics Co Ltd v Abbvie Biotechnology Ltd (Rev 1)* [2016] EWHC 425 (Pat) where claimants had invested many millions of pounds in obtaining regulatory approval for a product which was a biosimilar to the defendant's product which was covered by patents and pending divisional patent applications. In order to clear the way for product launch, they sought a declaration that their products were anticipated or obvious at the relevant priority dates, thereby avoiding their investment being put at risk by a period of uncertainty during the pendency of the divisional applications and until an EPO opposition was finally determined. The

defendants argued that *Arrow* was wrongly decided, that s.74 should not be interpreted to permit a patent merely to be declared invalid without being revoked, and that the requested declaration referred to features of the relevant patents and was merely a disguised declaration of invalidity. The court held [39], distinguishing *Organon Teknika Ltd v F. Hoffmann-La Roche AG* [1996] F.S.R. 383, that s.74 does not prohibit a declaration relating to a published application, that the relief sought did not amount to pre-grant opposition proceedings because the defendant would not be prevented by res judicata or issue estoppel from asserting any granted patent against other companies who were neither party nor privy to these proceedings, and that the underlying problem which *Arrow* confronted a very real issue. The proceedings should not be struck out because there was a realistic prospect that the trial judge would exercise his discretion to grant the declaration, which was limited to obviousness/anticipation in respect of particular characteristics of products which were clearly defined and was limited to the UK. The defendant's argument that it should not have to face the costs and burden of a UK trial in respect of the issues raised by the declaration were outweighed by the potential injustice to the claimant if it could not clear the way prior to the launch of its product. A similar conclusion was subsequently reached in *Fujifilm Kyowa Biologics Co Ltd v Abbvie Biotechnology Ltd* [2016] EWHC 2204 (Pat). Appeals were dismissed: *Fujifilm Kyowa Kirin Biologics Co Ltd v Abbvie Biotechnology Ltd* [2017] EWCA Civ 1; [2017] C.P. Rep. 16 (Floyd LJ, Longmore and Kitchin LJJ concurring). *Arrow* had been correctly decided. It was common ground that s.74 only applied to granted patents, not applications [18]. The Court of Appeal considered the general rules on grant of declarations and, at [60] cited *FSA v Rourke* [2002] C.P. Rep. 14 with approval:

> "... when considering whether to grant a declaration or not, the court should take into account justice to the claimant, justice to the defendant, whether the declaration would serve a useful purpose whether there are any other special reasons why or why not the court should grant the declaration."

■ A claim of right was no longer required, though its absence might show that a declaration was unlikely to be "useful" [61]. Nor was the existence of the statutory declaration under s.71 fatal—"it is not enough simply to point to an available statutory remedy, if the declaration sought serves a legitimate and useful purpose beyond that which could be achieved by that remedy" [63]. Under s.74, validity could only be put in issues in proceedings where the court or tribunal had power to revoke, thus serving the public interest in revocation of invalid patents [75]. It did not apply where there was no granted patent, i.e. to patent applications or to revoked patents [76]-[77]. Section 74(2) did not prohibit a claim to a declaration in conjunction with another remedy, e.g. revocation. Insofar as an *Arrow* declaration made it clear that "a future patent claim to that regimen would be invalid", it was not contrary to the scheme of the EPC or the 1977 Act [84]-[94]. Nor would it open floodgates [95] or undermine recast Brussels I—Regulation 1215/2012 (on civil jurisdiction and judgments) [96]-[97]. A parallel claim for a non-suit injunction would not be struck out. Note: Hugh Dunlop discusses the *Arrow* injunction, the *Fujifilm* appeal and relevance to the UPC at [2017] 4 *CIPA* 22; see also case note at p.43 of the same issue.

■ In subsequent proceedings *Fujifilm Kyowa Kirin Biologics Co Ltd v Abbvie Biotechnology Ltd* [2017] EWHC 395 (Pat), a declaration was sought that disposal of a biosimilar monoclonal antibody to the antibody adalimumab (Humira) in specific dosage regimes for arthritis treatment would have been anticipated and/or obvious at the date at which a relevant European patent was entitled to claim priority. However, the defendants had already disapproved the text of their patent, thereby revoking it centrally, and it was argued that this action together with certain offered undertakings gave at least as much protection to the claimants as the relief sought in their requested declarations. It was held that on the unusual facts of this case, there were special reasons which supported the grant of declarations. These included AbbVie's conduct of threatening infringement whilst abandoning proceedings at the last moment in order to shield their patent portfolio from scrutiny, the amount of money at stake for the claimants in terms of investment in clinical trials and potential damages if the claimants launched at risk and the need for commercial certainty, having regard to AbbVie's threats to sue for infringement throughout the world. Useful purposes would be served: necessary clarity for third parties, making grant of injunctive relief in other jurisdictions less likely which would be of direct benefit to the UK market, and the reasonable foreseeability that grant of the declarations would promote a settlement on a European or even a worldwide basis, in that it changed the parties' negotiating positions.

In *Stretchline Intellectual Properties Ltd v H&M Hennes & Mauritz* [2015] EWCA Civ 516, a settlement agreement precluded an attack on validity. The claimant succeeded in its claim for breach of contract. In a later hearing its applications for an injunction to prohibit further breaches of the settlement agreement, and *Island Records* disclosure to support election between damages and an account of profits, were refused: [2016] EWHC 162 (Pat).

Stay of proceedings pending determination of opposition at the EPO

Add new paragraphs at end: **74.07**

In *Eli Lilly v Janssen Sciences* [2016] EWHC 313 (Pat) Lilly sought a declaration of non-infringement of patents blocking the launch of its anti-Alzheimer's drug solanezumab. The court considered the guidelines on whether to stay proceedings as set out in *IPCom GmbH & Co KG v HTC Europe Co Ltd* [2013] EWCA Civ 1496 ("IPCom"), namely:

1. The discretion, which is very wide indeed, should be exercised to achieve the balance of justice between the parties having regard to all the relevant circumstances of the particular case.
2. The discretion is of the Patents Court, not of the Court of Appeal. The Court of Appeal would not be justified in interfering with a first instance decision that accords with legal principle and has been reached by taking into account all the relevant, and only the relevant, circumstances.
3. Although neither the EPC nor the 1977 Act contains express provisions relating to automatic or discretionary stay of proceedings in national courts, they provide the context and condition the exercise of the discretion.
4. It should thus be remembered that the possibility of concurrent proceedings contesting the validity of a patent granted by the EPO is inherent in the system established by the EPC. It should also be remembered that national courts exercise exclusive jurisdiction on infringement issues.
5. If there are no other factors, a stay of the national proceedings is the default option. There is no purpose in pursuing two sets of proceedings simply because the Convention allows for it.
6. It is for the party resisting the grant of the stay to show why it should not be granted. Ultimately it is a question of where the balance of justice lies.
7. One important factor affecting the exercise of the discretion is the extent to which refusal of a stay will irrevocably deprive a party of any part of the benefit which the concurrent jurisdiction of the EPO and the national court is intended to confer. Thus, if allowing the national court to proceed might allow the patentee to obtain monetary compensation which is not repayable if the patent is subsequently revoked, this would be a weighty factor in favour of the grant of a stay. It may, however, be possible to mitigate the effect of this factor by the offer of suitable undertakings to repay.
8. The Patents Court judge is entitled to refuse a stay of the national proceedings where the evidence is that some commercial certainty would be achieved at a considerably earlier date in the case of the UK proceedings than in the EPO. It is true that it will not be possible to attain certainty everywhere until the EPO proceedings are finally resolved, but some certainty, sooner rather than later, and somewhere, such as in the UK, rather than nowhere, is, in general, preferable to continuing uncertainty everywhere.

9. It is permissible to take account of the fact that resolution of the national proceedings, whilst not finally resolving everything, may, by deciding some important issues, promote settlement.

10. An important factor affecting the discretion will be the length of time that it will take for the respective proceedings in the national court and in the EPO to reach a conclusion. This is not an independent factor, but needs to be considered in conjunction with the prejudice which any party will suffer from the delay, and lack of certainty, and what the national proceedings can achieve in terms of certainty.

11. The public interest in dispelling the uncertainty surrounding the validity of monopoly rights conferred by the grant of a patent is also a factor to be considered.

12. In weighing the balance it is material to take into account the risk of wasted costs, but this factor will normally be outweighed by commercial factors concerned with early resolution.

13. The hearing of an application for a stay is not to become a mini-trial of the various factors affecting its grant or refusal. The parties' assertions need to be examined critically, but at a relatively high level of generality.

The undertakings offered by the patentee were similar to those in *Actavis Group PTC EHF v Pharmacia LLC* [2014] EWHC 2265 (Pat) and were (a) to support any application to the EPO Technical Board of Appeal to accelerate appeals proceedings, (b) not to seek a preliminary or final injunction against the claimant for the duration of the patent and (c) not to seek damages other than on a reasonable royalty basis if validity were upheld. In the outcome, balancing all the points considered relevant in the light of *IPCom*, the grant of a stay was refused and the English proceedings were allowed to go ahead. It might be that the EPO proceedings would produce a clear determination in Eli Lilly's favour rendering the English proceedings redundant and some costs in pursuing the English proceedings would be wasted between now and then. However, there was also a chance that even if the EPO proceedings were resolved before the English proceedings, they will not be determinative of all the issues between the parties. The infringement issues were important in this case and it was better that the English proceedings which were before the only forum in which the infringement issue could be decided should continue. Neither party was attracted by the idea of the English proceedings splitting out infringement from invalidity in some way.

An argument that *IPCom* had superseded the courts' jurisdiction exercised in *Arrow v Merck* [2007] EWHC 1900 (Pat); [2007] F.S.R. 39 and sought in *Fujifilm Kyowa Biologics Co Ltd v Abbvie Biotechnology Ltd (Rev 1)* [2016] EWHC 425 (Pat), was rejected in the latter case, at [52]-[55].

Opinions by Patent Office [Sections 74A–74B]

SECTION 74A —Opinions [as to validity or infringement] on matters prescribed in the rules

74A.00 *Add new paragraph 74A.00:*

74A.01   Statute
74A.02   Rule 92—Interpretation
74A.03   Rule 93—Request for an opinion under section 74A
74A.04   Rule 94—Refusal or withdrawal of request
74A.05   Rule 95—Notification and advertisement of request
74A.06   Rule 96—Submission of observations and observations in reply
74A.07   Rule 97—Issue of the opinion
74A.08   Submitting opinion observations by electronic means

RELEVANT RULES—RULES 92-97

Add new Note: **74A.05**

Note. Rule 95(1)(b) is prospectively amended by para.2(3) of the Patents (Amendment) Rules 2016 (SI 2016/517) to come into force on the date of entry into force of the Agreement on a Unified Patent Court.

COMMENTARY ON SECTION 74A

Scope of the section

Add new paragraph at end: **74A.09**

In *Intermune, Inc v Elkington and Fife LLP* BL O/163/16 the proprietor argued that the examiner should have refused the request for an opinion because it revisited issues already

105

determined by the EPO. However, the Hearing Officer found that, while the EPO did consider the question of inventive step, this did not bar an opinion being determined on the basis of new documents, nor did it prevent an opinion being determined on new questions relating to the same documents. The opinion examiner had found that the request for an opinion was allowable and the Hearing Officer agreed with this.

—Possible revocation of patent under s.73(1A)

74A.10   *Replace the final three paragraphs with:*

At the time of writing [September 2016] several patents have now been revoked under s.73(1A): see for example the patents in opinions 04/15, 05/15, 14/15 and 02/16. See also §73.08. Following opinion 07/15 (which related to a European patent in the UK) the Comptroller was minded to revoke the patent. However, this outcome was avoided after amendment of the claims under the central limitation procedure at the EPO.

In opinion 12/15, the requester asked the Comptroller to take action under s.73(1A) in the event the Examiner decided that the patent was invalid. There appears to be no mechanism in the Act for the UK-IPO to respond to such a request by a requester: either the Comptroller will decide to take action or not. If a requester wishes a patent to be revoked following an opinion of invalidity, the requester should make an application under s.72.

—Effect of s.74A on a European patent with unitary effect ("Unitary Patent")

74A.11   *Add new paragraph at the beginning:*

■ An Order (SI 2016/388) has now been made to implement the Agreement on a Unified Patent Court ("UPC Agreement") and the EU Regulations establishing the Unitary Patent. However, the Order will only come into force on the date of entry into force of the UPC Agreement. Schedule A3 of the Order sets out the provisions of the Patents Act that apply to Unitary Patents, and includes ss.74A and 74B, see §83A.01.

—Refusal of Request

74A.21   *Add new paragraph at end:*

■ In opinion 29/16, the requester asked for an opinion on infringement in view of two software products. The requester admitted that the products were missing certain features of claim 1 of the patent, but asked the Examiner to assume that those missing features were present for the purposes of the opinion. The observer alleged that the request should be refused as not sufficiently well-defined for a sensible opinion to be reached. The Examiner confirmed that, although this was an unusual starting point for an opinion on infringement, it is permissible to ask for an opinion as to whether a hypothetical product would infringe a patent, and proceeded to issue an opinion.

General provisions as to amendment of patents and applications [Sections 75-76A]

SECTION 75—Amendment of patent in infringement or revocation proceedings

75.00   *Add new paragraph 75.00:*

Contents

COMMENTARY ON SECTION 75

Discretion

To the end of the eighth paragraph (beginning "Delay in seeking amendment in court   **75.06**
proceedings can arise"), add:

The refusal to permit post-trial amendment was affirmed, notwithstanding that the proposed amendment was merely to excise from the claim that part which the court had been held to be invalid, see *Warner-Lambert Company LLC v Generics (UK) Ltd (t/a Mylan)* [2016] EWCA Civ 1006. The court of appeal held that when the patentee appreciated, or should have appreciated, that it had an amendment to make it should have drawn the matter to the attention of the court promptly so as not to appropriate to itself the case management implications of it making an amendment. It was wrong to postpone the decision as to whether it should make an amendment until after trial, when it had lost, and it was not fair to the defendants to treat a trial in which only the construction issue was in play as equivalent to one in which an amendment was in play as well. There was no reason to interfere with the decision of the trial court as to abuse of process.

Add new paragraph at end:

■ In *IPCom v HTC Europe* [2015] EWHC 1034 (Pat) Birss J held that it would not be proper exercise of the discretion under s.75 to refuse a valid claim amendment simply because it produced a claim with different scope from the one allowed by the EPO, even if, as here, the ostensible motive for the application to amend was to produce a claim with the same scope. All the more so when the difference (if it existed) arises in the context of a debate about translations. Allowance of the amendment was affirmed on appeal, [2017] EWCA Civ 90, the court observing that IPCom's intention to obtain a claim equivalent in scope to the German claim was simply irrelevant to the discretion to allow the amendment.

PRACTICE UNDER SECTION 75

Applications to the Comptroller

Add new paragraph at end: **75.13**

In certain, fairly exceptional, circumstances amendments need not be published under r.75(2). See §§123.08 and 123.66.

SECTION 76 [SUBSTITUTED]—Amendments of applications and patents not to include added matter

76.00   *Add new paragraph 76.00:*

Contents

COMMENTARY ON SECTION 76

The general test–explicit disclosure, implicit disclosure and obviousness

—Restriction to an intermediate generalisation

76.14   *After the eleventh paragraph (beginning "In Monsanto v Merck [2000] R.P.C. 709"), add new paragraph:*

■ A claim that had been amended in proceedings before the EPO Appeal Board was considered in *IPCom v HTC Europe* [2017] EWCA Civ 90 in a case where further amendments were before the UK court. The broad proposition that where a claim is based on a single embodiment it is not permissible to take certain features and not others was rejected, citing *Nokia v IPCom (No.3)* [2012] EWCA Civ 567; [2013] R.P.C. 5 at [57]–[60]. The court held that a reader of the amended claim would understand that it referred to the relevant embodiment as literally described, and minor variants. The reader was not taught any specific variant, but neither did the combination disclosed by that embodiment, so that the combination disclosed by the claim was no different from that disclosed by the embodiment itself.

Add new paragraphs at end:

The invention in T 1840/11 *HUANG/Perforated plastically deformable sheet* concerned a sheet which exhibited surface dryness and improved drainage velocity, and was formed with recesses in its upper and lower surfaces, each recess spanning a number of capillaries. The preferred but only disclosed embodiment had hexagonal recesses of two different sizes with larger recesses surrounded by a plurality of smaller ones, each larger recess spanning seven capillaries and each smaller recess spanning three capillaries. The patentee's main request in opposition proceedings introduced a requirement for the recesses to be of different sizes and to span different numbers of capillaries but did not specify recess shape or number of capillaries spanned. The description did not suggest that any of the particular characteristics of the described and illustrated structure could in some way be separated from the combination of features in that example. The skilled reader was therefore left with no indication of what particular aspect of the structure might in some sense be "preferred". The patentees argued that the omission of part of the features of the exemplary embodiment would not result in an unallowable intermediate generalisation, citing T 962/98 *ECOLAB/Antimicrobial additives* and T 879/09 *AFCO/Robotized device*. However, T 962/98 permitted an intermediate generalisation only if the skilled reader could recognise from the application as filed that some characteristics from a working example were not closely related to the other characteristics of that example and applied directly and unambiguously to the more general context. T 962/98 added nothing relevant. The essentiality test in T 331/87 *HOUDAILLE/Removal of feature* was not directly applicable since it related to removal of a feature from a claim, but if applicable would have made no difference. All the structural features were interrelated, none of these features could be considered as being dispensable in view of their drainage and surface dryness function, and the illustrated structure did not lend itself to easy alteration. Accordingly, the main request was open to objection under art.123(2) EPC.

■ It is accepted EPO practice that the disclosure of a quantitative range of values (e.g. for concentrations or temperatures) together with an included preferred narrower range also directly discloses the two possible part-ranges lying within the overall range on either side of the narrower range. Hence a simple combination of the preferred narrower range and one of these part-ranges is also unequivocally derivable and is supported by the disclosure, see T 2/81 *MOBAY/Methylenebis (phenyl isocyanate)* OJ EPO 1982, 394. However, the EPO approach to such amendments on occasions exhibits a degree of rigidity that arguably owes more to philology than to technical understanding. In T 1990/10 *BAVARIAN NORDIC/Virus propagation* a number of temperature ranges had been disclosed including "below 37°C" and the closed range "30°C to 35°C". An amendment to specify an open-ended temperature range "below 35°C" was refused on the ground that this merely amounts to the direct transfer of the term "below", which defines the openness of a disclosed broad range ("below 37°C"), to the upper end value of another temperature range disclosed in the application as filed ("30°C to 35°C"). In the absence of any indication in the application as filed to do so, this transfer of the term "below" to another temperature value or temperature range had no basis in the application as filed. It is noteworthy that the discussion in the Board's decision centres entirely on the language of the specification without reference to the significance of these temperatures for virus propagation and in particular for the resulting yields of virus particles.

—Disclaimers and added features making no technical contribution

Add new paragraphs at end: **76.15**

The controversy within the EPO concerning undisclosed disclaimers continues, see T 437/14 *THE TRUSTEES OF PRINCETON UNIVERSITY AND THE UNIVERSITY OF SOUTHERN CALIFORNIA/Complexes of form L2IrX*. The Board noted that in G 1/03 and G 2/03 the Enlarged Board of Appeal considered undisclosed disclaimers to be allowable under art.123(2) EPC. In G 2/10 the test for disclosed disclaimers according to the so-called "gold standard" was held to be whether the skilled person would, using common general knowledge, regard the remaining claimed subject-matter as explicitly or implicitly, but directly and unambiguously, disclosed in the application as filed. Although the question referred to the Enlarged Board in G 2/10 concerned "disclosed disclaimers" only, there were numerous passages in that decision which suggested that the so-called gold standard applied to any amendment (including undisclosed disclaimers) when assessing its compliance with art.123(2) EPC. Taking the Enlarged Board's remarks in G 2/10 to their logical conclusion, this would mean that there was only one test to be applied for assessing any amendment, including an undisclosed disclaimer, for its compliance with art.123(2) EPC, namely the gold standard. The most far-reaching argument brought forward in G 2/10 in favour of an undisclosed disclaimer was that it was a mere voluntary restriction by which the applicant abandoned part of the claimed subject-matter and that, therefore, an undisclosed disclaimer per se was not a technical feature of the claim, and thus could never infringe art.123(2) EPC. The Enlarged Board replied that any amendment to a claim is presumed to have a technical meaning, otherwise it would be useless to have it in the claim. The referring Board's view was that a disclaimer excluding undisclosed subject-matter almost by definition contravenes art.123(2) EPC, observing:

"If a whole is reduced by an undisclosed first part, the present board fails to see how the remaining second part could ever be regarded as explicitly or implicitly, but directly and unambiguously, disclosed in the application as filed. This can be illustrated by the following simple example: if one takes a bite out of an apple, what remains is recognisably no longer the same apple as the original one. Even though it is still an apple, the apple with the bite taken out of it cannot be regarded as explicitly or implicitly, but directly and unambiguously, "disclosed" in the original apple.

■ However, having regard to several allegedly conflicting decisions, the following questions were referred to the Enlarged Board, the case now proceeding under the reference G 1/16 *OLED/Disclaimer*, no decision having been handed down at the time of writing:

1. Is the standard referred to in G 2/10 for the allowability of disclosed disclaimers under art.123(2) EPC, i.e. whether the skilled person would, using common general knowledge, regard the subject-matter remaining in the claim after the introduction of the disclaimer as explicitly or implicitly, but directly and unambiguously, disclosed in the application as filed, also to be applied to claims containing undisclosed disclaimers?

2. If the answer to the first question is yes, is G 1/03 set aside as regards the exceptions relating to undisclosed disclaimers defined in its answer 2.1?

3. If the answer to the second question is no, i.e. if the exceptions relating to undisclosed disclaimers defined in answer 2.1 of G 1/03 apply in addition to the gold standard, may this standard be modified in view of these exceptions?

■ Comments of CIPA *amicus curiae* appear at [2017] 4 *CIPA* 14-18. In summary, the submission of CIPA, emphasizing the need to avoid an over-literal formalistic approach, is that:

In CIPA's view the approach adopted in G1/03 in relation to undisclosed disclaimers is the correct one. Thus, G1/03 has interpreted art.123(2) EPC in relation to the technical teaching of the claim including an undisclosed disclaimer. As noted above, the Enlarged Board in that case set out limited circumstances in which a disclaimer can be made for a legal, or non-technical reason and has provided clear guidance as to the circumstances in which a disclaimer has no bearing on the technical information in the application or does not contribute to the invention and thus is in compliance with art.123(2) EPC.

There is thus no need to apply the test of G2/10 to such disclaimers, as they are already regarded as complying with the requirement that the skilled person is not presented with any new technical information.

In relation to undisclosed disclaimers that do not meet the criteria of G1/03 the allowability of the amendment should be assessed according to the "gold standard" of G3/89, i.e. by determining whether the skilled person is provided with any new technical information. An assessment based only on the literal wording of the claim, as appears to be suggested in the referring decision, goes beyond the "gold standard" and is not the correct approach.

SECTION 76A [ADDED]—Biotechnological inventions

Add new paragraph 76A.00: **76A.00**

Contents

COMMENTARY ON SECTION 76A

The European Biotechnology Directive 98/44/EC

Add new paragraphs at end: **76A.03**

■ Following the decisions in G2/12 *Tomato II* and G2/13 *Broccoli II* holding that products derived from or using essentially biological processes might be patentable, even if the process used to obtain such a product (i.e. selecting and crossing the plants) was essentially biological and thus not patentable, it was appreciated that the patentability of such products might conflict with the legal protection provided to plant varieties under EU plant variety legislation as regards access to genetic resources. It was noted that Directive 98/44/EC does not state whether plants or plant material (fruits, seeds, etc.), or animals/animal material obtained through essentially biological processes, can be patented, the Enlarged Board deciding that they were eligible on the basis that exclusions from the general principle of patentability have to be narrowly interpreted. In December 2015, the European Parliament adopted a Resolution which asked the Commission to consider the patentability of products derived from essentially biological processes, and in consequence it published Notice C/2016/6997 concluding that the EU legislator's intention when adopting Directive 98/44/EC was to exclude from patentability products (plants/animals and plant/animal parts) that are obtained by means of essentially biological processes. In consequence, with effect from 1 July 2017, r.27 EPC *Patentable biotechnological inventions* has been amended at paragraph (b) by addition of a proviso that its provisions are without prejudice to a new paragraph added to r.28 EPC *Exceptions to patentability* which is prima facie in conflict with *Broccoli/Tomatoes II* and reads as follows:

(2) Under Article 53(b), European patents shall not be granted in respect of plants or animals exclusively obtained by means of an essentially biological process.

■ It may be noted that new r.28(2) does not change the position for claims in process format, on which the main authority remains *Broccoli/Tomatoes I*.

■ The need to introduce amendments of this kind was questioned by CIPA in its position paper of 6 July 2016, submitting that decisions G 2/12 and G 2/13 and the existing EU plant breeder's exemption and other rights represented a reasonable balance, and that any changes to the EPC might deter plant innovators from developing commercially or ethically valuable new plants or plant material. The legality of the changes has been questioned by CIPA, see Mike Snodin et al., "Are changes to rules 27 and 28 EPC illegal?" [2017] 7-8 *CIPA* 11-14. In summary, the paper refers to the EP preliminary reference procedure where interpretation of a provision of EU law is relevant to national proceedings and its interpretation is neither *acte éclairé* nor *acte clair*, see *Cilfit* (C-283/81). A decision that the products of essentially biological processes for the production of plants are not excluded from patentability had been handed down by the Court of Appeal of The Hague on 28 May 2013 in *Cresco v Taste of Nature*, Docket No.416501 / KG ZA 12-452. The Commission Notice represented an ongoing and as yet unresolved dispute as to the meaning of art.4(1)(b) of the Biotech Directive, which was neither the subject of a CJEU ruling nor *acte clair* and needs to be referred to CJEU under TFEU art.265 in accordance with CJEU opinions 1/09 and 2/13, see also in relation to the EPO as a non-EP body CJEU Judge Allan Rosas (in his article "The National Judge as EU Judge: opinion 1/09" in the book *Constitutionalising the EU Judicial System*):

"The added value of opinion 1/09 lies undoubtedly in its emphasis of the essential role played by national courts as integral parts of the Union judicial system. Just as the tasks of Union Courts cannot be transferred to non-EU bodies, the national courts of EU Member States have a constitutional mandate which cannot, in principle, be outsourced. Both Union Courts and national courts fulfil a 'duty entrusted to them both' of ensuring that in the interpretation and application of the Treaties law is observed."

■ It will be noted that it remains possible to obtain patent protection for transgenic plants or animals, plants or animals obtained by mutagenesis, and/or biotechnological methods of producing them, providing other patentability criteria are fulfilled, and also plant or animal derived products that are not propagation material, and in vitro plant or animal cell populations which are treated as microorganisms, but not plants produced by classical breeding techniques, see e.g. T 2365/13 *PROGENITOR LABS/Human pluripotent stem cells* where a claim was directed to the use of a progenitor cell in a drug screening assay to identify a regenerative drug. Readers should bear in mind that granted claims to plants or animals produced by classical breeding techniques may remain in other jurisdictions so that specifications filed in the UK should continue to include relevant disclosures where appropriate.

■ It is understood that examination of European applications potentially affected by the rule change resumed with effect from 3 July 2017.

—Divergent treatment in the US of exclusions from patentability

76A.03A   *Add new paragraph 76A.03A:*
Recent decisions both of the US Supreme Court and of the Court of Appeals for the

Federal Circuit suggest a divergence from the law as to eligibility as it is understood in the UK and Europe. In view of the importance of the US in the pharmaceutical, medical and biotechnological fields, UK and European practitioners need to be aware of these continuing and highly significant developments, and their implications for the drafting of patent specifications for inventions of UK and European origin.

Patent-eligibility under 35 USC 101 for the isolated BRCA1 gene defined in somewhat functional terms was denied by the Supreme Court in *Association for Molecular Pathology v Myriad Genetics, Inc* 133 S. Ct. 2107 (2013). In direct contrast, in a decision involving the European counterpart of the same patent the EPO Appeal Board upheld eligibility of nucleic acid probes comprised partial DNA sequences of the human BRCA1 gene which were held to be isolated elements of the human body as defined in r.29(2) EPC (formerly r.23e(2)) and thus patentable subject-matter, see T 1213/05 *UNIVERSITY OF UTAH/Breast and ovarian cancer*.

More recently in relation to an invention of UK origin, the Federal Circuit denied patent eligibility for a claim to a method for detecting a paternally inherited nucleic acid of fetal origin performed on a maternal serum or plasma sample from a pregnant female, which method comprised amplifying a paternally inherited nucleic acid from the serum or plasma sample and detecting the presence of a paternally inherited nucleic acid of fetal origin in the sample, see *Ariosa Diagnostics, Inc v Sequenom, Inc* 788 F.3d 1371 (Fed. Cir. 2015). In that case, a petition for *en banc* rehearing was denied 809 F.3d 1282 (Fed. Cir. 2015) as also was a petition for certiorari to the Supreme Court. In direct contrast, validity of a claim to essentially the same subject-matter was upheld by the EPO Appeal Board in T 146/07 *ISIS/Prenatal diagnosis* in the face of an objection as to lack of inventive step, and eligibility was challenged neither during examination nor during subsequent opposition proceedings.

The *Myriad* decision has been followed by Federal Circuit decisions divergent from expectation in the UK and Europe and using a two-step framework of analysis set out by the Supreme Court in *Mayo Collaborative Services v Prometheus Laboratories, Inc* 132 S. Ct. 1289 (2012) which in the view of many commentators is being applied with undue breadth.

A claim to a pair of single-stranded DNA primers for determination of a nucleotide sequence of a BRCA1 gene by a polymerase chain reaction was held ineligible in *In re BRCA1- & BRCA2-Based Hereditary Cancer Test* 774 F.3d 755 (Fed. Cir. 2014) on the grounds that the primers were held not to be distinguishable from the isolated DNA found patent ineligible in *Myriad* and are not similar to the cDNA found to be a patent-eligible composition of matter, compare T 1213/05 *UNIVERSITY OF UTAH/Breast and ovarian cancer* and T 666/05 *UNIVERSITY OF UTAH/Mutation*. The point that the claim was not to a single substance but to a pair of substances also clearly falling within the composition of matter category of 35 USC 101 as defined inter alia in *Diamond v Chakrabarty* 447 US 303 (1980) appears to have escaped the court.

A decision similar to that in *Ariosa* was reached recently in *Genetic Technologies v Merial* (Fed Cir. 2016) which resembled the fact pattern in that case insofar as the subject-matter held ineligible related to a method for detection of a coding region allele of a multi-allelic genetic locus by amplifying genomic DNA with a primer pair that spanned a non-coding region sequence to produce an amplified DNA sequence characteristic of said allele, and analysing the amplified DNA sequence to detect the allele. It was held that the product of the claimed method was information about a patient's natural genetic makeup and was directed to a law of nature, and was not saved when considered as an ordered combination because the recited steps were "well-understood, routine, conventional activity previously engaged in by researchers in the field" and insufficient to convert the natural law to a patent-eligible invention. It was observed that "to detect the allele" merely asked the user to compare the non-coding sequence he had amplified and analysed with a library of non-coding sequences known to be in linkage disequilibrium with certain coding region alleles. The instruction to undertake a simple comparison step did not represent an

PART I, SECTION 76A

unconventional, inventive application sufficient to make the claim patent-eligible. It may be noted that the corresponding European application was granted as EP-B-0414469 with a main claim like that in issue before the Federal Circuit. No eligibility issue was raised during examination and no opposition was filed. Corresponding applications were also granted inter alia in Australia, Canada and Japan.

What can be inferred from the decision of the Supreme Court not to grant certiorari in *Ariosa* in the face of a petition supported by some 22 *amici* including the Federal Circuit Bar Association, the New York and Boston Intellectual Property Law Associations, The Intellectual Property Owners' Association, the Biotechnology Innovation Organization, the BioIndustry Association, CIPA, the Institute of Professional Representatives before the EPO and corporations including Eli Lilly, Microsoft and Novartis? It is illogical to assume that the Justices of the Supreme Court treated a petition supported by such a multitude of amici dismissively and rejected the petition merely on the basis of workload. The more logical assumption is that they concluded that the correct principles of law had already been stated in their earlier decisions and did not need restatement, so that if error had arisen in the lower courts, that problem would be best resolved at that level.

The Australian *Myriad* decision discussed in the Main Work at §1.04 has been distinguished by the hearings section of IP Australia in *Arrowhead Research Corporation* [2016] APO 70 (13 October 2016). The claims at issue recited compositions comprising double-stranded interfering RNA molecules with specific, defined sequences that were complementary to a target mRNA sequence. By targeting naturally occurring mRNA sequences, the interfering RNA molecules effectively silenced gene expression, thereby treating certain diseases associated with that gene. It was held that consideration of "manner of manufacture" within s.18(1)(a) of the Australian Act should look beyond the form of words used in the claim to determine the substance of the claimed invention in the context of the specification as a whole. The applicants submitted that the substance of their invention was not genetic information but rather economically significant products and compositions with the capacity to attenuate the expression of the Syk gene. However, it was held that analysis of the subject-matter of the invention did not depend simply on the form of words used in the claim but on determination of its substance, consideration being given to the description and how the invention worked. The inventive contribution provided by the claimed invention resided in the identification of specific target sequences and the information embodied in the arrangement of nucleotides within the target sequences was crucial to the invention and could be considered to support the examiner's opinion that the substance of the invention was genetic information. However, when considering the invention as a whole, the dsRNA architecture of the claimed compositions was at least equally significant to the working of the invention, with the chemical and structural elements of the dsRNA being crucial for the recognition and digestion of the molecule by an enzyme called Dicer. Consequently, the informational, structural and chemical content of the dsRNA molecules should all be considered essential elements of the invention as claimed, so that the substance of the invention encompassed each of these elements and not merely genetic information. On balance, the substance of the invention was a pharmaceutical composition and not merely the genetic information that is contained in the composition. Consistent with the High Court decision in *Apotex Pty Ltd v Sanofi-Aventis Australia Pty Ltd* [2013] HCA 50 at [143] the claimed iRNA compositions were economically significant products that met the requirements of "manner of manufacture".

It is difficult to avoid the conclusion, supported in particular by the *Hereditary Cancer Test* decision, that much discussion and legal analysis in the USA is based on outcome rather than the sounder basis of identifying the relevant rule of law.

For example, the isolated BRCA1 genetic sequence considered in *Myriad* did not qualify in the "composition of matter" category, being neither a composition of two or more substances nor a composite article resulting from chemical union or mechanical mixture, see *Diamond v Chakrabarty* citing *Shell Development Co v Watson* 149 F.Supp. 279, 280 (DC 1957). It therefore qualified, if at all, in the category "manufacture" for which the decision in *Chakrabarty* was said to be central to the enquiry. It was explained that such a patent claim should not be to a hitherto unknown natural phenomenon but instead should be to a non-naturally occurring manufacture or composition of matter—a product of human ingenuity having a distinctive name, character and use, citing *Hartranft v Wiegmann* 121 U. S. 609, 615 (1887). The court held that the invention here was merely finding the hitherto unknown location of the gene and not the creation of a unique molecule. In contrast, the cDNA for BRCA1 was an exons-only molecule newly created by a laboratory technician, falling within the "composition of matter" category and distinct from the DNA from which it was derived. The court went on to hold that very short sequences of DNA that have no intervening introns to remove when creating cDNA might be indistinguishable from natural DNA and therefore not fall automatically within the "composition of matter" category. It is submitted that this reservation leaves open the question whether and if so when such sequences fall within the "manufacture" category and does not support the holding in *Hereditary Cancer Test*, especially given the caution with which the Supreme Court has expressed its opinion in each of its above mentioned decisions.

Some indication of an emerging more favourable approach is found in *Rapid Litigation Management Ltd v Cellzdirect, Inc* (Fed. Cir. 2016) where the court found that the claims were simply not directed to the ability of hepatocytes to survive multiple freeze-thaw cycles but instead were directed to a new and useful laboratory technique for preserving hepatocytes, emphasizing that the claims must be considered as a whole and as an ordered combination. It has been pointed out that here the claims were directed to the production of hepatocyte cultures which were a tangible thing and not merely to the production of diagnostic information.

Only a minority of the judges in the Federal Circuit have previously worked in the field of patents, and not all of them have a background in chemistry or biotechnology and in the pertinent case law in these specialised fields. It is therefore important where a dispute arises to ensure that briefs filed on behalf of the UK or European parties for whom we act fully explain the legal and technical background so that the judges can reach an informed decision. For that purpose, familiarity with the relevant statute and case law should not be confined to the US practitioners involved but should be shared by their UK and European colleagues.

A second point is that the claimed subject-matter should be defined so as to fall as positively as possible within one of the four categories of statutory subject-matter in s.101, see the US *Manual of Patent Practice* at 2106—Patent Subject Matter Eligibility, and to minimise the relevance of extra-judicial exceptions. The "process" category as defined in *Gottschalk v Benson*, 409 U.S. 63, 70, 175 USPQ 673, 676 (1972) relates to a mode of treatment of certain materials to produce a given *result* and is an act, or a series of acts, performed upon the subject-matter to be *transformed* and reduced to a different state or thing (emphasis added). The "manufacture" and "composition of matter" categories have been defined above. The skilled reader of a claim should be able to identify, directly or from context in the description, the result achieved and the transformational nature of what is claimed.

Further, although generalised functional expressions such as "isolating", "amplifying" and "detecting" may be justified for business and licensing reasons in the broadest claims, they may not be resistant to challenge as the cases above show. The feature of amplification, for example, in relation to DNA could usefully be qualified by specifying that amplification is to a level where fluorescence detection is possible, backed by a statement in the description and perhaps a subordinate claim as to the molarity that has to be reached before such detection is possible. Explicit statements of this kind either in a main claim or in a subordinate claim make it harder for the court to dismiss the amplified material as a mere product of nature since the naturally occurring material cannot itself be detected in this way.

The examples can usefully be a full and accurate record of the experimental procedures used rather than a mere generalised description, for example in the case of amplification both mentioning the length of sequence to be amplified and the number of moles of each nucleotide added, thereby enabling the amplification factor believed to have been achieved by the inventor(s) to be calculated and lending credibility to the claimed subject-matter.

■ A recent first instance decision in favour of eligibility is found in *Momenta Pharmaceuticals, Inc. v Amphastar Pharmaceuticals, Inc.* (D. Mass. 21 July 2017) which related to a method for analysing an enoxaparin sample for the presence or amount of a non-naturally occurring sugar. District Judge Gorton commented: "Because the '886 patent "[is] directed to a new and useful method" of ensuring the quality of enoxaparin and involves a series of laboratory steps rather than a law of nature or abstract idea, this Court concludes that the asserted claims involve patentable subject-matter. See *CellzDirect*, 827 F.3d at 1048". Further decisions for eligibility include a dehydrated laminated tissue graft in *MiMedx Group, Inc. v Liventa Bioscience, Inc.* (N.D. Ga. 2017) and a method of manufacturing a dental crown, see *Zircore v Straumann Manufacturing, Inc* (E.D. Texas, 2017).

■ Methods of medical testing continue to have a high risk of being held ineligible: see *Cleveland Clinic Foundation v True Health Diagnostics, LLC* (E.D. Va.,2017) which involved characterizing a test subject's risk of having atherosclerotic cardiovascular disease and relied heavily on the earlier *Sequenom* decision, and *Athena Diagnostics, Inc. v Mayo Collaborative Services, LLC*, (D. Mass2017) which concerned diagnosing neurotransmission or developmental disorders related to muscle specific tyrosine kinase (MuSK).

■ It will be apparent that broad functional features in claims issued by the USPTO especially in computer-related or life science arts can give US courts a pretext for holding that the subject-matter is "directed to" an arguably over-simplified invention which is then held to be ineligible. The more the "hand of man" is specified in such claims, supported where appropriate by detailed description and where available by examples, the better the prospect of avoiding judicial re-writing and consequential s.101 challenge.

Particular forms of claim applicable to biotechnology

—Recombinant DNA

76A.10   *Add new paragraph at end:*
As discussed in the *Examination Guidelines for Patent Applications relating to Biotechnological Inventions in the Intellectual Property Office* at [40], [41] genes that have been mutated artificially might be inventive if it is demonstrated that the mutated gene has an unexpected advantage over the naturally occurring gene. Such artificially mutated genes are considered to be a selection invention. The advantage of the mutated gene over the naturally occurring gene must be common to all of the mutations proposed for that particular gene. Furthermore, the advantage provided by the mutation(s) must be in respect of a specific feature of that particular gene, for example a particular sequence involved in a particular function of the corresponding protein. The "selection invention" criteria can also be applied to the specific combination of probes on a microarray. For example, if the exact combination of probes on a microarray meant a more accurate detection and/or a more precise diagnosis than the use of the probes individually, then the particular selection of probes may provide a surprising effect and inventive step. Moreover, this surprising effect may confer a unity of invention to the probe combination.

—Methods of culture of plants and of breeding animals and products obtained thereby

76A.12   *To the end of the third paragraph (beginning "However, the patentees in G 2/07 and G 1/08 were unwilling to concede defeat."), add:*
■ The principle that the process exclusion contained in art.53(b) EPC has no negative

impact on the allowability of product claims was reaffirmed in T 83/05 *PLANT BIOSCIENCE/Broccoli III*. The claim in issue was directed to an edible *Brassica* plant elevated in anticarcinogenic glucosinolates and produced by a defined method. The Board was satisfied, following the earlier ruling in G 2/13 that art.53(b) had no negative impact on the allowability of product claims in this form, and the case was remitted to the opposition division with an order to maintain the patent. Similarly, in T 1242/06 *STATE OF ISRAEL/Tomatoes III*. The main claim before the Board was directed to "A tomato fruit of the species *Lycopersicon esculentum* which is naturally dehydrated, wherein natural dehydration is defined as wrinkling of skin of the tomato fruit when the fruit is allowed to remain on the plant after a normal ripe harvest stage, said natural dehydration being generally unaccompanied by microbial spoilage." The Board was satisfied that the subject-matter of this claim was not excluded from patentability and the case was also remitted to the opposition division with an order to maintain the patent. However, following recent changes to the EPC Implementing Regulations the applicability of these decisions is now in doubt, see §76A.03.

Add new paragraphs at end:

The issue of whether a process, which merely includes a step of natural crossing and selection and also includes a step requiring human intervention, is patentable received consideration in T 915/10 *MONSANTO/Soybean event*. The claimed process was for the production of a soybean plant tolerant to glyphosate herbicide by introducing a particular sequence into the genome of the plant, and the introduced trait was due directly to the expression of the inserted DNA and was not the result of a plant breeding method characterised by crossing and selection. Accordingly, the Board was satisfied that the process was not excluded by art.53(b) EPC. There was also a product claim directed to a soybean plant containing the sequence and obtainable by crossing a plant obtained from soybean seed having particular inserted DNA and another plant. The Board was satisfied that the claimed group of plants embraced all the (indefinite number of) individual plants as defined by the presence of the sequence and was not defined by the expression of the characteristics that results from a given genotype or combination of genotypes. The claimed plants did not constitute a plant variety as defined by r.26(4) EPC, and technical feasibility with respect to improved yield applied not to one plant variety or group of plant varieties but to soybean plants in general.

■ In contrast, in T 2323/11 *BASF/Sequence expression* the claimed subject-matter concerned a method for the removal of unwanted sequences, e.g. antibiotic or herbicide marker sequences, from the genome of transgenic plants which also comprise an introduced gene for an agronomically valuable trait. The claimed method concerned the sexual crossing of two distinct transgenic parent plants, the first containing, besides sequences of interest conferring a particular trait on the plant, an undesired gene sequence in its genome ("target gene") and the second transgenic parent plant comprising a transgene encoding a particular sequence-specific DNA endonuclease that irreversibly excises this target gene from the genome. The Board held that the claimed method was ineligible because trait of the excision of the target gene was the result of the crossing of the parent plants and was determined by the underlying natural phenomenon of meiosis, applying G 2/07 *PLANT BIOSCIENCE/Broccoli* and G 1/08 *STATE OF ISRAEL/Tomatoes*. It was not accepted that the excision of the target gene was an additional step of a technical nature since it was simply the result of mixing of the genes of the plants chosen for sexual crossing.

Common general knowledge

—Claims to a desideratum or to matters "obvious to try"

Add new paragraph at end: **76A.16**

In *Richter Gedeon Vegyészeti Gyár Rt v Generics (UK) Ltd* [2016] EWCA Civ 410 the

Court of Appeal considered the effect of a prior disclosure that was clearly erroneous. A prior document disclosed the use of a hormone dose of 1.5 grams. The patent claimed use of a dose of 1.5 milligrams. The evidence was that the person in the art would understand that "1.5 grams" had to be an error—but not necessarily that the dose used must have been 1.5 milligrams. The judge held however that it would be obvious for the person skilled in the art to ring up the author of the paper and discover what the actual dose was. Accordingly, the invention was obvious. The Court of Appeal agreed, noting that "What the skilled person would do in the light of the state of the art is a pure question of fact". There is no reason to distinguish between looking up a physical constant in a textbook, and ringing up a colleague to obtain freely available information.

Warning against prior publication of a biotechnological invention

—Insufficiency issues in relation to biotechnology

76A.20 *After the fourteenth paragraph (beginning "In T 1466/05 SEREX/Pyridinoline it was held"), add new paragraphs:*

Assertions of utility in a patent specification must be "plausible". Carr J summarised the law on this in *GlaxoSmithKline v Wyeth* [2016] EWHC 1045 (Ch):

> "(i) In relation to sufficiency, the assertion that the invention will work across the scope of the claim must be plausible and in the case of claims involving a medical use, the patent must show that the claimed medical effect is plausible; *Regeneron Pharmaceuticals Inc v Genentech Inc* [2013] RPC 28 at [95]-[103].
>
> (ii) 'Plausible' means that there must be some real reason for supposing that the statement is true; *Human Genome Sciences Inc v Eli Lilly & Co* [2012] RPC 6 at [149]. This excludes speculative patents, based on mere assertion.
>
> (iii) Plausibility is a 'threshold test' which is satisfied by a disclosure which is 'credible', as opposed to speculative; *Actavis Group v Eli Lilly & Co* [2015] EWHC 3294 at [177]-[178]."

■ See also *Generics (UK) Ltd (t/a Mylan) v Warner-Lambert Co LLC* [2016] EWCA Civ 1006 discussed in more detail at §14.29.

PART II [SECTIONS 77-95]—PROVISIONS ABOUT INTERNATIONAL CONVENTIONS

European patents and patent applications [Sections 77-85]

SECTION 77—Effect of European patent (UK)

Notes

77.01 *Add at end:*

7. Various prospective insertions are made to subss.(4), (4A), (5)(a), (5A) and (9) by para.2(5) of the Patents (European Patent with Unitary Effect and Unified Patent Court) Order 2016 (SI 2016/388) to come into force on the date of entry into force of the Agreement on a Unified Patent Court.

SECTION 78—Effect of filing an application for a European patent (UK)

78.01 78.—(2) This section applies to the following provisions of this Act:—
section 2(3) and so much of section 14(7) as relates to section 2(3);
section 5;

section 6;

so much of section 13(3) as relates to an application for and issue of a certificate under that subsection;

sections 30 to 33;

section 36;

sections 55 to 69;

sections 70 to 70F;

section 74, so far as relevant to any of the provisions mentioned above;

section 111; and

section 125.

Notes

Add at end:

5. ■ Subsection (2) was amended by s.1(6) of the Intellectual Property (Unjustified Threats) Act 2017, with effect from 1 October 2017.

Add new Section 83A:

SECTION 83A—European patent with unitary effect and Unified Patent Court

83A.—(1) Schedule A3 contains provision about the application of this Act in relation to the European patent with unitary effect.   **83A.01**

(2) Schedule A4 contains provision about the jurisdiction of the Unified Patent Court in relation to the European patent (UK) and the European patent with unitary effect.

SCHEDULE A3

European Patent with Unitary Effect

MEANING OF "RELEVANT STATUTORY PROVISIONS"

1. In this Schedule "relevant statutory provisions" means—   **83A.02**

(a) the provisions of this Act which, by virtue of paragraph 2, apply in relation to the European patent with unitary effect, and

(b) the other provisions of this Act which, by virtue of the Unitary Patent Regulation, are to be treated as applying in relation to the European patent with unitary effect (see, in particular, Article 7 of that Regulation).

PROVISIONS APPLIED BY THIS SCHEDULE TO THE EUROPEAN PATENT WITH UNITARY EFFECT

2. The following provisions of this Act apply in relation to a European patent with unitary effect, subject to paragraphs 3 and 4—

section 48 (compulsory licences: general);

section 48A (compulsory licences: WTO proprietors);

section 48B (compulsory licences: other cases);

section 49 (provisions about licences under section 48);

section 50 (exercise of powers on applications under section 48);

section 50A (powers exercisable following merger and market investigations);

119

section 51 (powers exercisable in consequence of report of Competition and Markets Authority);

section 52 (opposition, appeal and arbitration);

section 53 (compulsory licences; supplementary provisions);

section 54 (special provisions where patented invention is being worked abroad);

section 55 (use of patented inventions for services of the Crown);

section 56 (interpretation, etc., of provisions about Crown use);

section 57 (rights of third parties in respect of Crown use);

section 57A (compensation for loss of profit);

section 58(1) to (6) and (9A) to (13) (references of disputes as to Crown use);

section 59 (special provisions as to Crown use during emergency);

section 60 (meaning of infringement);

section 64 (right to continue use begun before priority date);

sections 70 to 70F (unjustified threats);

section 73(2) to (4) (Comptroller's power to revoke patents on his own initiative);

section 74A (opinions on matters prescribed in the rules);

section 74B (reviews of opinions under section 74A);

section 76A (biotechnological inventions);

section 77(4) to (5A) (effect of European patent (UK));

section 80(1) (authentic text of European patents and patent applications);

sections 97 to 100 (legal proceedings) so far as they relate to proceedings which do not fall within the exclusive jurisdiction of the Unified Patent Court as set out in paragraph 1 of Schedule A4;

section 101 (exercise of comptroller's discretionary powers);

section 102 (right of audience, &c in proceedings before comptroller);

sections 103 (extension of privilege for communications with solicitors relating to patent proceedings) and 105 (extension of privilege in Scotland for communications relating to patent proceedings) so far as they relate to proceedings before the comptroller;

section 107 (costs and expenses in proceedings before the comptroller);

section 108 (licences granted by order of comptroller);

section 110 (unauthorised claim of patent rights);

section 116 (immunity of department as regards official acts);

section 118 (information about patent applications and patents, and inspection of documents);

section 123 (rules);

section 124 (rules, regulations and orders; supplementary);

section 125 (extent of invention);

section 128A (EU compulsory licences);

section 128B (supplementary protection certificates).

MANNER OF APPLICATION OF RELEVANT STATUTORY PROVISIONS

3. The relevant statutory provisions apply in relation to a European patent with unitary effect in the same way as they apply in relation to a European patent (UK).

4.—(1) In their application in relation to the European patent with unitary effect, the relevant statutory provisions which are referred to in this paragraph have effect subject to the modifications set out in this paragraph.

(2) In section 7(2)(b), the reference to the United Kingdom is a reference to any of the Participating Member States.

(3) In sections 30(7) and 31(7), references to proceedings by virtue of section 61 or 69 are references to equivalent proceedings in the Unified Patent Court.

(4) In sections 33(1)(a), 33(4), 37(2), 37(7), 38(2) and 38(3), the reference to registration is a reference to registration in the Register for unitary patent protection.

(5) In sections 48(1)(b), 48B(4), 50A(4), 51(3), 53(3), and 53(4), the reference to the register is a reference to the Register for unitary patent protection.

(6) In sections 48(2)(b), 50A(4), 51(3), 53(3), 53(4) and 53(5), the reference to making an entry is a reference to directing the making of an entry.

(7) In sections 48B(2)(b) and 50(2)(a), the reference to the journal is a reference to the European Patent Bulletin.

(8) In section 55(5)(b), the reference to the Patent Office is a reference to the European Patent Office.

(9) In section 59(2), the reference to section 69 includes a reference to Article 67 of the European Patent Convention.

(10) In section 60—

   (a) in subsections (1), (2), and (5)(d), (e) and (f), the references to the United Kingdom are references to the territory of a Contracting Member State in which the European patent with unitary effect has effect;

   (b) in subsection (7)—

        (i) in the definition of "relevant ship" and "relevant aircraft, hovercraft or vehicle", the reference to the United Kingdom is a reference to a Contracting Member State in which the European patent with unitary effect has effect; and

        (ii) in the definition of "exempted aircraft", the reference to an aircraft to which section 89 of the Civil Aviation Act 1982(9) applies is a reference to an aircraft other than an aircraft of a Contracting Member State in which the European patent with unitary effect has effect.

5. In this Schedule—

   (a) "Contracting Member State" has the same meaning as in Article 2(c) of the Agreement on a Unified Patent Court; and

   (b) the following expressions have the same meanings as in Article 2 of the Unitary Patent Regulation—

        Participating Member State;

        Register for unitary patent protection.

Note

Paragraph 2 of reference to ss.70 to 70F (unjustified threats) inserted by s.1(8) of the Intellectual Property (Unjustified Threats) Act 2017, with effect from 1 October 2017.

SCHEDULE A4

The Unified Patent Court

83A.03   1. The Unified Patent Court has exclusive jurisdiction in respect of an Article 32(1) action which relates to—

(a) a European patent with unitary effect, or

(b) a supplementary protection certificate(10) for which the basic patent is a European patent with unitary effect,

(c) subject to paragraph 2—

(i) a European patent (UK), or

(ii) a supplementary protection certificate for which the basic patent is a European patent (UK).

Transitional provisions

2.—(1) The transitional provisions in Article 83 apply in relation to an action referred to in Article 83(1).

(2) An opt out referred to in Article 83(3) may be exercised in accordance with that provision and any relevant Rules of Procedure.

(3) Such opt out may be withdrawn in accordance with Article 83(4) and any relevant Rules of Procedure.

(4) For the purposes of this paragraph, a reference to Article 83 is a reference to Article 83 of the Agreement on a Unified Patent Court.

Modifications of law applicable where UPC has jurisdiction

3.—(1) In the case of an Article 32(1) action relating to—

(a) a European patent with unitary effect, or

(b) a European patent (UK),

the provisions of this Act listed in sub-paragraph (2) do not apply in relation to the action where the Unified Patent Court has jurisdiction in accordance with paragraph 1.

(2) The provisions referred to in sub-paragraph (1) are—

section 58(7) to (9) (references of disputes as to Crown use);

section 61 (proceedings for infringement of patent);

section 62 (restrictions on recovery of damages for infringement);

section 63 (relief for infringement of partially valid patent);

section 65 (certificate of contested validity of patent);

section 66 (proceedings for infringement by a co-owner);

section 67 (proceedings for infringement by exclusive licensee);

section 68 (effect of non-registration on infringement proceedings);

section 69 (infringement of rights conferred by publication of application);

section 71 (declaration or declarator as to non-infringement);

section 72 (power to revoke patents on application);

section 73(1) to (1C) (comptroller's power to revoke patents on his own initiative);

section 74 (proceedings in which validity of patent may be put in issue);

section 75 (amendment of patent in infringement or revocation proceedings);

section 77(3) (effect of European patent (UK)).

(3) In the case of an Article 32(1) action relating to a supplementary protection certificate for which the basic patent is—

  (a) a European patent with unitary effect, or

  (b) a European patent (UK),

the provisions of this Act listed in sub-paragraph (4) do not apply in relation to the action where the Unified Patent Court has jurisdiction in accordance with paragraph 1.

(4) The provisions referred to in sub-paragraph (3) are—

  section 58(7) to (9) (references of disputes as to Crown use);

  section 61 (proceedings for infringement of patent);

  section 62 (restrictions on recovery of damages for infringement);

  section 63 (relief for infringement of partially valid patent);

  section 65 (certificate of contested validity of patent);

  section 66 (proceedings for infringement by a co-owner);

  section 67 (proceedings for infringement by exclusive licensee);

  section 68 (effect of non-registration on infringement proceedings);

  section 69 (infringement of rights conferred by publication of application);

  section 71 (declaration or declarator as to non-infringement);

  section 74 (proceedings in which validity of patent may be put in issue);

  section 75 (amendment of a patent in infringement or revocation proceedings).

ENFORCEMENT

4.—(1) For the purposes of enforcement of a decision or order of the Unified Patent Court—

  (a) the decision or order has the same force and effect,

  (b) proceedings for or with respect to enforcement of the decision or order may be taken, and

  (c) the enforcing court, or in a relevant Northern Ireland case the Enforcement of Judgments Office, has the same powers in relation to the enforcement of the decision or order,

as if the decision or order had originally been made by the enforcing court.

(2) The enforcing court, or in a relevant Northern Ireland case the Enforcement of Judgments Office, may enforce a mediation settlement in the same manner as a judgment or order of the enforcing court.

(3) In this paragraph—

  "enforcing court" means—

  (a) as respects England and Wales, the High Court,

  (b) as respects Scotland, the Court of Session, and

  (c) as respects Northern Ireland, the High Court in Northern Ireland;

    "mediation settlement" means a settlement reached through mediation using the facilities of the patent mediation and arbitration centre established under Article 35 of the Agreement on a Unified Patent Court;

    "relevant Northern Ireland case" means a case where—

  (a) the decision or order of the Unified Patent Court would, if it had been given by the High Court in Northern Ireland, or

   (b) the mediation settlement would, if enforced in the same manner as a judgment or order of the High Court in Northern Ireland, be enforced by the Enforcement of Judgments Office under the Judgments Enforcement (Northern Ireland) Order 1981(11).

INTERPRETATION

5. In this Schedule—

   (a) "Article 32(1) action" means an action listed in Article 32(1) of the Agreement on a Unified Patent Court;

   (b) "basic patent" has the same meaning as in Article 1(c) of Regulation (EC) No 469/2009 of the European Parliament and of the Council of 6th May 2009 concerning the supplementary protection certificate for medicinal products(12); and

   (c) "Rules of Procedure" has the same meaning as in the Agreement on a Unified Patent Court."

Footnotes

  (1) Section 58(6) was amended by the Patents Act 2004 (c.16), section 2(2)(a).

  (2) Section 60(5) was amended by S.I. 2000/2037 and S.I. 2005/2759.

  (3) Section 60(6G) was inserted by S.I. 2014/1997.

  (4) Section 77 was amended by the Copyright, Designs and Patents Act 1988 (c.48), Schedule 5, paragraphs 8 and 21; the Patents Act 2004 (c.16), Schedule 1, paragraph 2; S.I. 2005/687; the Intellectual Property Act 2014 (c.18), Schedule, paragraph 6.

  (5) Section 91 was amended by the Patents Act 2004 (c.16), Schedule 2, paragraph 20.

  (6) Section 92 was amended by S.I. 1979/1714 (N.I. 19).

  (7) Section 130(1) was amended by the Armed Forces Act 1981 (c.55), section 22(1) and (3); the Copyright, Designs and Patents Act 1988 (c.48), Schedule 5, paragraph 5, Schedule 7, paragraph 23 and Schedule 8; S.I. 2000/2037; the Patents Act 2004 (c.16), Schedule 1, paragraph 9(1) and (2), Schedule 2, paragraph 27, and Schedule 3; S.I. 2004/2357; S.I. 2006/1028; Crime and Courts Act 2013 (c.22), Schedule 9, Part 2, paragraph 27; S.I. 2013/2602.

  (8) OJ No L 361, 31.12.2012, p1.

  (9) 1982 c.16.

  (10) Section 128B(2) of the Patents Act 1977 (c.37), as amended by S.I. 2014/2411, defines "supplementary protection certificate".

  (11) S.I. 1981/226 (N.I. 6).

  (12) OJ No L152, 16.6.2009, p.1.

Note

Prospectively added by the Patents (European Patent with Unitary Effect and Unified Patent Court) Order 2016 (SI 2016/388) (not yet in force, and coming into force on the date of entry into force of the Agreement on a Unified Patent Court signed at Brussels on 19 February 2013, cm 8653).

International applications for patents [Sections 89-89B]

SECTION 89 [SUBSTITUTED]—Effect of international application for patent

RELEVANT RULES—RULES 64, 65, 71 AND 72

89.04   *Replace r.65(1)-(2) with:*

    65.—(1) An international application for a patent filed at the Patent office as a

124

competent receiving office under the Patent Co-operation Treaty must be filed **in English or Welsh [—**

    (a) *in English or Welsh; and*

    (b) *in triplicate.*

(2) *Where fewer than three copies of the application are filed, the comptroller may direct the applicant to pay any copying costs.]*

Add new Note:

Note. Amended (effective 1 October 2016) by para.11 of the Patents (Amendment) (No. 2) Rules 2016 (SI 2016/892).

COMMENTARY ON SECTION 89

United Kingdom Intellectual Property Office as an international authority

—Number of copies (r.65)

Add new paragraph at end: **89.18**
As the UK-IPO now transfers all international applications to the International Bureau and the European Patent Office electronically, there is no longer any need for three copies to be filed whether the application is filed with the UK-IPO on paper or electronically (see the UK-IPO publication "Proposed Changes to the Patents Rules" dated February 2016). Amendments to r.65 have therefore been introduced in to remove the requirement for international applications to be filed in triplicate and to remove the provision to demand a fee to make copies.

PRACTICE UNDER SECTION 89

International phase

In the third paragraph, after "For paper-based filing, all documents, other than the fee **89.31** *calculation sheet, should be filed in triplicate (r.65(1))", add:*
, but see proposed changes discussed in §89.18:

SECTION 89A [ADDED]—International and national phases of application

RELEVANT RULES — RULES 66-70

Add new paragraph 89A.02A: **89A.02A**

Rule 66A—Amendment of International application before grant

66A.—(1) This rule applies to an international application for a patent (UK) which has begun the national phase of the application.

(2) The period within which an applicant may amend his application under section 19(1) is as follows.

(3) Where during the international phase of the application, the International Searching Authority has sent to the applicant the International Search Report relating to the invention, the period within which the applicant may amend his application is the period beginning with the date on which the national phase of the application begins and ending with the date on which the comptroller sends the applicant the first substantive examination report.

(4) Where during the international phase of the application, the International

Searching Authority has not sent to the applicant the International Search Report relating to the invention, the period during which the applicant may amend his application is the first to commence of—

(a) the period prescribed by rule 31(3); and

(b) the period beginning with the date on which the International Searching Authority sends the International Search Report to the applicant and ending with the date on which the comptroller sends the applicant the first substantive examination report.

Note. New r.66A is inserted effective 1 October 2016; para.12 of the Patents (Amendment) (No.2) Rules 2016 (SI 2016/892).

COMMENTARY ON SECTION 89A

Valid entry into the UK phase (subss.(2) and (3)(a))

—General

89A.12   *Replace the fourth paragraph with:*

By virtue of s.20A(1), reinstatement may be available for international applications which are taken to be withdrawn as a result of an unintentional failure to satisfy the requirements for entry to the UK national phase. The period within which reinstatement must be requested is now twelve months from the date on which the application was terminated. The alternative of two months from the date on which the removal of the cause of non-compliance occurred has been removed with effect from 1 October 2016 by amendment of r.32, see §20A.02.

PRACTICE UNDER SECTION 89A

Prosecution and amendment

89A.36   *In the fourth paragraph, after "The substantive examiner considers the international search report", add:*

and any supplementary international search reports

To the end of the fourth paragraph, add:

Where the International Searching Authority has issued a declaration under art.17(2) of the PCT that no international search report has been established, but the substantive examiner considers that the claims relate to a patentable invention, a full search is performed but no additional fee may be requested from the applicant (see the *MOPP* para.89B.12.2).

Add new paragraphs at end:

Where third party observations have been filed in the international phase, the substantive examiner considers them in the same way as they would consider third party observations filed on a domestic application (see the *MOPP* para.89B.16).

New r.66A (reprinted at §89A.02A) has been introduced with the intention of "clarifying" existing practice at the UK-IPO (IPO Guidance of 1 September 2016).

The rule envisages two situations. In the first (where an International Searching Authority has issued an International Search Report) an applicant may amend its application at any time before the IPO issues its first substantive examination report. In the second situation (where no International Search Report has been issued) amendment may be made during the period either commencing from the issuance of a UK-IPO Search Report or the International Search Report (which issues first) until the IPO first substantive examination report.

SECTION 89B [ADDED]—Adaptation of provisions in relation to international application

COMMENTARY ON SECTION 89B

Amendment in the UK phase

In the first paragraph, after "Thus,", add: **89B.17**
subject to the comments further below,

Add new paragraphs at end:

It is stated in r.31(3) that "the applicant may amend his application only within the period beginning with the date on which the applicant is informed of the examiner's report under s.17(5) and ending with the date on which the Comptroller sends him the first substantive examination report". However, for most international applications no report is sent under s.17(5) because the UK-IPO uses the results of the search performed by the International Searching Authority. Consequently, it has been considered to be unclear from the current r.31 whether it is possible to amend international applications at the time of, or after, entry into the national phase and prior to examination of the application (see the UK-IPO publication "Proposed Changes to the Patents Rules" dated February 2016).

■ A new r.66A has therefore been brought into force to make it clear that where during the international phase of the application, the International Searching Authority has sent to the applicant the International Search Report relating to theinvention, the period within which the applicant may amend his application is the period beginning with the date on which the national phase of the application begins and ending with the date on which the Comptroller sends him the first substantive examination report.

Where a PCT application enters the national phase early and a full search is performed by a UK examiner, a search report under s.17(5) will be issued. In these circumstances, the existing provisions of r.31(3) will apply, meaning that the applicant can amend their application once the search report under s.17(5) has been issued and before the first examination report is issued (see the UK-IPO publication "Proposed Changes to the Patents Rules" dated February 2016).

Miscellaneous [Sections 91-95]

SECTION 91—Evidence of conventions and instruments under conventions

■ **91.**—(1) Judicial notice shall be taken of the following, that is to say—   **91.01**
   (a) the European Patent Convention, the Community Patent Convention, **the Agreement on a Unified Patent Court** and the Patent Co-operation Treaty (each of which is hereafter in this section referred to as the relevant convention);
(6) In this section—
   "convention institution" means an institution established by or having functions under the relevant convention;
   "relevant convention court" does not include a court of the United Kingdom or of any other country which is a party to the relevant convention **but does include the Unified Patent Court**; and
   "legal proceedings", in relation to the United Kingdom, includes proceedings before the comptroller.

Add new paragraph at end of Note:

■ Subsections (1)(a) and (6) amended by the Patents (European Patent with Unitary Effect and Unified Patent Court) Order 2016 (SI 2016/388) (not yet in force).

127

SECTION 92—Obtaining evidence for proceedings under the European Patent Convention

92.01   *Add new paragraph at end of Note:*

■ Prospective insertions are made in subss.(1) and (5):

After "European Patent Convention" insert "or proceedings before the Unified Patent Court".

This change is to be effected by the Patents (European Patent with Unitary Effect and Unified Patent Court) Order to come into force on the date of entry into force of the Agreement on a Unified Patent Court.

PART III [Sections 96-132]—MISCELLANEOUS AND GENERAL

Legal proceedings [Sections 96-108]

SECTION 96 [REPEALED]—The Patents Court

COMMENTARY ON SECTION 96 [REPEALED]

Subject-matter jurisdiction of the Patents Court

96.07   *Add new paragraph at end:*

However, a dispute about royalties due under a patent licence agreement does not need to be heard in the Patents Court, see *Medical Research Council v Celltech R&D Ltd* [2015] EWHC 2139 (Ch) since it was not obvious that the defendant would argue that the relevant product fell outside the claims of the licensed patents, and other judges were competent to construe a licence which was simply a permission to do something and did not call for technical expertise such as would be required to decide a patent action. On the scope of the jurisdiction of the Patents Court under CPR r.63.2(1) the court observed:

> "In my judgment, s.62(1) [of the Senior Courts Act] does not preclude the Patents Court from taking such other proceedings as may be appropriate to be heard. What it does is it sets out the central business of the Patents Court, and when read with CPR 63.2, the combination provides that certain claims must be started in the Patents Court, but they do not, taken together, preclude other appropriate claims from being started in or transferred to the Patents Court."

SECTION 97—Appeals from the comptroller

RELEVANT RULES

97.02   *Add at end:*

■ CPR Pt 52 was substantially revised and re-structured in October 2016 pursuant to the Civil Procedure (Amendment No.3) Rules 2016 (SI 2016/788). The changes to CPR Pt 52 came into effect on 3 October 2016. A consequence of the re-structuring is that the CPR rule numbers used in the commentary to s.97 of the Main Work are no longer correct. The references to the CPR in the Main Work should now be read as follows:

- Replace "CPR 52.3(6)" with "CPR 52.7(2)"
- Replace "CPR 52.4(a)" with "CPR 52.12(2)(a)"
- Replace "CPR 52.4(3)" with "CPR 52.12(2)"
- Replace "CPR 52.4(3)(b)" with "CPR 52.12(3)(b)"

- Replace "CPR 52.4(6)(1)" with "CPR 52.12(2)(a)"
- Replace "CPR 52.5" with "CPR 52.13"
- Replace "CPR 52.5(4)" with "CPR 52.13(4)"
- Replace "CPR 52.5(5)" with "CPR 52.13(5)"
- Replace "CPR 52.5(6)" with "CPR 52.13(6)"
- Replace "CPR 52.6(1)" with "CPR 52.15(1)"
- Replace "CPR 52.11" with "CPR 52.21"
- Replace "CPR 52.11(1)" with "CPR 52.21(1)"
- Replace "CPR 52.11(1)(a)" with "CPR 52.21(1)(a)"
- Replace "CPR 52.11(1)(b)" with "CPR 52.21(1)(b)"
- Replace "CPR 52.11(2)" with "CPR 52.21(2)"
- Replace "CPR 52.11(3)" with "CPR 52.21(3)"
- Replace "CPR 52.12A" with "CPR 52.25"
- Replace "CPR 52.13" with "CPR 52.7"
- Replace "CPR 52.13(2)" with "CPR 52.7(2)"

Further appeals from the Patents Court after appeal from the Comptroller (subs.(3))

Replace the first paragraph with: **97.06**

■ Subsection (3) concerns further appeals from the Patents Court in relation to appeals from the Comptroller, other than those where the proceedings were held in Scotland (for which see §97.07). The subsection is expressed in terms that no further appeal shall lie from a decision of the Patents Court on appeal from the Comptroller except (a) where the Comptroller's decision was given under certain listed sections of the Act; or (b) where the ground of appeal is that the decision of the Patents Court was wrong in law. However, in all cases, such further appeal lies only if specific leave to appeal is given either by the Patents Court or by the Court of Appeal itself.

■ It is noted that the Access to Justice Act 1999 s.55, together with the CPR, specifically precludes "second appeals" unless permitted only by the Court of Appeal under strict circumstances. This seems to be in contradiction to s.97(3) which also permits permission to appeal to be given by the Patents Court. In *Smith International v Specialised Petroleum Services* [2005] EWCA Civ 1357; [2006] F.S.R. 25 at 487; [2006] I.P. & T. 534, the Court of Appeal held that the strict second appeals provisions in s.55 of the 1999 Act and the CPR (r.52.13 at the time) do not apply to appeals under s.97(3). Following that, the Court of Appeal was able to treat Smith's appeal as a "first appeal" and apply the less strict test for such first appeals provided in the then CPR r.52.3. That rule said that permission for "first appeals" may only be given where the court considers that the appeal would have a real prospect of success (or there is some other compelling point of principle or practice), so that such a first appeal was not subject to the stricter requirement that it must raise an important point of principle or practice. The court went on to decide that permission should be granted as Smith's appeal did have a real prospect of success.

■ The revision of CPR Pt 52 in October 2016 increased the threshold for "second appeals". In particular, a further requirement has been added: the Court of Appeal must now be satisfied either that the a second appeal has "a real prospect of success" (CPR r.52.7(2)(a)(i)) and that it raises an important point of principle or practice (CPR r.52.7(2)(a)(ii)), or there is some other compelling reason to hear it (CPR r.52.7(2)(b)). Despite this change to the CPR, it appears that the reasoning in *Smith* still applies: permission to appeal under s.97(3) may be granted by the Patents Court or Court of Appeal, and if permission is sought from the latter, treatment as a "first appeal" under CPR r.52.6(1) should be expected so that the threshold for permission is merely "real prospect of success" or "other compelling reason".

SECTION 99—General powers of the court

COMMENTARY ON SECTION 99

99.02   *Add new paragraph at end:*

In the case of entitlement disputes, however, it may be desirable for the Comptroller to decline to exercise her original jurisdiction before the court rules. In *Angle Ring Ltd v ASD Westok Ltd* [2015] EWHC 2779 (IPEC) HHJ Hacon declined to award summary judgment on a claim to entitlement but held that it should go to trial under the court's inherent jurisdiction along with other issues. To have separate hearings on entitlement in the IPO would be "unsatisfactory and wasteful". Nonetheless the parties formally invited the IPO to decline to hear the entitlement dispute. The IPO issued a "with consent" decision from the papers: BL O/595/15.

SECTION 102 [SUBSTITUTED]—Right of audience, etc. in proceedings before comptroller

102.01   *Add new paragraph at end of Note:*

In the event that arrangements for the European patent with unitary effect come into force in the UK, the Patents (European Patent with Unitary Effect and Unified Patent Court) Order 2016 (SI 2016/388), para.2(10) will apply s.102 to these patents.

SECTION 102A [REPEALED]—Right of audience, etc., in proceedings on appeal from the comptroller

COMMENTARY ON SECTION 102A

102A.02   *In the fourth paragraph, after "an Appointed Person appointed to hear appeals under s.76 of the Trade Marks Act 1994", add:*

or s.27A of the Registered Designs Act 1949

SECTION 106—Costs and expenses in proceedings before the court [under section 40]

106.01   ■ **106.**—(1A) This section applies to proceedings before the court (including proceedings on an appeal to the court) which are—

    (a) proceedings under section 40;

    (b) proceedings for infringement;

    (c) **in respect of an actionable threat under section 70A**; or

    (d) proceedings on an application for a declaration or declarator under section 71.

Notes

Add at end:

■ 3. Subsection (1A)(c) was amended by s.1(7) of the Intellectual Property (Unjustified Threats) Act 2017, with effect from 1 October 2017.

SECTION 107—Costs and expenses in proceedings before the comptroller

Notes

Add at end:

5. In the event that arrangements for the European patent with unitary effect come into force in the UK, the Patents (European Patent with Unitary Effect and Unified Patent Court) Order 2016 (SI 2016/388), para.2(10) will apply s.107 to these patents.

107.01

Commentary on Section 107

The general rule for exercising the Comptroller's powers

—Departures from the standard scale of costs

Add new paragraphs at end:

107.04

The principal grounds advanced by the defender in *Robert Wilson v Enviromax* BL O/004/16 for departing from the standard scale were, firstly, that the defender was forced to respond to evidence filed by the pursuer in respect of grounds which were ultimately not pursued at the hearing, and secondly, that the pursuer commenced or maintained his case without a genuine belief that there was an issue to be tried, essentially in light of the pursuer's admission under cross-examination that he had agreed to the patent being filed in the defender's name. In contrast to *Farr v Orbis* BL O/469/11 the pursuer had been legally represented throughout the case. The Hearing Officer held that the pursuer very clearly put the defender to proof of a significant point of fact when all along he knew that it was true, which was a paradigm example of forcing the defender to waste time and money. It was unreasonable behaviour justifying a departure from the scale to compensate the defender for the expenses incurred in attempting to prove this fact. However, the pursuer's conduct only reached the necessary levels of unreasonableness after it had become clear that whether or not he had agreed to the patent application being filed in the defender's name was a key fact at issue that he required the defender to prove. If awarding scale costs, the Hearing Officer would not usually break costs down by issue, but this was more just when making a higher off-scale award. In the outcome, costs of £7,646 were awarded.

■ In *Caterpillar Inc and Joseph Vogele AG* BL O/274/16, off-scale costs were not awarded, despite the claimant having presented arguments unacceptably late, because the defendant's costs did not seem to have been significantly increased as a result.

■ In *University of Warwick v Dr Geoffrey Graham Diamond* BL O/441/16, both sides sought to rely upon Dr Diamond's choice to represent himself (despite urging from the IPO to seek legal advice and warning that "his refusal to do so increased the expense of the proceedings as a whole"). Hopeless arguments had been advanced by both sides, which effectively offset each other so that off-scale costs would not be awarded.

Supplemental [Sections 122-132]

SECTION 123—Rules

Add new paragraph 123.00:

123.00

Contents

RELEVANT RULES—RULES 1, 2, 4, 73-88, 102, 106-115, 117-120

Replace r.75 with: 123.08

Rule 75—Publication of notices

75.—(1) Subject to paragraph (2) and rule 105(5) the comptroller must advertise in the journal any event to which it is possible to object under any of the provisions mentioned in Part 2 or 3 of Schedule 3.

(2) Where an amendment to the specification of a patent is proposed by the proprietor under section 75(1) the comptroller may, if he thinks fit, advertise in the journal the proposed amendment.

Add new Note:

Note. Amended (effective 1 October 2016) by para.13 of the Patents (Amendment) (No.2) Rules 2016 (SI 2016/892).

SCHEDULE 4

Extension of time limits

Add new Note: 123.26

Note. Schedule 4 has been amended as follows, effective 1 October 2016; para.16 of the Patents (Amendment) (No.2) Rules 2016 (SI 2016/892):

(a) in Pt 1, omit the entry in respect of r.104(2); and

(b) in Pts 2 and 3, after each entry in respect of r.68, insert the following entry—rule 104(2) (period for furnishing an address for service), in relation to an application for a patent.

These amendments permit a two-month extension for furnishing an address for service. See §32.23.

COMMENTARY ON SECTION 123

Scope of the section

Add new paragraphs at end: 123.38

Many changes are proposed to be introduced by the Patents (European Patent with

Unitary Effect and Unified Patent Court) Order 2016 (SI 2016/388) to come into force on the date of entry into force of the Agreement on a Unified Patent Court. The Brexit vote has introduced uncertainty whether, and if so when, that Agreement will enter into force and whether it will cover the UK. Accordingly, its provisions are not discussed in detail in this supplement.

As noted at numerous places in this supplement, changes have been introduced by the Patents (Amendment) (No.2) Rules 2016 (SI 2016/892).

123.44B *Add new paragraph 123.44B:*

Proceedings heard before the Comptroller (Part 7, rr.73-88)

—Powers of the Comptroller concerning striking out

In *HAPSS Ltd v J. G. Bowen* BL O/076/16 the defendant applied under r.83 to strike out a reference under s.12 (entitlement to grant of European patent application) for the following reasons:

(a) he was barred from entering the UK, which would prevent him from having a fair and just hearing contrary to the European Convention on Human Rights;

(b) none of the shareholders in the claimant was resident in the UK, the claimant had no business in the UK and has not filed accounts with Companies House;

(c) an agreement to transfer ownership of the patent application from the defendant to the claimant was invalid; and

(d) the proper jurisdiction for deciding this matter was the US, and an action for declaratory relief had already been filed in the US Federal Court in Los Angeles.

It was held that there was insufficient evidence to decide whether the defendant would be denied a fair hearing or could e.g. use videoconferencing facilities if unable to enter the UK. The Comptroller had jurisdiction under s.12 because the claimant had its principal place of business in the UK, and there was no written evidence that the parties had agreed to submit to the jurisdiction of the competent authority of a relevant contracting state other than the United Kingdom. The invention the subject of the European patent application was not before the US court. The claimant's reference met the requirements of the Act, and the defendant's application should be refused.

—Onus and standard of proof

123.46 *To the end of the second paragraph, add:*

It was held in T 2451/13 *NUTRICIA/Sensoric imprinting* that this yardstick means "beyond reasonable doubt" rather than "absolute certainty". The relevant document was addressed to parents, giving them instructions on how to feed their infants. It would be contrary to life experience to assume that the document was not published but rather kept in the drawer for about four years, until after the priority date of the patent, and this was corroborated by other subsequent publications. Accordingly, the document constituted prior art under art.54(2) EPC.

123.55A *Add new paragraph 123.55A:*

—Powers of the Comptroller concerning striking out

The powers of the Comptroller to strike out a statement of case or to give summary judgment are set out in r.83. In *HAPSS Ltd v J. G. Bowen* BL O/076/16, Mr Bowen failed to strike out the HAPSS Ltd reference under s.12 because he was not able to demonstrate that the HAPSS Ltd statement of case disclosed no reasonable grounds (r.83(2)(a)).

Miscellaneous

—Irregularity in procedure

After the first paragraph, add new paragraph: **123.62**

■ The *MOPP* indicates (by reference to *Cypress Semiconductor Corp's Application* BL O/326/16) that an action made under earlier *MOPP* guidance does not always amount to an error which contributed to an irregularity of procedure. In *Cypress Semiconductor Corp's Application*, an application was reinstated in 2009 following a failure to respond to an examination report. The Office followed its practice at the time and did not provide a new period for compliance. The applicant was not therefore able to amend their application. In 2010, the practice changed such that applicants were given an opportunity to amend in such circumstances. In 2015, the applicant noticed that the application had not been terminated and argued that, given the change in practice, the compliance period should be treated as being amended such that the previously proposed amendments could be considered. The Hearing Officer held that no new period for compliance could be set.

Add new paragraph at end:

■ Rule 107 was invoked in *Fisher-Rosemount Systems' Application* BL O/490/16 because the Hearing Officer had found that the case had not been flagged as being urgent when it was nearing the end of its compliance period and considered this to be an Office irregularity that could have resulted in the late filing of Form 52. The compliance period was retrospectively extended under r.107(1) by three days to allow a first request for extension under r.108 to be made in time. The compliance period had expired on 11 July 2016. An e-mail was sent to the applicant on 14 September 2016 to advise them that the period for requesting an extension had expired but a late filing would be accepted providing that adequate reasons were given, such as the forthcoming hearing. The extension request was filed the same day with the reasons.

Advertisements (subs.(2)(e))

Add new paragraph at end: **123.66**

New r.75(2) (§123.08) permits that the Comptroller "may, if he thinks fit" advertise amendments in s.75(1) proceedings (i.e. amendment of patent in infringement or revocation proceedings). This relaxation of the mandatory requirement for publication is expected to be exercised only in fairly unusual circumstances. The IPO Guidance of 1 September 2016 suggests that publication should be made unless the amendments "would be those which are so insignificant that no-one could be expected to want to oppose them".

—Extensions arising from delays in communication services (r.111)

Add new paragraph at end: **123.79**

■ Rule 111 was successfully invoked to permit the extension of the period for requesting restoration (the r.40(1) period) in *AEB SRL's Patent* BL O/288/17. In that case evidence showed that the relevant patent number had been incorrectly transcribed on the responsible attorneys' renewal system and that they had therefore been paying the renewal fee on the incorrect patent. Those attorneys stated that they had never received renewal or notification of lapse notices on the correct patent and were able to provide proof of the system they had in place for dealing with them had they been received. The Hearing Officer found on the balance of probabilities (observing that proof of a negative is a difficult one) that had any of these notices been received then action would have been taken and since it had not been it was reasonable to conclude that the notices had not been received and not received by reason of a failure in the postal system. He therefore permitted the application to extend the restitution period under r.111.

SECTION 125—Extent of invention

125.00   *Add new paragraph 125.00:*

Contents

Commentary on Section 125

Introduction and scope of the section

125.04   *Add new paragraphs at the beginning:*
■ On 12 July 2017, the President of the Supreme Court (Lord Neuberger) gave judgment in *Actavis UK Ltd v Eli Lilly* [2017] UKSC 48. The judgment represents a fundamentally different approach to "scope of protection" and can only be seen as meaning that the House of Lords previous decision as to doctrine of equivalents in *Kirin-Amgen Inc v Hoechst Marion Roussel* [2004] UKHL 46; [2005] R.P.C. 9 (and all those case that follow it) are no longer good law.

■ *Actavis* makes clear that there *is* a doctrine of equivalents which cannot be correctly applied by conflating the issue into one of construction. That said, nothing in the case necessarily means that the *Kirin-Amgen* principles of contextual construction are no longer good. But one cannot now stop there.

■ The first three paragraphs in the commentary in the Main Work should therefore no longer be seen as representing the law.

Add new paragraphs at end:

■ UK practitioners having applications before the USPTO or involved in post-grant proceedings before the Patent Trial and Appeal Board (PTAB) may be puzzled by the difference between the "broadest reasonable interpretation" (BRI) standard applied by the USPTO and the *Phillips* standard applied by the US district and appellate courts, see *Phillips v Awh Corp*, 415 F.3d 1303 (Fed. Cir. 2005). A paper by Suzannah K. Sundby, "Examining Examiners: I Say Potato and You Say Vegetable, BRI and the Unexpected Results of Interviews", delivered at the 2017 AIPLA annual meeting and available on the AIPLA website provides useful guidance for UK and European practitioners who routinely encounter the difficulties created by the BRI approach in connection with European-originating applications for which they are responsible. That standard was approved by the US Supreme Court in *Cuozzo Speed Techs, LLC v Lee*, 136 S.Ct. 2131 (2016) where it was explained that the use of the BRI standard which had been used by the USPTO for over 100 years helps protect the public because the BRI standard "helps ensure precision while avoiding overly broad claims, and thereby helps prevent a patent from tying up too much knowledge, while helping members of the public draw useful information from the disclosed invention and better understand the lawful limits of the claim." However, the USPTO recognises that BRI is not the broadest "possible" interpretation, see *MPEP* 2111. It is not reasonable to simply select the broadest dictionary definition to construe the common and ordinary meaning of a claim term, *PPC Broadband, Inc v Corning Optical Commc'ns*, 815 F.3d 747, 752 (Fed. Cir. 2016). Instead, the BRI must be reasonable in view of the specification. The BRI of a claim term must not exceed its plain meaning, *Cutsforth, Inc v Motivepower, Inc* (Fed. Cir. 2016) (nonprecedential). Additionally, the general principles of claim construction should be followed. The construction of a claim term must reasonably reflect the language and disclosure of the specification, see *Microsoft v Proxyconn*, 789 F.3d at 1300 and *In re Suitco Surface, Inc*, 603 F.3d 1255, 1260 (Fed. Cir. 2010). It cannot result in something that is illogical and contrary to other claim limitations, it cannot be inconsistent with the specification and other claim features or render claim terms superfluous, cannot read claim limitations out of the claims, and cannot make a method claim ineffective to achieve the desired result. A relative term has a meaning that depends on context so that its interpretation cannot be based on some unrelated disclosure or context.

■ It follows that the ambit of BRI should not be arbitrary or unlimited. UK and European practitioners facing seemingly arbitrary and over-broad claim interpretations in US cases that they are handling may therefore wish to consult US colleagues who may be able to identify more reasonable interpretations and useful counter-arguments.

General principles

Replace with: **125.05**

■ To ascertain the scope of protection, the following two-step procedure is necessary following the decision of the Supreme Court in *Actavis UK Ltd v Eli Lilly* [2017] UKSC 48, 54:

> "(i) does the variant infringe any of the claims as a matter of normal interpretation; and, if not,
>
> (ii) does the variant nonetheless infringe because it varies from the invention in a way or ways which is or are immaterial?
>
> If the answer to either issue is 'yes', there is an infringement; otherwise, there is not. Such an approach complies with article 2 of the Protocol, as issue (ii) squarely raises the principle of equivalents, but limits its ambit to those variants which contain immaterial variations from the invention. It is also apparent that the two issues comply with article 1 of the Protocol in that they involve balancing the competing interests of the patentee and of clarity, just as much as they seek

to balance the encouragement of inventions and their disclosure with the need for a competitive market. In my view, issue (i) self-evidently raises a question of interpretation, whereas issue (ii) raises a question which would normally have to be answered by reference to the facts and expert evidence."

■ In respect of the first of these steps Lord Neuberger (perhaps wisely) used the somewhat virgin term "normal interpretation". It is submitted that what was meant was purposive construction of the type contemplated in *Kirin-Amgen* and it seems illogical to manufacture some alternative construction which is contextual yet somehow narrower in approach. Hence it is submitted that the cases concerning such "normal" construction remain good law at least insofar as they omit any recourse to the three *Improver* questions in order to determine such a construction.

■ A reasonable summary of the first of these steps, but no longer of the entire process, is "what would the person skilled in the art have understood the patentee to be using the language of the claim to mean".

■ In respect of the second of these steps, the once familiar *Improver* questions may be adopted. This is subject to some reformulation most notably in respect of the second question. The reformulated questions are set out in §125.08.

■ For an interesting and informative take on the road to the decision in *Actavis* see Gordon Harris, "*Actavis v Eli Lilly*—Should we have seen this coming?" *https:// gowlingwlg.com/GowlingWLG/media/UK/pdf/170914-actavis-v-eli-lilly-should-we-have-seen-it-coming.pdf.*

Article 69 and the Protocol

125.06 *Delete the second, third and fourth paragraphs (from "Lord Hoffmann points out" to "was intending to claim".) and replace with:*

■ The importance of Article 69 and the Protocol should also impact on validity vis-a-vis (at least) the assessment of novelty and inventive step. In the Editors' view it can only be right that the scope of the claims (i.e. the extent of protection) is the same regardless of whether one is assessing validity or infringement. So far as the Act is concerned s.125(1) and (3) tie the Protocol to the definition of "invention". The corresponding provisions concerning novelty and inventive step (ss.1 to 3) likewise make reference to an "invention".

■ It is therefore the Editors' view that the "extent of protection" is analogous to and not wider than any extent of the invention. That said it is not entirely without doubt that the "construction" of the claim, i.e. its normal interpretation, is the be all and end all when one assesses novelty/inventive step.

■ Somewhat unfortunately therefore some decisions of the Boards of Appeal of the EPO have stated that the Protocol is "primarily for use by the judicial organs which deal with infringement cases". For this reason, whilst the Boards will take into account that the terms of claims need to be interpreted in context, this does not permit using the Protocol to determine a claim scope for the purposes of assessing novelty and inventive step. At least one Board (see T1279/04 *XEROX/Modular charging device*) has ameliorated the approach by rationalising its job at the opposition stage as giving legal certainty. The Board stated that "there was no case for anything other than a strict definitional approach, given that in this procedural stage the claim could and should be amended to ensure legally certain patentability, in particular novelty and inventive step over any known prior art" (decision §3). This rationale (at least) does not lead to a divergence as to whether or not, as a matter of law, the Protocol is applicable when assessing novelty and inventive step, merely that the different function of examination or opposition means that it is not applicable for it to be considered at that stage. See especially *Caselaw Book* II.A. at 6.3.2 Relevance of Article 69 EPC.

Normal construction

125.07 *Change heading to "Normal construction" and add new paragraphs at the beginning:*

■ Following the Supreme Court decision in *Actavis UK Ltd v Eli Lilly* [2017] UKSC 48, the speech of Lord Diplock in *Catnic* should no longer be treated as entirely good law; nor should the remainder of the commentary in the Main Work relating to this section.

■ As to the relevance of the three questions, and their reformulation, see §125.05 and §125.08 respectively.

■ As discussed in §125.05, the post-*Kirin-Amgen* cases at least, and those which do not require the assistance of the *Improver* questions would appear to remain good law in reaching a "normal" meaning of claim terms for the purposes of the first step of assessing the scope of protection.

■ In *Actavis UK Ltd v Eli Lilly* [2017] UKSC 48 the Supreme Court referred to the applicable principles of interpretation required to reach a normal construction as being the same as those used in construing a document, these being as recently affirmed by the Supreme Court itself in *Wood v Sureterm Direct Ltd* [2017] UKSC 24 in which it said the following:

"10. The court's task is to ascertain the objective meaning of the language which the parties have chosen to express their agreement. It has long been accepted that this is not a literalist exercise focused solely on a parsing of the wording of the particular clause but that the court must consider the contract as a whole and, depending on the nature, formality and quality of drafting of the contract, give more or less weight to elements of the wider context in reaching its view as to that objective meaning. In *Prenn v Simmonds* [1971] 1 WLR 1381 (1383H-1385D) and in *Reardon Smith Line Ltd v Yngvar Hansen-Tangen* [1976] 1 WLR 989 (997), Lord Wilberforce affirmed the potential relevance to the task of interpreting the parties' contract of the factual background known to the parties at or before the date of the contract, excluding evidence of the prior negotiations. When in his celebrated judgment in *Investors Compensation Scheme Ltd v West Bromwich Building Society* [1998] 1 WLR 896 Lord Hoffmann (pp 912-913) reformulated the principles of contractual interpretation, some saw his second principle, which allowed consideration of the whole relevant factual background available to the parties at the time of the contract, as signalling a break with the past. But Lord Bingham in an extra-judicial writing, *A new thing under the sun? The interpretation of contracts and the ICS decision* Edin LR Vol 12, 374-390, persuasively demonstrated that the idea of the court putting itself in the shoes of the contracting parties had a long pedigree.

11. Lord Clarke elegantly summarised the approach to construction in *Rainy Sky* at para 21f. In *Arnold* all of the judgments confirmed the approach in *Rainy Sky* (Lord Neuberger paras 13-14; Lord Hodge para 76; and Lord Carnwath para 108). Interpretation is, as Lord Clarke stated in *Rainy Sky* (para 21), a unitary exercise; where there are rival meanings, the court can give weight to the implications of rival constructions by reaching a view as to which construction is more consistent with business common sense. But, in striking a balance between the indications given by the language and the implications of the competing constructions the court must consider the quality of drafting of the clause (*Rainy Sky* para 26, citing Mance LJ in *Gan Insurance Co Ltd v Tai Ping Insurance Co Ltd (No 2)* [2001] 2 All ER (Comm) 299 paras 13 and 16); and it must also be alive to the possibility that one side may have agreed to something which with hindsight did not serve his interest: *Arnold* (paras 20 and 77). Similarly, the court must not lose sight of the possibility that a provision may be a negotiated compromise or that the negotiators were not able to agree more precise terms.

12. This unitary exercise involves an iterative process by which each suggested interpretation is checked against the provisions of the contract and its commercial consequences are investigated: *Arnold* para 77 citing *In re Sigma Finance Corpn* [2010] 1 All ER 571, para 10 per Lord Mance. To my mind once one has read the language in dispute and the relevant parts of the contract that provide its context, it does not matter whether the more detailed analysis commences with the factual background and the implications of rival constructions or a close examination of the relevant language in the contract, so long as the court balances the indications given by each.

13. Textualism and contextualism are not conflicting paradigms in a battle for exclusive occupation of the field of contractual interpretation. Rather, the lawyer and the judge, when interpreting any contract, can use them as tools to ascertain the objective meaning of the language which the parties have chosen to express their agreement. The extent to which each tool will assist the court in its task will vary according to the circumstances of the particular agreement or agreements. Some agreements may be successfully interpreted principally by textual analysis, for example because of their sophistication and complexity and because they have been negotiated and prepared with the assistance of skilled professionals. The correct interpretation of other contracts may be achieved by a greater emphasis on the factual matrix, for example because of their informal-

ity, brevity or the absence of skilled professional assistance. But negotiators of complex formal contracts may often not achieve a logical and coherent text because of, for example, the conflicting aims of the parties, failures of communication, differing drafting practices, or deadlines which require the parties to compromise in order to reach agreement. There may often therefore be provisions in a detailed professionally drawn contract which lack clarity and the lawyer or judge in interpreting such provisions may be particularly helped by considering the factual matrix and the purpose of similar provisions in contracts of the same type. The iterative process, of which Lord Mance spoke in *Sigma Finance Corpn* (above), assists the lawyer or judge to ascertain the objective meaning of disputed provisions."

The "Improver" questions

125.08   *Replace with:*

■ The entirety of the commentary of the Main Work may no longer be good law and needs at least consideration in view of the questions being definitely restated (with particular reformulation of the second question) in *Actavis UK Ltd v Eli Lilly* [2017] UKSC 48:

"i) Notwithstanding that it is not within the literal meaning of the relevant claim(s) of the patent, does the variant achieve substantially the same result in substantially the same way as the invention, ie the inventive concept revealed by the patent?

ii) Would it be obvious to the person skilled in the art, reading the patent at the priority date, but knowing that the variant achieves substantially the same result as the invention, that it does so in substantially the same way as the invention?

iii) Would such a reader of the patent have concluded that the patentee nonetheless intended that strict compliance with the literal meaning of the relevant claim(s) of the patent was an essential requirement of the invention?

In order to establish infringement in a case where there is no literal infringement, a patentee would have to establish that the answer to the first two questions was "yes" and that the answer to the third question was 'no'."

■ The immediately foreseeable issue with the approach now to be taken in respect of equivalents is how precisely is one to determine the "inventive concept" if one is not to rely on the wording used in the claims. This is relevant both to the first and third questions.

■ This, one may assume, was what exercised Lord Hoffmann when rejecting any scope of protection outside of a contextual construction of the claim. Hence Lord Hoffmann's reasoning included the facts that: "there is no window into the mind of the patentee"; "a patent may, for one reason or another, claim less than it teaches or enables"; and "the conventions of word meaning and syntax enable us to express our meanings with great accuracy and subtlety and the skilled man will ordinarily assume that the patentee has chosen his language accordingly" (these at least being the thoughts of Sir Hugh Laddie, a distinguished patents judge, in his article "Kirin Amgen—the end of equivalents in England?" [2009] *IIC* 3 citing from *Kirin-Amgen* at 32-34).

■ Laddie argued that if one only adopts a contextual construction, then one is doing nothing more than giving the narrowest scope of protection applicable under the Protocol, ie. one is at the "reasonable degree of certainty for third parties" extreme. This is essentially the same reasoning as that of Lord Neuberger. When one goes any wider however, the question immediately becomes, how much wider? The Protocol implies that one can answer this question by considering fair protection to the patentee and reasonable degree of certainty for third parties, reintroducing perhaps concepts of colourable imitation and pith and marrow. Such concepts can perhaps be summarised in the words of Lord Reid in *Van der Lely v Bamfords* [1963] R.P.C. 61:

"Copying an invention by taking its 'pith and marrow' without textual infringement of the patent is an old and familiar abuse which the law has never been powerless to prevent. It may be that in doing so there is some illogicality, but our law has always preferred good sense to strict logic. The illogicality arises in this way. On the one hand the patentee is tied strictly to the invention which he claims and the mode of effecting an improvement which he says is his invention. Logically it would seem to follow that if another person is ingenious enough to effect that improvement by a slightly different method he will not infringe. But it has long been recognised that there 'may be an essence or substance of the invention underlying the mere accident of form; and that invention, like every other invention, may be pirated by a theft in a disguised or mutilated form, and it will be in every case a question of fact whether the alleged piracy is the same in substance and effect, or is a substantially new or different combination' [Per James, L.J., in *Clark v. Adie* (1873) L.R. 10 Ch. 667.]"

■ One aspect that may go to the identification of the inventive concept, relevant potentially to both the first and third questions is the content of the file wrapper which is discussed at §125.17.

■ As for the second question, there was substantial reformulation of the assessment required. In its original formulation, the Court considered that the question imposed too high a burden on the patentee, because it required that addressee to work out for himself whether the variant would work:

"62. In my opinion, the second question is better expressed as asking whether, on being told what the variant does, the notional addressee would consider it obvious that it achieved substantially the same result in substantially the same way as the invention. In other words, it seems to me that the second *Improver* question should be asked on the assumption that the notional addressee knows that the variant works to the extent that it actually does work. That, I think, would be a fair basis on which to proceed in terms of balancing the factors identified in article 1 of the Protocol, and it is, I think, consistent with the approach of the German, Italian and Dutch courts. It is also consistent with the fact that the notional addressee is told (in the patent itself) what the invention does.

63. This reformulated second question should also apply to variants which rely on, or are based on, developments which have occurred since the priority date, even though the notional addressee is treated as considering the second question as at the priority date. Such an approach is supported by the desirability of both consistency of approach and pragmatic justice. It seems right in principle to have the same question, including the same assumption (ie that the variant works) for all cases. As to pragmatism, the point is touched on by Judge Kalden in the passage quoted at the end of para 51 above: while the notional addressee may answer the reformulated second question affirmatively even where the variant was unforeseeable at the priority date, he is less likely to do so than in relation to a variant which was unforeseeable as at that date."

Purpose not the be-all and end-all

Replace with: **125.09**

■ The entirety of the commentary of the Main Work may no longer be good law in view of the judgment in *Actavis UK Ltd v Eli Lilly* [2017] UKSC 48 to the effect that there is a doctrine of equivalents. Reference should be made to the commentary in this supplement.

Equivalents

Add new paragraphs at the beginning: **125.10**

■ The entirety of the commentary in the Main Work, being to the effect that there is no doctrine of equivalents should no longer be considered to be good law consequent upon the Supreme Court's decision in *Actavis UK Ltd v Eli Lilly* [2017] UKSC 48. The Editors note their previously expressed opinion that the former non-existence of such a doctrine was "despite what seems to be wording to the contrary in the second paragraph of the Protocol".

■ The observations of Mr Justice Arnold (from the first instance hearing of *Actavis*) remain interesting reading. It is the Editors' view that these scenarios may now become relevant to any consideration of whether the doctrine of equivalents can be invoked and still yet give fair protection to the patentee. It is the first of these categories (unfortunate drafting) where the biggest difficulties may arise. In the second class (technology moved on), as Arnold J observed the law is more sympathetic and the change in the expression of the second *Improver* question will likely extend that sympathy further. As for the third (patentee regrets decision taken during prosecution) the Editors agree with the observation of Arnold J that "there is no reason why the law should be sympathetic". As to the extent to which the Supreme Court appear to be sympathetic to a factual situation in which an

Examiner's view was accepted (which the Court believed was overly strict) the opinion of the Editors is that this is far from the balance sought by the Protocol. They say this on the basis that a patentee has fair protection in that it can force an appealable decision from an Examining Division. Likewise, insofar as the law now requires third parties to consult the prosecution history because it is publicly available, reasonable certainty cannot be achieved by seemingly allowing a patentee to gain a patent on one basis and yet assert it on a broader one.

■ The problems that can arise from the need to consider prosecution history, in that instance following oral proceedings before the EPO TBA were considered in *IPCom v HTC Europe* [2017] EWCA Civ 90, where Floyd LJ explained:

"The enquiry before the judge into what happened before the TBA involved receiving evidence from no less than five witnesses, including four who attended the TBA hearing and an expert, independent translator, who did not. The parties were not agreed about what happened at the hearing, or about the significance of those events. The debate extended to the question of what the TBA had in mind when it accepted the final form of amended claim, having rejected earlier ones. The judge was right not to place any reliance on this material. It is an illustration of the impossible burden it places on a skilled reader if it were to be recognised as a legitimate aid to construction."

"File wrapper estoppel"

125.17 *Add new paragraphs at the beginning:*

■ Although yet again rather half-hearted, the Supreme Court confirmed in *Actavis UK Ltd v Eli Lilly* [2017] UKSC 48 that the file wrapper may, on occasions, be relevant to the extent of protection of a patent.

■ Thus [88] contemplates two particular circumstances whilst making clear that these are non-exhaustive:

"While it would be arrogant to exclude the existence of any other circumstances, my current view is that reference to the file would only be appropriate where (i) the point at issue is truly unclear if one confines oneself to the specification and claims of the patent, and the contents of the file unambiguously resolve the point, or (ii) it would be contrary to the public interest for the contents of the file to be ignored. The first type of circumstance is, I hope, self-explanatory; the second would be exemplified by a case where the patentee had made it clear to the EPO that he was not seeking to contend that his patent, if granted, would extend its scope to the sort of variant which he now claims infringes."

■ Various of the first set of circumstances are discussed in the Main Work.

■ The *Actavis* case itself gives an indication of when the second circumstances might occur. During prosecution, the patentee had limited the claims in response to the examiner's objections. These claim limitations were at least arguably more than necessary (yet the patentee chose not to argue the point with the examiner). One might suspect that this was a circumstance in which it could be said that the patentee entered into the limitations with its eyes open; if it chose not to fight the point it had effectively disclaimed that which it now seeks to claim.

■ The court did not agree, or at least held the point to be a neutral one. It suggested that it was open to a patentee take what it was offered yet argue for more subsequently, stating:

"The whole point of the doctrine is that it entitles a patentee to contend that the scope of protection afforded by the patent extends beyond the ambit of its claims as construed according to normal principles of interpretation." *Actavis* at [89].

■ It could be said that this is consistent with the attitude taken by the Boards of Appeal to the applicability of the Protocol and the consideration of equivalent. See the discussion relating to §125.06.

■ In view of this stated "whole point" of the doctrine the case in which the second of Lord Neuberger's stated circumstances for consulting the filewrapper may be vanishingly small. This is because, in the Editors' experience, a patentee seldom comments on the extent of protection during prosecution (inter alia because the EPO are not interested) and so any comments as to the scope of the claims are likely to have referred to the scope with no consideration given to any equivalents doctrine. This is hardly a desirable state of affairs (or one in which third parties have any certainty) if what appears to be a disclaimer of extent of protection is to be treated instead as a disclaimer of claim scope reserving an option to maintain a monopoly with the disclaimed scope under an equivalents doctrine.

■ Moreover the "take what you can and argue for more later" approach seems in the Editors' view contrary to two of the established laws of construction affirmed in *Wood v Capita* to which specific reference was made by Lord Neuberger in his *Actavis* judgment. In *Wood* it was suggested that a more literal analysis could be taken to a document whose "sophistication and complexity... [had] been negotiated and prepared with the assistance of skilled professionals." In addition, it was also recognized that a party might have (presumably knowingly) have agreed to something which with hindsight did not serve his interests. See §125.07. Moreover, in the Editors' view it is difficult to see how if at least the second of these points fail at the normal construction stage, they can be circumvented at the equivalents stage and yet maintain either fair protection to the patentee or a reasonable degree of certainty for third parties.

Geometric terms

—The need for a uniform construction of the extent of protection

Add new paragraph at the beginning: **125.20**

■ Following *Actavis UK Ltd v Eli Lilly* [2017] UKSC 48 the equating of claim construction with extent of protection can no longer be considered good law. That said, it is the Editors' view that there should remain a uniform "extent" regardless of whether one is considering validity or infringement. See §125.06.

—Claims containing numerical limits

Change heading to "Claims containing numerical limits" and, to the end of the fourth **125.23**
paragraph (beginning "After a substantial amount of analysis and consideration"), add:
The above decision and the issue of interpretation of numerical ranges is discussed by Isabel Teare and Alasdair Poore, "Fuzzy boundaries" [2015] 7 *CIPA* 28.

In *Napp Pharmaceutical Holdings v Dr Reddy's Laboratories (UK) and Sandoz* [2016] EWHC 1517, Arnold J applied the principles set out in *Smith & Nephew* in order to construe numerical limits. He rejected a broad interpretation on the basis that a different component had been specified as 10 to 15% and had the patentee wished something along these lines, it should have said so. The word "about"' should be taken to mean a "a small degree of permitted imprecision over and above that implied by the usual rounding convention". The term "about 10%" was therefore interpreted to cover ≥ 9.0 to $<11.0\%$, which was not enough to encompass the quantity of ingredient in the defendant's product. The Court went on to consider the de minimis principle, finding that if only 1 in 10,000 products infringed, this would amount to de minimis infringement. The decision has been affirmed, see [2016] EWCA Civ 1053.

Claims containing a statement of purpose

To the end of the sixth paragraph (beginning "In FH Brundle v Perry [2014] EWHC **125.24**
475 (IPEC)"), add:
Jim Boff, "Adapted, constructed or suitable for confusion?" [2015] 1 *CIPA* 12 discusses changes in *MOPP* at 2.12.3 and in the immediately following paragraph consequential upon *Brundle v Perry* and with further reference to *Schenck Rotec GmbH v Universal Balancing Ltd* [2012] EWHC 1920. He argues that the IP Office appears to be constructing new "generalised drafting conventions" that are not general, and then adopting them without reference to the particular case.

SECTION 128B [ADDED]—Supplementary protection certificates

128B.00   *Add new paragraph 128B.00:*

Contents

COMMENTARY ON SECTION 128B AND SUPPLEMENTARY PROTECTION CERTIFICATES
GENERALLY

Scope of the section

Add new paragraph at end: **128B.58**
A review of recent decisions is found in a two-part review Daniel Wise et al., "SPCs—navigating rocky waters" [2016] 8-9 *CIPA* 14 and [2016] 10 *CIPA* 40.

The legal basis for supplementary protection certificates

Add new paragraphs at end: **128B.62**
■ On two occasions (once in December 2015 and again June 2016), the European Commission has called for tenders in connection with a "Study on the legal aspects of the supplementary protection certificates in the EU". After no qualifying bids were received in response to the first call, the breadth of the proposed study was narrowed significantly. This led to the Max Planck Institute for Innovation and Competition being awarded the contract for the second call. The Commission intends to use the results of the study "for an overall evaluation of the SPC system in the EU and to inform the decision on whether to revise the existing SPC legislation". It is also understood that the Commission has awarded a separate contract for a second study (on the economic impact of supplementary protection certificates (SPCs), pharmaceutical incentives and rewards in Europe) to Copenhagen Economics. That second study was due to be completed by the end of 2017. The Commission has indicated that, amongst other things, it intends to use the results of that second study "as one of the inputs into an evaluation report of the SPC system in the EU and to inform the decision on whether to come forward with a revision (notably with an option of establishing common SPC titles covering the entirety of the internal market)/ scope and term/modification of the existing SPC acquis".

■ A discussion of the likely impact of Brexit on SPCs (and other, "regulatory" exclusivities) is found in the article by Julia Florence in [2017] 5 *CIPA* 16.

In view of the result of the referendum on 23 June 2016, it appears that the UK will on or about 19 March 2019 cease to be a member state of the European Union. If and when this happens, the EU Regulations will cease to have direct legal effect in the UK, and the UK courts will no longer be obliged to follow the judgments of the Court of Justice of the EU. It is possible that arrangements could be made wherein some or all of the provisions of the EU Regulations continue to apply in the UK, for example if the UK becomes a member state of European Economic Area. However, another possibility is that the UK will create its own law on SPCs (or another, similar IP right). In the latter event, it may prove necessary (e.g. in view of issues relating to legal certainty and legitimate expectations) for the UK to ensure that transitional arrangements are put in place that effectively continue to apply the provisions of the EU Regulations to "pre-Brexit" SPCs and SPC applications.

Scope of the Community Regulations under United Kingdom law and practice

In the last paragraph, replace "The hearing office found that the SPC application failed   **128B.64**
to comply with Article 2, and that the product defined in the application was outside of the scope of Reg.469/2009. A reason for finding Leibniz-Institut's SPC application non-compliant with art.2 (instead of art.3(b), as for Cerus' SPC application discussed in § 128B.73) was that the device in the Leibniz-Institut case did not include "a substance which, if used separately, may be considered to be a medicinal product". Instead, it was held that the device exercised its activity by physical means alone. A similar finding based upon an EC Design Examination Certificate was made in Angiotech Pharmaceuticals v University of British Columbia BL O/466/15." with:
The Hearing Officer found that the SPC application failed to comply with art.2, and that

the product defined in the application was outside of the scope of Reg.469/2009. A reason for finding *Leibniz-Institut's SPC application* non-compliant with art.2 (instead of art.3(b), as for *Cerus' SPC application* discussed in §128B.73) was that the device in the *Leibniz-Institut* case did not include "a substance which, if used separately, may be considered to be a medicinal product". Instead, it was held that the device exercised its activity by physical means alone. Similar reasoning, as supported by the CJEU's commentary on art.1(b) in *Forsgren* (C-631/13, discussed in more detail in §128B.66), was relied upon by the German Federal Patent Court (BPatG, case 14 W (Pat) 45/12) to uphold the rejection of Leibniz's corresponding German SPC application. Non-compliance with art.2 was also found by the IPO in *Angiotech Pharmaceuticals and University of British Columbia* BL O/466/15, on the grounds that the products in question had not been "subject to an administrative procedure as laid down in Directive 2001/83/EC" (instead being "authorised" by way of an EC Design Examination Certificate, which was held to not be equivalent to an authorsiation under Directive 2001/83/EC).

Conditions for obtaining an SPC

128B.65 *After the twenty-first paragraph (beginning "Thus, if Mr Justice Warren's judgment is followed by the IPO"), add new paragraphs:*

■ However, it is unclear whether even other judges at the Patents Court will be persuaded to follow Warren J's judgement in *Eli Lilly*. Indeed, in his judgement in *Teva UK Ltd v Gilead Sciences Inc* [2017] EWHC 13 (Pat), Arnold J took issue with certain aspects of of Warren J's reasoning. Having done so he also decided to seek further guidance from the CJEU, by referring (yet again) the question "What are the criteria for deciding whether 'the product is protected by a basic patent in force' in Article 3(a) of the SPC Regulation?" That question is now pending before the CJEU in *Teva UK and Others* (C-121/17).

■ It is not immediately apparent why the CJEU would answer the question referred in C-121/17 any differently than on the two previous occasions on which an essentially identical question has been referred (in C-322/10 and C-493/12). Nevertheless, Arnold J has attempted to assist the CJEU by explaining that, in his view, a combination product must not only fall within the extent of protection provided by the claims, but it must also "embody the inventive advance of the basic patent".

■ It is important to note that C-121/17 derives from a dispute relating to an SPC for a combination product. This is because Arnold J's proposal to assess the "inventive advance" of a patent may not have a direct impact upon the assessment of art.3(a) for at least some SPCs relating to single active ingredients. This is illustrated by Arnold J's ruling in *Sandoz Ltd v GD Searle LLC* [2017] EWHC 987 (Pat), in which he stated that the CJEU's ruling in C-493/12 "suggests that it is sufficient for the claim to specify the product by means of a Markush formula which covers it".

■ Whether Arnold J is justified in emphasising the importance of the "inventive advance" for assessing compliance with art.3(a) remains to be seen. In the meantime, Arnold J's judgment in *Teva UK Ltd v Merck Sharp & Dohme Corp* [2017] EWHC 539 (Pat) serves as a reminder of the continued importance of the wording of the claims. In that case, an SPC to a triple combination was found to be invalid under art.3(a) on the grounds that a claim to a combination of one active ingredient with "*a* nucleoside analog" could not be construed to "protect" (in the art.3(a) sense) a combination of that active ingredient with *two* such nucleoside analogs.

To the end of the twenty-fifth paragraph (beginning "The ruling in University of Queensland was also relied upon"), add:

Indeed, extent of protection appears to have been a key issue in a later, contrary decision from the Dutch patent office. In that decision, the examiner rejected Mount Sinai's corresponding Dutch SPC application for failure to comply with art.3(a)), on the grounds that all claim limitations must be taken into account when determining what is "protected" by the basic patent. Withdrawal of an appeal against the Dutch decision means that the CJEU is unlikely to be provided with an early opportunity to provide a ruling that will harmonise national patent office practices in connection with the assessment of art.3(a) for claims in process format.

After the twenty-ninth paragraph (beginning "As regards (b) above, a full "marketing autorisation" is required"), add new paragraph:

■ In *Merck Sharp & Dohme Corp* BL O/117/16, the Hearing Officer at the IPO considered whether the date of authorisation in the UK could be taken as the date of an "End of Procedure Communication of Approval" issued by the Reference Member State in connection with a "decentralised" approval procedure. Compliance with art.3(b) for the product in question hinged upon this issue, as the basic patent had expired in the period between the date of the "End of Procedure Communication of Approval" and the date of the formal authorisation granted by the MHRA. In rejecting the SPC application for failing to satisfy art.3(b), the Hearing Officer noted that considerations relating to determining the duration of the SPC ruled out accepting either that the date of a valid authorisation in the UK was that of End of Procedure Communication or that the absence of a valid UK authorisation prior to patent expiry was an "irregularity" that could be cured under art.10(3). An appeal against the Hearing Officer's conclusions on these points has led to the Patents Court referring questions to the CJEU ([2016] EWHC 1896 (Pat)), largely upon the grounds that other national patent offices have reached contrary (i.e. diverging) conclusions when granting corresponding SPC applications. The questions referred, which are now pending in case C-567/16, are as follows.

1. Is an end of procedure notice issued by the reference member state under art.28(4) of the Medicinal Products Directive equivalent to a granted marketing authorisation for the purposes of art.3(b) of the SPC Regulation?
2. If the answer to question (1) is no, is the absence of a granted marketing authorisation at the date of the application for a certificate an irregularity which can be cured under art.10(3) of the SPC Regulation once the marketing authorisation has been granted?

In the last paragraph, replace "The current practice of the IPO is to only grant SPCs to combinations that include an active ingredient for which an SPC has already been obtained "if the combinations are themselves the subjects of separate patents or separate core inventive advances within the same patent" (see MOPP para.SPM2.03)." with:

Indeed, in *Merck Sharp & Dohme Corp* (discussed above) the Hearing Officer at the IPO, relying upon commentary in *Actavis v Boehringer*, effectively concluded that it was not necessary to have "a new patent", and that a second SPC based upon the same patent could be granted if the product for the first SPC did not represent the "sole subject-matter of the invention" of that patent. This decision is consistent with the current practice of the IPO, which is to grant SPCs to combinations that include an active ingredient for which an SPC has already been obtained "if the combinations are themselves the subjects of separate patents or separate core inventive advances within the same patent" (see *MOPP* para.SPM2.03).

Add new paragraph at end:

■ In *Teva UK Ltd v Merck Sharp & Dohme Corp* [2017] EWHC 539 (Pat) discussed above, Arnold J also considered whether the SPC in question, directed to a combination of three active ingredients, satisfied the provisions of art.3(c) in the light of the prior grant of an SPC based upon the same patent and directed to one of the three active ingredients (efavirenz). In order to answer the question of whether the triple combination qualified for further SPC protection, Arnold J held that it was necessary to decide whether that combination represented "a distinct invention protected by the patent", for which purpose it could be assumed that the subject-matter of the earlier SPC (efavirenz and its biological activity) was known to the skilled person at the priority date. Arnold J justified adopting such an unusual approach to assessing validity of a patent claim on the grounds that the relevant question under art.3(c) was "whether, given the invention of efavirenz, claim 16 represents a distinct invention such that it could in principle form the subject-matter of a separate patent". Using this approach, Arnold J concluded that there was nothing in the basic patent to suggest that the triple combination represented a distinct invention. He also considered that the expert evidence supported a lack of independent validity for the claim protecting the triple combination.

Definition of "product" for which a supplementary protection certificate can be granted

128B.66   *After the seventeenth paragraph (beginning "In Yeda Research and Development Co Ltd v BIE"), add new paragraph:*

On its own, the common name or INN given to a biological active ingredient might not provide a clear distinction over a similar but structurally distinct active ingredient. The *MOPP* does not contain any comments upon which (if any) objections under art.3(c) or art.3(d) the IPO might raise in cases where this issue arises. However, objections have been raised in certain cases in other jurisdictions. In a recent example, the Paris Court of Appeal confirmed the rejection of an SPC directed towards HPV Type 16 L1 protein and based upon the authorisation for Cervarix® (Paris Court of Appeal, Section 5, Chamber 1, 12 April 2016, case 15/12234, *The government of the United States of America v General Director of the French IP Office* ("INPI")). The SPC application in question (FR08C0003) had been rejected by INPI for non-compliance with art.3(c), on the grounds that the applicant had already obtained an SPC (FR07C0020) for a product having the same definition, but based upon a different marketing authorisation (that for Gardasil®). Attempts by the applicant to amend the definition of the product and to rely upon differences in glycosylation and primary structure (due to production in insect cells as opposed to yeast cells) were unsuccessful, as it was held that the definition of the product for the earlier SPC encompassed all such variants of HPV Type 16 L1 protein. For comparison, the IPO simultaneously granted UK equivalents of both SPCs (SPC/GB07/030 and SPC/GB08/001, though only after the product definition for the latter was amended to specify that the protein was "made in insect cells"). In the light of such divergent decisions, it appears that only a ruling by the CJEU on this topic, or on the related topic of the scope of protection afforded to SPCs to biological products, can harmonise practice across the member states of the EU.

After the nineteenth paragraph (beginning "In its judgment (C-130/11), the CJEU agreed with Jacob L.J."), add new paragraphs:

The CJEU's decision in *Neurim* has been interpreted and applied in variety of different ways by national patent offices and courts. To date, the IPO in the UK appears to interpret it as permitting the grant of a new SPC in circumstances where there is both a new indication (or "application" in the words of the CJEU) and a new patent that has claims directed towards that indication. Indeed, the *MOPP* at SPM3.05.2 states that "In cases similar to *Neurim* it may be necessary to ask the applicant to show that the indication in the marketing authorisation is within the scope of protection of the basic patent, in accordance with paragraph 26 of the judgment. The scope of an SPC granted having regard to the *Neurim* judgment will extend only to the authorised use, paragraph 25 of the judgment".

In the case of *William J Binder* (Case 34 R 104/15), the Higher Regional Court of Vienna considered the question of whether it is necessary for the new use of the product to be the subject of a of a "stand-alone" marketing authorisation. In that case, the basic patent protected the use of botulinum toxin for the reduction of pain associated with a migraine headache. However, this new use of botulinum toxin was only authorised by way of a so-called "type II variation", which effectively added "chronic migraine" to the list of authorised indications for botulinum toxin. In deciding that the type II variation represented the first authorsiation for the purposes of art.3(c) and art.3(d), and therefore granting the SPC application, the court emphasised the fact that the basic patent protected the newly-added indication (but not the other, earlier-authorised indications for botulinum toxin). It also held that the earlier authorisations could be ignored for the purposes of art.3(c) and art.3(d) even though, in contrast to the situation in *Neurim*, they were for human use.

■ The question of whether a new formulation of an active ingredient could count as a new "application" of that ingredient in the sense of the *Neurim* decision was the subject of a decision of the Hearing Officer in *Abraxis BioScience LLC* BL O/410/16. In that case, the Hearing Officer rejected the SPC application (to a new formulation of paclitaxel) on the grounds that "*Neurim* instructs me, in the context of this decision, to interpret the meaning of a 'new application' of a medicinal product as a new therapeutic application". On appeal, see *Abraxis Bioscience v Comptroller* [2017] EWHC 14 (Pat), Arnold J appeared to be inclined to concur with the Hearing Officer's conclusions. Nevertheless, he agreed that it was necessary to seek further guidance from the CJEU on the correct interpretation of art.3(d). The CJEU received a preliminary reference in the *Abraxis* case (which is now pending as C-443/17) on 24 July 2017. Whilst the question(s) referred had not been published at the time of writing, Arnold J indicated that he intended to refer a question to the CJEU that essentially asked:

> "Is Article 3(d) of the SPC Regulation to be interpreted as permitting the grant of an SPC where the marketing authorisation referred to in Article 3(b) is the first authorisation within the scope of the basic patent to place the product on the market as a medicinal product and where the product is a new formulation of an old active ingredient?"

Definition of "basic patent" upon which a supplementary protection certificate can be granted

Add new paragraph at end: **128B.67**

As also discussed at §127B.65, the IPO has relied upon the CJEU's reasoning in *Actavis v Boehringer* to justify the grant an SPC to a combination (ezetimibe and atorvastatin) despite the prior grant, based upon the same patent, of an SPC to one component of that combination (ezetimibe). In that instance, the Hearing Officer at the IPO was satisfied that "the combination of ezetimibe and atorvastatin is protected as such by the basic patent and that the monotherapy is not the sole subject-matter of the invention".

Subject-matter of protection

Add new paragraph at end: **128B.68**

■ Taking the EFTA Court's opinion into account, the Oslo court found the SPC in question to be valid, as well as to be infringed by the sale of a vaccine containing a variant of the virus strain present in the originally authorised product. This decision was reversed on appeal, with the Borgarting Court of Appeal finding Intervet's SPC to be invalid on the grounds that it had been granted "with a scope of protection that is inconsistent with Article 4 of the SPC Regulation". This seemingly establishes a rather surprising precedent, namely invalidation of an SPC for contravention of the provisions of art.4. This is surprising because art.4 is not a ground of invalidity under the SPC Regulation. However, it is possible to interpret the Court of Appeal's decision as actually meaning that the SPC was invalid for contravention of art.3(b) (i.e. on the grounds that not all of the active ingredients covered by the definition of the product for the SPC were the subject the marketing authorisation relied upon for the purposes of satisfying art.3(b)).

Deadline for filing the application for a certificate

Replace the last paragraph with: **128B.70**

■ The CJEU's decision in *Seattle Genetics* (C-471/14), discussed in more detail in §128B.73) ought to also affect the calculation of the deadline for filing an SPC application based upon a "centralised" marketing authorisation. That is, the deadline ought to be set as 6 months from the date of notification of that authorisation, as opposed to the (typically 2 to 4 days earlier) deadline of 6 months from the date of the European Commission's decision to issue the authorisation. However, as the CJEU did not comment on this specific point there is perhaps some (small) room for doubt that this is indeed the correct interpretation of the filing deadline.

Duration of the certificate and meaning of "Community"

128B.73   *After the ninth paragraph (beginning "In a judgment issued by reasoned order on November 14, 2013"), add new paragraphs:*

In the light of the CJEU's decisions, the date of the first (relevant) marketing Authorisation in the Community is clearly determinative for the duration of SPCs filed and granted under the provisions of Community law. However, the situation was less clear for SPCs filed and/or granted at a time when a Community law did not apply in the country in question. If taken at face value, the transitional provisions of art.21 apply different standards to pre-accession SPCs in Austria and Finland (art.21(1)) and those in the Czech Republic, Estonia, Cyprus, Latvia, Lithuania, Malta, Poland, Slovenia, Slovakia and Romania (art.21(2)). That is, whilst art.21(2) purports to apply Community law retroactively to pre-accession SPCs in the 2004 and 2007 accession countries, art.21(1) adopts the opposite approach for Austria and Finland. These divergent approaches reflect differences between the relevant Treaties of Accession to the EU. However, because the approach adopted in art.21(2) could have the effect of retroactively curtailing the duration of pre-accession SPCs, the Supreme Court (*Riigikohus*) of Estonia referred the following questions to the CJEU in *F. Hoffmann-La Roche* (C-572/15).

1. Must art.21(2) of Regulation No.469/2009 of the European Parliament and of the Council of 6 May 2009 concerning the supplementary protection certificate for medicinal products (codified version) be interpreted as shortening the duration of a supplementary protection certificate issued in a Member State which was issued under national law before the accession of the State in question to the European Union and whose duration in relation to an active substance, as stated in the supplementary protection certificate, would be longer than 15 years from the time when the first marketing authorisation in the Union was granted for a medicinal product consisting of the active substance or containing it?

2. If the answer to the first question is in the affirmative, is art.21(2) of Regulation No.469/2009 of the European Parliament and of the Council of 6 May 2009 concerning the supplementary protection certificate for medicinal products (codified version) compatible with European Union law, in particular the general principles of European Union law on the protection of acquired rights, the principle of the prohibition of retroactive effect of law, and the Charter of Fundamental Rights of the European Union.

■ Whilst the CJEU answered question 1 in the affirmative, it declined to answer question 2 (on the grounds of lack of jurisdiction to rule on the validity of a provision deriving from a Treaty of Accession). At this point, it is unclear whether the retroactive curtailment of SPC duration that can result from applying the CJEU's answer to question 1 is consistent with the right to peaceful enjoyment of property enshrined in Article 1 of Protocol 1 to the European Convention of Human Rights (in relation to which see the discussion in the article by Mike Snodin in *Bio-Science Law Review* 15(6), 248).

In the eleventh paragraph (beginning "The issue of whether the appeal under art.17(2) of the Plant Protection Regulation"), replace "Thus, art.17(2) must be interpreted such that the appeal aimed at rectifying the duration of the certificate is not subject to a time limit." with:

■ Thus, the view of the Council of State was that art.17(2) must be interpreted such that the appeal aimed at rectifying the duration of the certificate is not subject to a time limit.

Nevertheless, patent offices of other EU Member States remain reluctant to accept the resoning of the Dutch Council of State. As a result, a court in Hungary (*Fővárosi Törvényszék*) has referred the following questions to the CJEU, which are now pending in *Incyte Corporation* (C-492/16):

1. Must art.17(2) of Regulation (EC) No.1610/96 of the European Parliament and of the Council of 23 July 1996 concerning the creation of a supplementary protection certificate for plant protection products be interpreted as meaning that "the date of the first authorization to place the product on the market in the Community" is incorrect in an application for a supplementary protection certificate, within the meaning of that regulation and of Regulation (EC) No.469/2009 of the European Parliament and of the Council of 6 May 2009 concerning the supplementary protection certificate for medicinal products, where that date was determined without taking account of the Court of Justice's interpretation of the law in the judgment in *Seattle Genetics* (C-471/14), with the result that it is appropriate to rectify the date of expiry of the supplementary protection certificate even if the decision to grant that certificate was made prior to that judgment and the time limit for appealing against that decision has already expired?

2. Is the industrial property authority of a Member State which is entitled to grant a supplementary protection certificate required to rectify, of its own motion, the date of expiry of that certificate in order to ensure that that certificate complies with the interpretation of the law set out in C-471/14?

Replace the final two paragraphs with:

■ For determining the date of a "centralised" marketing authorisation (i.e. an authorisation issued by the European Commission, following receipt of a positive opinion from the European Medicines Agency), the standard practice of almost all national patent offices was to rely upon the date specified on the authorisation document, which is the date that the European Commission issued its decision to grant a marketing authorisation. However, it was argued that this standard practice was incorrect, and that the relevant date for the purposes of art.13(1) was instead that upon which the Commission's decision is notified to the applicant for marketing authorisation (see the article "Every day counts: why pharmaceutical companies in the EU need to make sure they get the right SPC term" by Snodin (M.) [2011] *Scrip Regulatory Affairs*, September 23). The basis for preferring the notification date is that the authorisation only becomes valid upon that date (in the light of art.297(2) TFEU). Whilst not appearing on the authorisation document, the notification date for each authorised medicinal product is nevertheless published in the *Official Journal of the EU*. In a decision issued on 22 October 2013 (*Genzyme Corporation* BL O/418/13), the IPO accepted arguments in favour of use of the notification date and subsequently changed its practice regarding calculation of the duration of SPCs for which a "centralised" authorisation was the first in the Community (see the discussion of the IPO's practice note in §128B.73). Despite this development, patent offices in other jurisdictions resisted changing their standard practices, which ultimately led to the Appellate Court in Vienna (*Oberlandesgericht Wien*) referring the following questions to the CJEU in *Seattle Genetics* (C-471/14):

1. Is the date for the first authorisation to place the product on the market, pursuant to art.13(1) of Regulation No.469/2009 concerning the supplementary protection certificate for medicinal products determined according to Community law, or does that provision refer to the date on which the authorisation takes effect in the law of the member state in question?

2. If the court determines that the answer is that the date is determined by Community law, is this the date of authorisation or the date of notification?

■ In a decision that essentially followed the (more detailed) opinion of the Advocate-General, the CJEU ruled that the date of authorisation is determined by EU law, with the consequence that the "date of the first authorisation" in art.13(1) is the date of *notification* of the decision granting the authorisation to the addressee of that decision.

PRACTICE CONCERNING SUPPLEMENTARY PROTECTION CERTIFICATES

Procedure for challenge of grant or refusal of a supplementary protection certificate

128B.79   *Add new paragraph at end:*
■ The IPO will, upon request (using patents form 17) and upon payment of the prescribed fee (currently £200), provide an opinion on whether particular compositions or acts infringe a granted SPC, or upon the validity of a granted SPC (see *MOPP* paras SPM5.04 and 15.05). However, any such opinion is non-binding. Also, documents submitted in connection with any such request, including descriptions of particular compositions or acts, will not be viewed as confidential by the IPO. Thus, copies of such documents will be sent to "other interested parties", including the SPC holder, and will be published together with details of the request for an opinion.

Procedure for obtaining an extension to a supplementary protection certificate

128B.81   *Replace the third paragraph with:*
MOPP at SPM10.09 indicates that the IPO will examine whether the product has already been the subject of the alternative reward set out in Reg.1901/2006. In this respect, it is understood that the IPO will check whether the product is designated as an orphan medicinal product (on the grounds that art.36(4) of Reg.1901/2006 stipulates that the reward of a six-month extension of SPC term "shall not apply to medicinal products designated as orphan medicinal products pursuant to Regulation (EC) No 141/2000"). It is also understood that the IPO will establish whether the product has benefited from the alternative reward mentioned in art.36(5) of Reg.1901/2006, namely an additional year of regulatory data protection (stemming from the authorisation of a new paediatric indication that, in comparison with existing therapies, brings a significant clinical benefit).

SECTION 130—Interpretation

Notes

130.01   *Add at end:*
■ 15. In s.130 (interpretation)—
(a) in subsection (1), insert the following definitions at the appropriate places—
""Agreement on a Unified Patent Court" means the Agreement on a Unified Patent Court signed at Brussels on 19th February 2013;
"European patent with unitary effect" has the same meaning as in Article 2 of the Unitary Patent Regulation;
"Unified Patent Court" means the court established under the Agreement on a Unified Patent Court;
"Unitary Patent Regulation" means Regulation (EU) No 1257/2012 of the European Parliament and of the Council of 17 December 2012 implementing enhanced cooperation in the area of the creation of unitary patent protection 8.;"
(b) in subsection (1), in the definition of "court", after paragraph (c) insert—
"or the Unified Patent Court, as respects the jurisdiction which it has by virtue of Schedule A4;";
(c) in subsection (6), after paragraph (c), insert—
"(d) The Agreement on a Unified Patent Court;".
■ Prospectively inserted by the Patents (European Patent with Unitary Effect and Unified Patent Court) Order 2016 (SI 2016/388) (not yet in force).

SECTION 132—Short title, extent, commencement consequential amendments and repeals

RELEVANT STATUTORY INSTRUMENTS

Add new paragraph at end:

132.02

The Patents (Isle of Man) (Amendment) Order 2016 amends the Patents (Isle of Man) Order 2013 to make further modifications to the Patents Act 1977 in its application to the Isle of Man.

Application of the CDPA 1988 to the Isle of Man

Add new paragraph at end:

132.03

Paragraph 1 of the Schedule to the 2016 Order refers to the relevant Act of Tynwald on perjury which applies in the Isle of Man instead of the Perjury Act 1911 which applies in England and the Perjury (Northern Ireland) Order 1979 which applies in Northern Ireland. The other amendments in the Order correspond to the amendments made to the Act (as it has effect in the UK) by the Copyright (Public Administration) Regulations 2014 (SI 2014/1385) and the Patents (Supplementary Protection Certificates) Regulations 2014 (SI 2014/2411).

COMMENTARY ON SECTION 132

Extension of the Act beyond the United Kingdom

—Extension of the Act to the Isle of Man (subs.(2))

Add new paragraph at end:

132.07

■ Note the provisions of the Patents (Isle of Man) (Amendment) Order 2017 (SI 2017/162) which provides provision to extend the Unified Patents Court to the Isle of Man (not yet in force).

Copyright, Designs and Patents Act 1988 (c.48)

["the CDPA 1988"]

PART V [SECTIONS 274-281]—PATENT AGENTS AND TRADE MARK AGENTS

Patent Agents [Sections 274-281]

SECTION 274—Persons permitted to carry on business of a patent agent

RELEVANT RULE—RULE 101

Replace r.101(1) with:

Rule 101—Agents

101.—(1) Any act required or authorised by the Act or these Rules to be done by or to any person in connection with an application for a patent, or any procedure relating to a patent, may be done by or to an agent authorised by that person orally or in writing—

  (a) where an agent is appointed when a person starts or joins any proceeding under the Act, once the comptroller has been notified of his appointment in writing; or

  (b) where an agent is appointed after a person has started or joined any proceeding under the Act, once Patents Form 51 has been filed [*in duplicate*].

Add new Note:

Note. Amended, effective 1 October 2016; para.13 of the Patents (Amendment) (No.2) Rules 2016 (SI 2016/892).

Representation by an agent

—Change of agency

Replace the first sentence with: **274.06**

Rule 101(1) requires that, where an agent is appointed for the first time, the Comptroller must be notified of his appointment in writing before that agent can act, and where an agent is appointed after the commencement of proceedings, a declaration of authorisation must be filed on PF 51 (for which no fee is required), the requirement for filing in duplicate being abolished with effect from 1 October 2016, see the amendment to r.101 at §274.02.

SECTION 280—Privilege for communications with patent agents

COMMENTARY ON SECTION 280

Extent of the privilege extended to patent attorneys (subss.(1) and (2))

Add new paragraph at end: **280.03**

In the US decision *In re Queen's University at Kingston* (Fed. Cir. 2016) it was held that legal professional privilege extended to a US patent agent in respect of communications reasonably necessary and incident to prosecuting patents before the USPTO. Anthony Tridico and Erin Sommers, "Privilege for US Patent Agents" [2016] 6 *CIPA* 18 argued that US district courts could find foreign practitioner-client privilege based on the policy considerations undergirding the Federal Circuit's analysis in *Queen's University*.

Appendices

APPENDIX D—THE TREATY ON THE FUNCTIONING OF THE EUROPEAN UNION (TFEU)

COMMENTARY ON THE EU TREATY

Key concepts in the TTBE

—Scope

After the second paragraph, add new paragraphs:

The concept of a market is not always easy to define. In the case of patents, the view sometimes taken by competition authorities is that the market is defined by reference to the claims of the relevant patent. However, in *Genzyme Ltd v OFT* [2004] CAT 4, Sir Christopher Bellamy QC at paras 197-221 said that the question was one of fact. *Genzyme* was followed in *Chemistree Homecare Ltd v Abbvie Ltd* [2013] EWHC 264, Roth J, where he said at [27]:

"It is, of course, very possible for a single patented drug to be dominant in a market and it is conceptually possible for such a drug to constitute a distinct market of its own, although that is rare (see, for example, the discussion [in *Genzyme*]). Everything depends on the facts."

Chemistree was affirmed on appeal [2016] EWCA Civ 1338, CA. Readers are advised to conduct a proper market definition analysis bearing in mind that the proper market operators may need to be identified. In the case of *Chemistree* the market operators were said to be pharmacists. However, they were claimed to be under dispensing constraints since they had to dispense in accordance with a prescription and, where specific drugs were prescribed, they had no alternatives: in the case of the drug in question there was no other which could be used, dispensed or prescribed. These considerations may suggest exclusivity and market clearing rather than co-existence. However, each case turns on its facts.

Abuse of a dominant position (TFEU art.102)

To the end of the last paragraph, add:

Birss J, was upheld (in that respect) [2016] EWCA Civ 489; [2016] E.C.C. 21, CA (though reversed in other respects).

■ The legal notion of FRAND and its history and purpose were reviewed at length by Birss J in *Unwired Planet International Ltd v Huawei Technologies Co Ltd* [2017] EWHC 711. The concept originated in US anti-trust law (see Jorge Contreras, "A Brief History of FRAND: Analyzing Current Debates in Standard Setting and Antitrust Through a Historical Lens" 80 *Antitrust Law Journal* 39 (2015)). The first public formulation by the Commission of a specific requirement for FRAND terms in the context of IP and standardisation had been in a paper *Communication on Intellectual Property Rights and Standardisation* on 27 October 1992 (COM (92) 445 final at 4.3.3). Cases where the FRAND undertaking had been considered included *InterDigital v Nokia and ZTE*, US ITC Investigations 337-TA-868 and 337-TA-613), the IP High Court of Japan (see *Apple v Samsung* Case No. 2013 [Ne] 10043) and China (see *Huawei v InterDigital* (2013) Guangdong High Ct. Civ. Third Instance

No 305), see also *Huawei Technologies Co LTD v (1) ZTE Corp; (2) ZTE Deutschland GmbH* (C-170, 2015).

■ The concept that there is only a single set of FRAND terms for a given situation was workable. It will promote certainty and would enhance the normative aspect of FRAND, would make the enforcement of the ETSI FRAND undertaking conceptually straightforward, and would allow a court to hold the parties to their FRAND obligations arising from the FRAND undertaking since both parties would be entitled to insist on FRAND terms and neither would be entitled to insist on anything other than FRAND terms, and the *Veringo* problem would be eliminated. If parties presented rival FRAND terms to a court, then the court has to decide what terms would be FRAND in the given circumstances and could grant a declaration to that effect.

■ Unwired offered royalty rates e.g. for 4G or LTE infrastructure of 0.42% and for mobile devices 0.55%, whereas Huwei's August 2016 offer was 0.036% for infrastructure aand 0.04% for mobile devices. After lengthy and detailed consideration of the relevant law and evidence, the court settled on a rate of 0.064% for both infrastructure and handsets in major markets, and in China and other non-major markets the lesser rates of 0.032% for infrastructure and 0.016%for handsets.

■ Furthermore, a UK portfolio licence was not FRAND: a FRAND licence between Unwired Planet and Huawei would be a worldwide licence. Where a proprietor of a standards essential patent (SEP) was in a position to licence a global portfolio (because the technology was usually only licenced on a global basis, the parties being globally orientated) then it was not a breach of competition law for the proprietor of an SEP to insist upon a licence which does that.

■ The terms of the eventual settled licence are attached to a further judgment of Birss J at [2017] EWHC 1304 (Pat). For other issues relevant to the "non-technical" trial see §§61.21, 61.34 and 61.59.

—Mere exercise of rights

To the end of the first paragraph, add: **D27**

However, this doctrine should be applied with care in cases where the patent has SEP status and the proprietor has offered licences on FRAND terms. Under English common law principles this may amount to a unilateral offer which when accepted amounts to an enforceable contract at least in so far as the declared offer terms are concerned (which may not be much since the offer terms may be incomplete, vague or so general as to amount to an offer of nothing) or, more likely, the law of competition would regard it is an abuse of a dominant position to resile from that undertaking— *Huawei Technologies Co Ltd v ZTE Corp* (C-170/13) EU:C:2015:477; [2015] Bus. L.R. 1261, CJEU, though the same problems of certainty may arise; this latter issue has yet to be determined as a matter of EU law (the position, post Brexit, will likely be no different under UK competition law).

SUPPLEMENTARY INDEX

This Index is supplementary to that at the back of the Main Work and refers to the section (§) numbers therein. Thus both Indexes should be consulted and then the indicated sections studied in both the Main Work and this Supplement.